MECHANICAL ENG

MW01519820

EDITORS

S. Paolucci   M. Sen

Undergraduate Lectures on Statics
Dynamics
CAD/Engineering Graphics
Measurements and Data Analysis
Solid Mechanics
Mechanical Vibrations
Control Systems
Kinematics
Machine Design
Thermodynamics
Intermediate Thermodynamics
Fluid Mechanics
Heat Transfer

The books in this Mechanical Engineering Series educate readers on critical subjects included in undergraduate mechanical engineering curricula. Each topical volume is concise, written specifically for students new to the material, and complete in presenting the essentials covered in a one term course. The books are highly readable in style, rigorous in detail of underlying concepts, and emphasize the basic principles needed for engineering applications. The chapters of each volume are discrete units that instructors can present as individual lessons and students can use to accompany the lectures.

S. Paolucci
University of Notre Dame

Undergraduate

Lectures on

Heat Transfer

BreviLiber

First published 2019

Library of Congress Cataloguing in Publication data
Names: S. Paolucci, author.
Title: Undergraduate Lectures on Heat Transfer / S. Paolucci, University of Notre Dame.
Description: South Bend, IN : BreviLiber, 2019. | © 2019 | Includes illustrations, examples and index.

Typeset in LaTeX
Printed by KDP

ISBN 978-1-098-53096-9 Paperback

Series Preface

Commonly used engineering textbooks have usually undergone through many editions since they were first written by the primary author(s). They have usually grown considerably in size; from perhaps 300 pages in the first edition to three times as many in a current edition. Books just seem to grow while the number of hours spent in the classroom has not. The real downside is that such lengthy books are not read as much as the authors expect or hope. Indeed, much of the contents of a typical textbook are not even included in a course but are there for possible future reference. A student who is just learning the material quite often has difficulty identifying the "wheat" from the "chaff" in such voluminous tomes. Furthermore, it is common to have a large number of unsolved problems at the end of each chapter, and physical property tables and charts that take up considerable space at the end of a book. This leads to a culture of not reading the material that is essential for a course.

This volume is part of a series of books that are disposable, inexpensive and brief, and ones that the student should read, write notes on, and dog-ear to get an understanding of the subject matter. These books are written for the student rather than for the instructor, and are intended to be used in conjunction with in-class lectures. The material covered in each book is presented as a series of lectures, where each lecture includes at least one example. As such, we hope that instructors will also find the present book useful in the classroom. The content of each lecture can actually be covered in a standard lecture period. The books in the Series do not have lots of examples and a long list of unsolved exercises or problems at the end of each chapter. Neither do the books have a list of physical properties of materials. Solved and/or unsolved problems can be easily obtained from other sources for classroom purposes (there are even books in many areas that specialize entirely in problems). In addition, most physical properties are easily obtainable from the Internet (as an example, for the thermodynamic properties of water one can download an open-source code which will do the job). Such searches enhance the students' learning since actual learning is an active and not a passive process. Integrals, trigonometric identities and similar information that can be obtained from the Internet are also eliminated.

Lastly, and to be clear, books in this Series are not watered down in terms of the level of physics and mathematics used in an engineering curriculum and the effort needed by the student to master the topics; no change is expected in either of those fronts from what is currently expected from the student.

South Bend, Indiana   S. PAOLUCCI AND M. SEN

Preface

The present book covers essential material in heat transfer. It is aimed at those students who desire a fundamental understanding of the subject of heat transfer and provides them with the ability of solving engineering problems related to heat transfer. It is assumed that the student is familiar with differential equations, thermodynamics and fluid mechanics. The material covered in the book is in four parts.

Part I consists of Lectures 1 and 2. These lectures provide a brief overview of the three modes of heat transfer: conduction, convection and radiation. Dimensions and units of various quantities, the fundamental laws, and the role that energy balance plays in addressing heat transfer problems are also covered in these lectures.

Part II, consisting of Lectures 3 through 11, deals with conduction heat transfer. First, the general problem of heat conduction is discussed in Lecture 3. Subsequently, simplifications dealing with steady one-dimensional problems are covered in Lectures 4 and 5, heat sources in Lecture 6, fins in Lecture 7, steady two-dimensional problems in Lecture 8, and transient problems of various dimensions in Lectures 9 through 11.

Part III consists of Lectures 12 through 25 and deals with convection heat transfer. Basic concepts, such as the boundary layer approximation, non-dimensionalization and similarity, are covered in Lectures 12 through 14. Further discussion of boundary layer theory, including effects of turbulence and use of the Reynolds analogy is presented in Lectures 15 and 16. Lectures 17 through 20 cover forced convection (laminar, mixed, and turbulent) in external flows under different heating conditions; heat transfer associated with banks of tubes is also discussed. Convection heat transfer (also under different heating conditions) associated with flows inside tubes is covered in Lectures 21 through 23. Lastly, Lectures 24 and 25 discuss free convection and corresponding applications associated with different geometries.

Part IV, consisting of Lectures 26 through 31, deals with the subject of thermal radiation. Basic concepts, such as spectral emissive powers, blackbody radiation, Kirchhoff's law and solar radiation are discussed in Lectures 26 through 28. Subsequently, Lectures 29 through 31 cover radiation exchange. In these lectures, view factors, grey surfaces, exchange between surfaces and in enclosures, radiation shields and participating media are discussed.

I would like to conclude by thanking my colleague Mihir Sen (without his collaboration this volume would not have been possible) and the many students who learned heat transfer using this essential material. In particular, I would like to thank my son, Alex Paolucci, for drawing the figures in the text.

South Bend, Indiana   S. PAOLUCCI

Contents

Part I

Introduction

1 Modes of Heat Transfer

Heat transfer is very important in today's technology and environment. It plays a prominent role in energy production and conversion, insulation, electronic cooling, global warming, etc.

Heat transfer deals with energy. In general energy is transferred from the interaction of a system with its surroundings by either work or heat. More specifically,

Thermodynamics (or more appropriately *Thermostatics*) — deals with end states (or equilibria) of processes; it does not concern itself with the nature of interactions or methods of computing such interactions or how long it takes to reach an end state.

Heat Transfer — deals with the rate of energy transfer; it deals with time and non equilibrium phenomena, thus it gives an idea of how long it takes to reach an end state; it is the study of different modes of thermal energy transfer due to *temperature differences*.

1.1 Dimensions and Units

Throughout this text we use the dimensions of length, mass, time and temperature with appropriate units in the Système International (SI) given in Table 1.1:

Dimension	SI
length (L)	meter (m)
mass (M)	kilogram (kg)
time (t)	second (s)
temperature (T)	Kelvin (K)

Table 1.1: Dimensions and units.

For time we also use minutes (min), hours (hr), and days (day), and for temperature we also use degrees centigrade (°C), where

$$T(\text{K}) = T(^{\circ}\text{C}) + 273.15. \qquad (1.1)$$

All other units can be derived. For example:

force (= mass·acceleration): 1 Newton $=$ 1 N $=$ 1 kg·m/s^2

pressure (= force/area): 1 Pascal $=$ 1 Pa $=$ 1 kg/m·s^2 ($=$ 1 N/m^2)

energy (= force·distance): 1 Joule $=$ 1 J $=$ 1 kg·m^2/s^2 ($=$ 1 N·m)

power (= energy/time): 1 Watt $=$ 1 W $=$ 1 kg·m^2/s^3 ($=$ 1 J/s)

1.2 Modes of Heat transfer

The three modes of heat transfer, illustrated in Fig. 1.1, are:

conduction — energy transfer across a (macroscopic) *stationary* medium; diffusion of energy due to random molecular motion;

convection — energy transfer between a surface and a moving fluid; diffusion of energy due to random molecular motion plus energy transfer due to (macroscopic) advection by fluid motion;

(thermal) radiation — energy transfer by electromagnetic waves between two surfaces; it is most effective in the *absence of a medium.*

Figure 1.1: Modes of heat transfer.

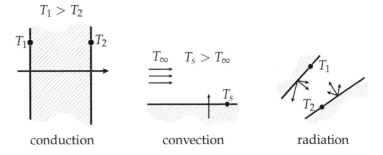

conduction   convection   radiation

1.3 Physical Mechanisms of Heat Transfer

Conduction — Transfer of energy by random molecular activity (also called thermal diffusion). Temperature at a material point is proportional to the kinetic energy of gas molecules near the point. The energy is mostly the result of translational, rotational, and vibrational motions of molecules. As illustrated in Fig. 1.2, when molecules collide (like billiard balls), energy is transferred from more energetic to less energetic molecules. The fundamental equation of conduction is given by

Fourier's law: the heat flux (W/m^2) is proportional to the negative of the temperature gradient, i.e.

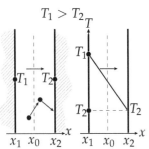

Figure 1.2: Energy transfer by molecular collisions.

$$q''_x \propto -\frac{dT}{dx}$$

or

$$q''_x = -k\frac{dT}{dx}. \qquad (1.2)$$

The quantity k (W/m·K) is called the thermal conductivity and is viewed as a proportionality "constant" ≥ 0. It is a transport property that is a function of the medium and accounts for all molecular motions. It is generally a function of temperature and it indicates how fast heat will flow in a given material.

Magnitude of k:	
Gases	Smallest
Non-Metallic Liquids	
Non-Metallic Solids	↓
Liquid Metals	
Metallic Solids	Largest

The total heat transfer, or heat rate through a plane wall of area A, is the product of heat flux and the area:

$$q_x = q''_x \cdot A \ \ (\text{W}). \qquad (1.3)$$

If the heat flux and the thermal conductivity are constant, then the temperature distribution is linear as shown in Fig. 1.3 and given by

$$T = T_1 + (T_2 - T_1)\left(\frac{x - x_1}{x_2 - x_1}\right) \qquad (1.4)$$

and

$$q''_x = -k\frac{T_2 - T_1}{x_2 - x_1}. \qquad (1.5)$$

Notes:

- A subscript x indicates the coordinate direction of heat transfer.

- The quantities a''', a'', and a' denote the quantity a per unit volume, per unit area, and per unit length, respectively.

- Similar processes occur in liquids and solids where molecular translational motion plays a lesser role and vibrational motion a larger role.

- The measure for the rate of heat transfer is called the heat flux. It is the energy transfer per unit area perpendicular to the direction of energy transfer (W/m^2).

- In the presence of a temperature gradient, energy transfer by conduction is in the direction of decreasing temperature.

- Under steady conditions, for constant heat flux and thermal conductivity, the temperature distribution is always linear in a plane wall.

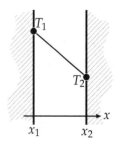

Figure 1.3: Conduction.

Example 1.1:

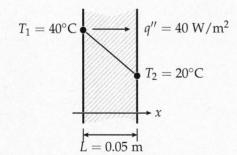

Known: The heat flux and surface temperatures associated with a wood slab of prescribed thickness.

Find: The thermal conductivity of the wood.

Assumptions: One-dimensional (1-D), steady-state, and constant thermal conductivity.

Analysis: From (1.2) and (1.5) we have that

$$q''_x = -k\frac{dT}{dx} = -k\frac{T_2 - T_1}{x_2 - x_1}$$

and now using $L = x_2 - x_1$ and solving for k,

$$k = \frac{q''_x L}{T_1 - T_2} = \frac{40 \text{ W/m}^2 \cdot 0.05 \text{ m}}{(40 - 20)°\text{C}} = 0.1 \text{ W/m} \cdot \text{K}.$$

Comments: °C or K may be used interchangeably when evaluating a *temperature difference*.

Convection — Energy transfer by random molecular motion (conduction) and by bulk, or macroscopic, motion (advection). As illustrated in Fig. 1.4, due to the viscosity of a fluid, the heat flux at a wall whose normal is in the y direction is by *conduction* (since $u = 0$ there), but

$$q''_y = f\left(\frac{dT}{dy}\right)\bigg|_{wall}$$

and $(dT/dy)|_{wall}$ is dependent on the flow field. So to evaluate it we need a relation between $(dT/dy)|_{wall}$ and the flow field. Convection heat transfer depends on viscosity as well as other properties of the fluid. We distinguish two types of convection: *forced*, where heat transfer is due to an imposed velocity field, and *natural or free*, where there is no imposed velocity, but fluid motion arises from density gradients in the fluid near the surface. The fundamental equation of convection is given by

Newton's law of cooling: the convection heat flux is proportional to the difference between the surface and the fluid temperatures:

$$q''_y \propto (T_s - T_\infty)$$

or

$$q''_y = h(T_s - T_\infty). \tag{1.6}$$

The *convection heat transfer coefficient* (also called *film conductance* and *film coefficient*) h (W/m$^2 \cdot$ K) is viewed as a proportionality "constant" ≥ 0. Estimated values are given in Table 1.2.

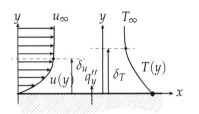

Figure 1.4: Convection with velocity and temperature boundary layers.

Notes:

- Convection is only possible in a fluid (gas or liquid), but not in a solid.

- h accounts for fluid/wall interactions.

- You will not find a table for values of h, but typical estimates are given in the table below.

- In many problems one is provided an estimated value of h.

Mode	h (W/m$^2 \cdot$ K)
free convection in air	5 − 25
forced convection in air	10 − 500
forced convection in water	100 − 15,000

Table 1.2: Typical values of h.

Example 1.2:

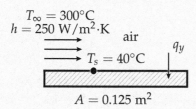

Known: Forced convection heat transfer between the plate and air stream.

Find: Heat transfer rate from air to plate.

Assumptions: 1-D, steady-state, uniform temperature over plate, and h is uniform over the plate (the flow is uniform).

Analysis: From (1.3) and (1.6) we have

$$q_y = q_y'' \, A = hA \, (T_s - T_\infty)$$

or

$$q_y = 250 \, \frac{\text{W}}{\text{m}^2 \cdot \text{K}} \cdot 0.125 \text{ m}^2 \cdot (40 - 300)^\circ \text{ C} = -8125 \text{ W}.$$

Comments: i) Newton's law of cooling implies a direction for the heat transfer rate; negative means that the heat flows from the air to the plate. ii) Note the canceling of K and °C.

(Thermal) Radiation — As illustrated in Fig. 1.5, it is the energy emitted by matter that is at a finite temperature. The fundamental equation of radiation is given by

Stefan–Boltzmann law: A *blackbody* (an ideal radiator) emits energy at a rate proportional to the fourth power of the *absolute* temperature of the body:

$$q'' \propto T_s^4$$

or

$$q'' = \sigma \, T_s^4. \tag{1.7}$$

The quantity σ is called the Stefan-Boltzmann constant and is an *absolute constant* approximately equal to 5.6716×10^{-8} (W/m^2·K^4). For

Notes:

- Radiation is due to changes in electron configuration of atoms.

- Energy is transported by electromagnetic waves and photons.

- In a vacuum they travel in straight lines.

- Does not require a medium for transfer; it is most efficient in a vacuum.

- The law does not apply to other forms of radiation.

realistic or *gray* surfaces:

$$q'' = \epsilon \, \sigma \, T_s^4, \tag{1.8}$$

where the dimensionless quantity $0 \le \epsilon \le 1$ is called the *emissivity* which is a radiative property of the surface. Not all radiation leaving a surface "1" reaches a second surface "2", thus the net radiation between the two surfaces is given by

$$q'' = \epsilon \, F_{12} \, \sigma \left(T_1^4 - T_2^4 \right), \tag{1.9}$$

where the dimensionless quantity $0 \le F_{12} \le 1$ is called the *view factor* (it is a geometric factor). For the special case of a small surface with temperature T_s in a large enclosure with surface temperature T_{sur} we have that $F_{12} = 1$, and so

$$q'' = \epsilon \, \sigma \left(T_s^4 - T_{sur}^4 \right). \tag{1.10}$$

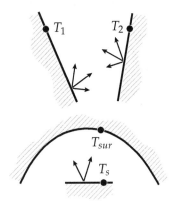

Figure 1.5: Thermal radiation.

Notes:

- In general ϵ and F_{12} are not independent of one another.

- It is possible to write $q'' = h_r(T_s - T_{sur})$, where $h_r \equiv \epsilon\sigma(T_s + T_{sur})(T_s^2 - T_{sur}^2)$ is the "radiation heat transfer coefficient," but doing so is only useful in numerical computations when we need to *linearize* the equations in an iterative procedure.

- Note that h_r depends strongly on temperature, while h depends weakly on temperature.

- We focus on radiation from solid surfaces, although emission from liquids and gases also occur, but they are much smaller.

- Black dull surfaces approximate a blackbody. In this case q'' is the maximum radiation emitted by the body.

Example 1.3:

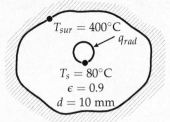

Known: Spherical object maintained at a prescribed temperature within an oven at given temperature.

Find: The heat transfer rate from the oven walls to the object.

Assumptions: Object completely surrounded by oven walls ($F_{12} = 1$), steady-state, sphere and oven walls have uniform temperatures, oven is evacuated and large compared to the sphere, and sphere has gray surface.

Analysis: Using (1.3) and (1.10) we have that

$$q = q'' \cdot A$$
$$= \epsilon \sigma A \left(T_s^4 - T_{sur}^4 \right)$$
$$= 0.9 \cdot 5.6716 \times 10^{-8} \frac{W}{m^2 \cdot K^4} \left(\pi \cdot 0.01^2 \right) m^2 \left(353^4 - 673^4 \right) K^4$$
$$= -3.04 \ W.$$

Comments: i) The equation is valid only for a small object completely surrounded by a large surface. ii) The law implies a direction for the heat transfer rate; negative means the heat flows from the large surface into the object. iii) *Always* use absolute temperature in radiation calculations. iv) The problem is really unsteady since the sphere temperature will change due to heat gain; at steady state $T_s = T_{sur}$.

Exercises 1:

1. The thermal conductivity in a particular plane wall of thickness L depends as follows on the wall temperature: $k = a + bT$, where a and b are constants. The temperatures are T_1 and T_2 on either side of the wall. Develop an expression for q.

2. A 2 m long, 0.3 cm diameter electrical wire extends across a room at 15°C. Heat is generated in the wire as a result of resistance heating, and the surface temperature of the wire is measured to be 152°C in steady operation. Also, the voltage drop and electric current through the wire are measured to be 60 V and 1.5 A, respectively. Disregarding any heat transfer by radiation, determine the convection heat transfer coefficient for heat transfer between the outer surface of the wire and the air in the room.

3. Consider a person standing in a room maintained at 21°C at all times. The inner surfaces of the walls, floors, and the ceiling of the house are observed to be at an average temperature of 11°C in winter and 24°C in summer. Determine the rates of radiation heat transfer between this person and the surrounding surfaces in both summer and winter if the exposed surface area, emissivity, and the average outer surface temperature of the person are 1.6 m², 0.95, and 32°C, respectively.

2 Methods of Heat Transfer

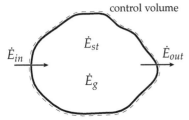

Figure 2.1: Control volume energy balance.

Notes:

- $\dot{E}_{st} = q_{st} = \rho\, V\, c_p\, \dot{T}$ is the rate of energy stored in the control volume; it is proportional to the size of control volume; ρ (kg/m³) is the density, V (m³) is the volume, and c_p (J/kg·K) is the specific heat at constant pressure.

- $\dot{E}_{in}$ and $\dot{E}_{out}$ are rates of thermal and mechanical energies coming in and going out of the control volume; they only occur on the boundary so they are proportional to the surface area of the control volume.

- The quantity $\dot{E}_g = q_g''' V$ is the rate of heat generation in the control volume; it is proportional to the size of control volume; q_g''' (W/m³) is the energy generation rate per unit volume.

2.1 Conservation of Energy

From thermodynamics we have that energy in a control volume is conserved, and so

$$\dot{E}_{st} = \dot{E}_{in} - \dot{E}_{out} + \dot{E}_g, \qquad (2.1)$$

where we use the notation

$$\dot{E} = \frac{dE}{dt},$$

and where $\dot{E}_{st}$, $\dot{E}_{in}$, $\dot{E}_{out}$, and $\dot{E}_g$ denote the rates of energy stored in, coming into, going out of, and generated in a control volume, respectively, as indicated in Fig. 2.1. The choice of a control volume is indicated by dashed lines enclosing the volume. It is noted that generally $\dot{E}_{in}$ and $\dot{E}_{out}$ include thermal and mechanical energy: conduction, convection, radiation, potential, kinetic, and thermal energy of fluid, and mechanical work.

Steady-state is possible only if $\dot{E}_{st} = 0$ or $\dot{E}_{in} + \dot{E}_g = \dot{E}_{out}$.

For a surface energy balance, the dashed lines will enclose a surface, in which case $\dot{E}_{st} = \dot{E}_g = 0$ and

$$\dot{E}_{in} - \dot{E}_{out} = 0. \qquad (2.2)$$

Equation (2.1) is valid at any instant of time so (integrating):

$$E_{st} = E_{in} - E_{out} + E_g. \qquad (2.3)$$

Hints for solving problems:

1. identify the control volume or surface;

2. recognize the different processes that contribute to the control volume or surface;

3. substitute the appropriate energy transfer rate expressions.

Example 2.1:

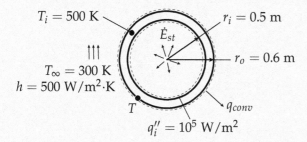

$T_i = 500$ K

$r_i = 0.5$ m

$\dot{E}_{st}$

$r_o = 0.6$ m

$T_\infty = 300$ K

$h = 500$ W/m²·K

T

q_{conv}

$q_i'' = 10^5$ W/m²

Known: Inner surface heating and new environmental conditions associated with a spherical canister of prescribed material (stainless steel AISI 302) and dimensions.

Find: i) The governing equation for the variation of the outside wall temperature with time and its initial rate of temperature change; ii) the steady-state outer wall temperature.

Assumptions: Negligible temperature gradient within the canister, constant thermal properties, and uniform time-independent heat flux at the inner surface.

Properties: For stainless steel AISI 302 at $T \approx 400$ K: $\rho = 8055$ kg/m³, $c_p = 512$ J/kg·K.

Analysis: Take the spherical canister as the control volume; for the canister $\dot{E}_g = 0$, but inside the canister we have

$$q_g''' = \frac{q_g'' A}{V} = \frac{3 q_i''}{r_i} = 6 \times 10^5 \ \frac{\text{W}}{\text{m}^3}.$$

i) Now $\dot{E}_{st} = \dot{E}_{in} - \dot{E}_{out}$ or

$$\rho \left[\frac{4}{3} \pi \left(r_o^3 - r_i^3 \right) \right] c_p \frac{dT}{dt} = q_i'' \left(4 \pi r_i^2 \right) - h \left(4 \pi r_o^2 \right) (T - T_\infty)$$

or

$$\frac{dT}{dt} = \frac{3}{\rho c_p \left(r_o^3 - r_i^3 \right)} \left[q_i'' r_i^2 - h r_o^2 (T - T_\infty) \right].$$

Initially $T = T_i$, so

$$\frac{dT}{dt}\bigg|_i = \frac{3}{8055\,\text{kg/m}^3 \cdot 512\,\text{J/}(\text{kg} \cdot \text{K})\,(0.6^3 - 0.5^3)\,\text{m}^3} \times$$

$$\left[10^5\,\frac{\text{W}}{\text{m}^2} \cdot 0.5^2\,\text{m}^2 - 500\,\frac{\text{W}}{\text{m}^2 \cdot \text{K}} \cdot 0.6^2\,\text{m}^2\,(500 - 300)\,\text{K} \right]$$

$$= -0.088\,\text{W} \cdot \text{K/J}$$

$$= -0.088\,\text{K/s}.$$

ii) At steady-state $dT/dt = 0$, so

$$q_i'' \, r_i^2 - h\, r_o^2 \, (T - T_\infty) = 0$$

or

$$T = T_\infty + \frac{q_i''}{h} \left(\frac{r_i}{r_o} \right)^2$$

$$= 300\,\text{K} + \frac{10^5\,\text{W/m}^2}{500\,\text{W/}(\text{m}^2 \cdot \text{K})} \left(\frac{0.5\,\text{m}}{0.6\,\text{m}} \right)^2$$

$$= 439\,\text{K}.$$

Comments: Let

$$\theta = T - T_\infty, \quad S = \frac{3\,q_i''\,r_i^2}{\rho\,c_p\,(r_o^3 - r_i^3)}, \quad \text{and} \quad R = \frac{3\,h\,r_o^2}{\rho\,c_p\,(r_o^3 - r_i^3)}.$$

Then

$$\frac{d\theta}{dt} = S - R\,\theta$$

with initial condition $\theta\,(t = 0) = \theta_i = T_i - T_\infty$. This is a first order, non-homogenous, constant coefficients, initial value, ordinary differential equation (ODE). The solution is given by

$$\theta = \theta_i\,e^{-Rt} + \frac{S}{R} \left(1 - e^{-Rt} \right).$$

Now it is easy to see that

$$\frac{d\theta}{dt}\bigg|_i = S - R\,\theta_i \quad \text{and} \quad \theta\,(t \to \infty) = \frac{S}{R}.$$

Example 2.2:

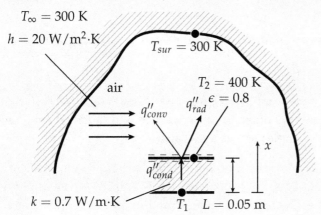

$T_\infty = 300$ K

$h = 20$ W/m²·K

$T_{sur} = 300$ K

air

$T_2 = 400$ K

q''_{rad} $\epsilon = 0.8$

q''_{conv}

x

q''_{cond}

$k = 0.7$ W/m·K

T_1 $L = 0.05$ m

Known: Thickness and thermal conductivity of a wall; wall surface temperature, emissivity, and convection heat transfer coefficient with air; temperature of air; temperature of large surroundings.

Find: Temperature T_1 at back surface of wall.

Assumptions: 1-D, steady-state, radiation exchange with large surroundings ($F_{12} = 1$), constant k and h, and uniform temperatures.

Analysis: Use a surface energy balance of front surface of wall as indicated in the figure, so

$$\dot{E}_{in} = \dot{E}_{out}$$

or

$$q_{cond} = q_{conv} + q_{rad}$$

and thus, per unit area,

$$-k\frac{T_2 - T_1}{L} = h(T_2 - T_\infty) + \epsilon\,\sigma\left(T_2^4 - T_{sur}^4\right)$$

which upon substituting known information gives

$$0.7\,\frac{W}{m\cdot K}\cdot\frac{(T_1 - 400)\,K}{0.05\,m} = \underbrace{20\,\frac{W}{m^2\cdot K}\cdot(400 - 300)\,K}_{q''_{conv}\ =\ 2000\,W/m^2} +$$

$$\underbrace{0.8\cdot 5.6716\times 10^{-8}\,\frac{W}{m^2\cdot K^4}\cdot\left(400^4 - 300^4\right)K^4}_{q''_{rad}\ =\ 794\,W/m^2}$$

or

$$T_1 = 600 \, \text{K}.$$

Comments: Radiation heat transfer is smaller but significant.

Exercises 2:

1. Can a medium involve (a) conduction and convection, (b) conduction and radiation, or (c) convection and radiation simultaneously? Give examples for the "yes" answers.

2. An ice chest whose outer dimensions are 30 cm $\times$40 cm $\times$40 cm is made of 3 cm thick Styrofoam ($k = 0.033 \, \text{W/m·}^\circ\text{C}$). Initially, the chest is filled with 40 kg of ice at 0°C, and the inner surface temperature of the ice chest can be taken to be 0°C at all times. The heat of fusion of ice at 0°C is 333.7 kJ/kg, and the surrounding ambient air is at 30°C. Disregarding any heat transfer from the 40 cm $\times$40 cm base of the ice chest, determine how long it will take for the ice in the chest to melt completely if the outer surfaces of the ice chest are at 8°C.

3. A thin metal plate is insulated on the back and exposed to solar radiation at the front surface. The exposed surface of the plate has an absorptivity of 0.6 for solar radiation. If solar radiation is incident on the plate at a rate of 700 W/m^2 and the surrounding air temperature is 25°C, determine the surface temperature of the plate when the heat loss by convection and radiation equals the solar energy absorbed by the plate. Assume the combined convection and radiation heat transfer coefficient to be 50 W/m^2·$^\circ$C.

Part II

Conduction

3 The Problem of Heat Conduction

3.1 Equation of Heat Conduction

Examine the 1-D differential control volume shown in Fig. 3.1 with volume $dV = A\,dx$. Now the energy balance gives

$$\dot{E}_{st} = \dot{E}_{in} - \dot{E}_{out} + \dot{E}_g$$

or

$$q_{st} = q_x - q_{x+dx} + q_g.$$

Using a Taylor series expansion about x, we can write

$$q_{x+dx} = q_x + \frac{\partial q_x}{\partial x}\,dx + O\left(dx^2\right),$$

so that the above equation becomes

$$q_{st} = -\left[\frac{\partial q_x}{\partial x}\,dx + O\left(dx^2\right)\right] + q_g.$$

But

$$q_{st} = \rho\,(A\,dx)\,c_p\,\frac{\partial T}{\partial t}, \quad q_x = -k\,A\,\frac{\partial T}{\partial x} \quad \text{and} \quad q_g = q_g'''\,(A\,dx),$$

so that upon substituting into the above equation, canceling $A\,dx$, and taking the limit $dx \to 0$, we obtain

$$\rho\,c_p\,\frac{\partial T}{\partial t} = \frac{\partial}{\partial x}\left(k\,\frac{\partial T}{\partial x}\right) + q_g'''. \tag{3.1}$$

Analogously, in three dimensions (3-D), examining the energy balance over the differential control volume $dV = dx\,dy\,dz$, we have

$$q_{st} = \left(q_x + q_y + q_z\right) - \left(q_{x+dx} + q_{y+dy} + q_{z+dz}\right) + q_g,$$

where

$$q_{x+dx} = q_x + \frac{\partial q_x}{\partial x}\,dx + O\left(dx^2\right), \quad \text{etc.,}$$

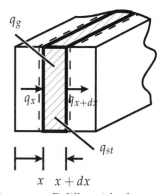

Figure 3.1: 1-D differential volume.

Note:

- $O(dx^2)$ indicates terms that are of the order dx^2.

so that upon substituting, we have

$$q_{st} = -\left\{ \left[\frac{\partial q_x}{\partial x} dx + O\left(dx^2\right)\right] + \left[\frac{\partial q_y}{\partial y} dy + O\left(dy^2\right)\right] + \left[\frac{\partial q_z}{\partial z} dz + O\left(dz^2\right)\right] \right\} + q_g.$$

Now since

$$q_{st} = \rho\,(dx\,dy\,dz)\,c_p\,\frac{\partial T}{\partial t}, \quad q_x = -k\,dy\,dz\,\frac{\partial T}{\partial x}, \quad \text{etc.,} \quad q_g = q_g'''\,(dx\,dy\,dz),$$

upon substituting, dividing through by $dx\,dy\,dz$, and taking the limits $(dx, dy, dz) \to 0$ we obtain

$$\rho\,c_p\,\frac{\partial T}{\partial t} = \frac{\partial}{\partial x}\left(k\,\frac{\partial T}{\partial x}\right) + \frac{\partial}{\partial y}\left(k\,\frac{\partial T}{\partial y}\right) + \frac{\partial}{\partial z}\left(k\,\frac{\partial T}{\partial z}\right) + q_g''', \quad (3.2)$$

or in vector notation

$$\rho\,c_p\,\frac{\partial T}{\partial t} = \nabla \cdot (k\,\nabla T) + q_g'''. \quad (3.3)$$

Note:

- While we have derived the equation of heat conduction in Cartesian coordinates, the vector form of the equation applies to any coordinate system providing that use is made of appropriate forms for the gradient and divergence operators.

Special cases:

i) $k = \text{const.}$:

$$\frac{1}{\alpha}\,\frac{\partial T}{\partial t} = \nabla^2 T + \frac{q_g'''}{k}, \quad (3.4)$$

where $\alpha = k/\rho\,c_p$ (m^2/s) is called the *thermal diffusivity*. The operator ∇^2 is called the Laplacian operator.

ii) Steady-state:

$$\nabla \cdot (k\,\nabla T) + q_g''' = 0. \quad (3.5)$$

iii) 1-D:

$$\rho\,c_p\,\frac{\partial T}{\partial t} = \frac{1}{x^n}\,\frac{\partial}{\partial x}\left(k\,x^n\,\frac{\partial T}{\partial x}\right) + q_g''', \quad (3.6)$$

where $n = 0$ for Cartesian coordinates, $n = 1$ for cylindrical coordinates with $x \to r$, and $n = 2$ for spherical coordinates with $x \to r$.

iv) 1-D Cartesian coordinates, steady-state, $k = \text{const.}$:

$$\frac{d^2 T}{d x^2} + \frac{q_g'''}{k} = 0. \quad (3.7)$$

3.2   Initial and Boundary Conditions

Consider the 1-D Cartesian coordinates case where $T = T(x, t)$. A typical initial condition where the temperature is uniform within the body is $T(x, 0) = T_0$, where T_0 is a constant. Typical boundary conditions applied at a surface located at $x = 0$ are illustrated in Fig. 3.2 and are given explicitly as follows:

(a) Isothermal (or constant temperature):

$$T(0,t) = T_s.$$ (3.8)

(b) Constant heat flux:

$$-k \left. \frac{\partial T}{\partial x} \right|_{x=0} = q_s''.$$ (3.9)

If $q_s'' = 0$ then the surface is an *insulated* or *adiabatic surface* and

$$\left. \frac{\partial T}{\partial x} \right|_{x=0} = 0.$$

(c) Convection condition:

$$-k \left. \frac{\partial T}{\partial x} \right|_{x=0} = h \left[T_\infty - T(0,t) \right].$$ (3.10)

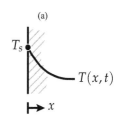
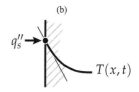
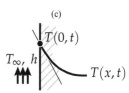

Figure 3.2: Boundary conditions: (a) isothermal, (b) constant heat flux, and (c) convection.

Note:

- Boundary conditions (b) and (c) are obtained by energy balances on the surface $x = 0$.

Example 3.1:

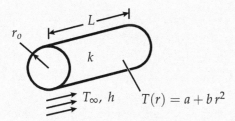

Known: Temperature distribution in a thin solid cylinder of length L and radius r_0 immersed in a fluid; convection coefficient at the cylinder surface.

Find: Heat rate at the surface and the fluid temperature.

Assumptions: 1-D in cylindrical coordinates, $r_0/L \ll 1$, steady-state, and $k = $ const..

Analysis: Since $T(r) = a + br^2$, then for any value of r the heat rate in the r-direction is

$$q_r(r) = -kA\frac{dT}{dr} = -k(2\pi rL)(2br) = -4\pi kbLr^2,$$

so that at $r = r_0$ we have

$$q_r(r_0) = -4\pi kbLr_0^2.$$

From the surface energy balance at $r = r_0$:

$$q_r(r_0) = q_{conv} = h A \left[T(r_0) - T_\infty\right],$$

or

$$-4\pi k b L r_0^2 = h(2\pi r_0 L)\left[\left(a + b r_0^2\right) - T_\infty\right],$$

and thus

$$T_\infty = a + b r_0 \left(r_0 + \frac{2k}{h}\right).$$

Exercises 3:

1. Show that the steady state 1-D heat conduction differential equation with constant properties in Cartesian coordinates may be satisfied by expressions of the following forms: i) $T = a$, ii) $T = a + b x$, and iii) $T = a + b x + c x^2$, where a, b, and c are constants. In each case, state whether the solution corresponds to heat generation or not, and suggest what real problem might give rise to these solutions. Repeat the question, but for the transient 1-D equation without heat generation and the expression $T = a e^{-bx} \sin(\omega t - b x) + c$. How is b related to the thermal diffusivity?

2. A short cylindrical metal billet of radius R and height H is heated in an oven to a temperature T_i throughout and is then taken out of the oven and allowed to cool in ambient air at T_∞ by convection and radiation. Assuming the billet is cooled uniformly from all outer surfaces and the variation of the thermal conductivity of the material with temperature is negligible, obtain the differential equation that describes the variation of the temperature in the billet during this cooling process along with the corresponding initial and boundary conditions.

3. A spherical metal ball of radius R is heated in an oven to a temperature T_i throughout and is then taken out of the oven and allowed to cool in ambient air at T_∞ by convection and radiation. The thermal conductivity of the ball material is known to vary linearly with temperature. Assuming the ball is cooled uniformly from the entire outer surface, obtain the differential equation that describes the variation of the temperature in the ball during cooling along with the corresponding initial and boundary conditions.

4 Steady 1-D Conduction

The governing equation for steady 1-D conduction is

$$\frac{1}{x^n}\frac{d}{dx}\left(k\,x^n\,\frac{dT}{dx}\right)+q_g'''=0. \qquad (4.1)$$

To fully specify a problem, we require two boundary conditions of type (3.8)–(3.10).

Example 4.1:

With $k=$ const., $q_g'''=0$, and a plane wall of thickness L with prescribed surface temperatures T_1 and T_2, we have

$$\frac{d^2 T}{dx^2}=0, \qquad T(0)=T_1, \qquad T(L)=T_2.$$

Subsequently, upon integrating and applying the boundary conditions to obtain the constants,

$$T(x)=C_1\,x+C_2, \qquad T(0)=C_2=T_1, \qquad T(L)=C_1\,L+T_1=T_2,$$

we obtain the solution

$$T(x)=(T_2-T_1)\frac{x}{L}+T_1.$$

Note that:

a)
$$q_x''=-k\frac{dT}{dx}=-k\frac{T_2-T_1}{L}=\text{ const.;}$$

b) for 1-D, steady-state, $k=$ const., the temperature distribution in a plane wall is always linear.

4.1   Variable Area

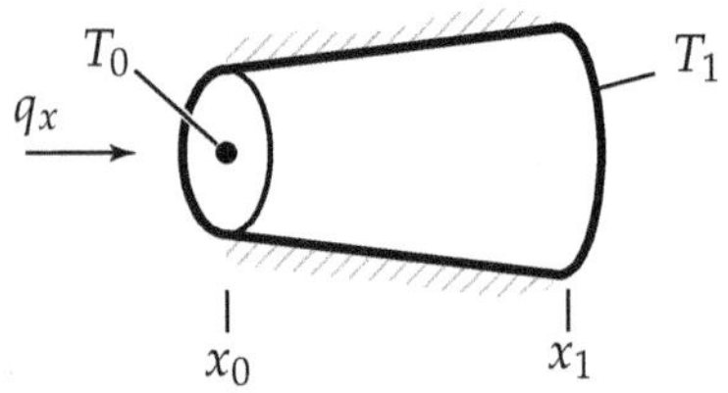

Figure 4.1: Variable area region.

If we have a region whose variation in the x-direction in Cartesian coordinates is not large and we have no heat losses from the sides and no heat generation in the region, as illustrated in Fig. 4.1, then a 1-D analysis is approximately applicable:

$$q_x = -k(T) \, A\,(x) \, \frac{dT}{dx},$$

and since $q_x = $ const.,

$$q_x \int_{x_0}^{x} \frac{dx}{A\,(x)} = - \int_{T_0}^{T} k\,(T)\,dT. \tag{4.2}$$

We need to specify $A\,(x)$, $k(T)$, T_0, and T_1 to solve a problem, and the temperature variation will *not* be linear, unless A and k are constant.

4.2   Thermal Resistance

The concept of thermal resistance is useful only when $q_x'' = $ const. or $q_g''' = 0$. The general definition of a resistance is given by

$$\text{resistance} = \frac{\text{difference in driving potential}}{\text{transfer rate}}.$$

For example, in electrical conduction we have that the electrical resistance R_e (ohm) over an electrically conducting wire of cross-sectional area A between $x = 0$ and $x = L$ is given by

$$R_e = \frac{E_1 - E_2}{I} = \frac{L}{\sigma A},$$

where E (volt) is the electrical voltage, so that $E_1 = E\,(x = 0)$ and $E_2 = E\,(x = L)$, I (amp) is the electrical current flowing in the wire, and σ (1/ohm·m) is the electrical conductivity. Note that in writing the second relation we have used Ohm's law (note similarity with Fourier's law)

$$I = -\sigma\,A\,\frac{E_2 - E_1}{L}.$$

Analogously, in thermal conductivity we have that the thermal conductive resistance $R_{T,cond}$ (K/W) over a thermally conductive plane layer of cross-sectional area A between $x = 0$ and $x = L$ is given by

$$R_{T,cond} = \frac{T_1 - T_2}{q_x} = \frac{L}{k\,A}, \tag{4.3}$$

where T (K) is the temperature, so that $T_1 = T\,(x = 0)$ and $T_2 = T\,(x = L)$, q_x (W) is the thermal current (heat transfer rate), and k

(W/m·K) is the thermal conductivity. Note that in writing the second relation we have used (1.3) and Fourier's law (1.5) applied to the plane layer. Similarly, we can define the thermal convective resistance

$$R_{T,conv} = \frac{T_s - T_\infty}{q_{conv}} = \frac{1}{h\,A},\qquad (4.4)$$

where the second relation is obtained upon using Newton's law of cooling (1.6).

Quite often we also have to deal with heat transfer between two surfaces that are not in perfect contact, as illustrated in Fig. 4.2. In such a case, we can also define a *thermal contact resistance* to the heat transfer as

$$R_{T,cont} = \frac{T_a - T_b}{q_x}.\qquad (4.5)$$

In general, $R_{T,cont}$ is obtained experimentally. The magnitude of $R_{T,cont}$ is affected by the roughness of surfaces, the pressure applied to the surfaces, and the fluid present between the surfaces. Thermally conducting gels are often used between surfaces to reduce the contact resistance.

Figure 4.2: Contact resistance.

4.3   Composite Wall

Now, as in electrical conductivity, we can add resistances in series and in parallel. To illustrate, if we have thermal convection on both sides of a conductive layer, as illustrated in Fig. 4.3, we can write

$$q_x = \frac{T_{\infty,1} - T_{s,1}}{1/h_1 A} = \frac{T_{s,1} - T_{s,2}}{L/k\,A} = \frac{T_{s,2} - T_{\infty,2}}{1/h_2 A}.$$

Subsequently, since we have resistances in series we can write

$$q_x = \frac{T_{\infty,1} - T_{\infty,2}}{R_{tot}},$$

where

$$R_{tot} = \frac{1}{h_1 A} + \frac{L}{k\,A} + \frac{1}{h_2 A}.$$

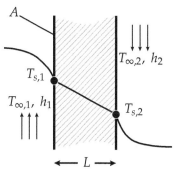

Figure 4.3: Conductive-convective layer.

In general, for the thermal resistances in series and parallel illustrated in Figs. 4.4 and 4.5, we have

$$q_x = \frac{T_{\infty,1} - T_{\infty,2}}{R_{tot}},\qquad (4.6)$$

where for resistances in series

$$R_{tot} = \sum_i R_{T,i},\qquad (4.7)$$

while for resistances are in parallel

$$R_{tot} = \left(\sum_i \frac{1}{R_{T,i}} \right)^{-1}. \qquad (4.8)$$

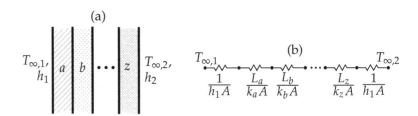

Figure 4.4: Composite wall in (a) series and (b) equivalent circuit.

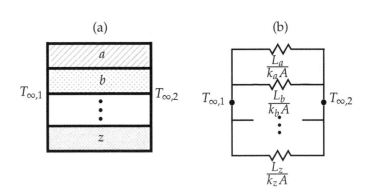

Figure 4.5: Composite wall in (a) parallel and (b) equivalent circuit.

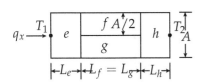

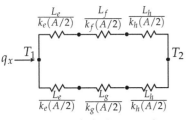

Figure 4.6: Bounds for heat transfer in 2-D walls.

In any case, and in analogy to Newton's law of cooling, we can also write

$$q_x = U \, A \, \Delta T, \qquad (4.9)$$

where U is the *overall heat transfer coefficient*,

$$U = \frac{1}{R_{tot} A}, \qquad (4.10)$$

and $\Delta T = T_{\infty,1} - T_{\infty,2}$ is the *overall temperature difference*.

We can use the series and parallel resistances in 1-D to bound the heat transfer in regions in which the transfer is clearly two-dimensional (2-D). To illustrate this, consider the region shown in Fig. 4.6. Then, we can alternatively estimate the heat transfer by considering the surfaces normal to the heat flux direction to be isothermal, in which case we have

$$R_{tot,1} = R_e + \left(\frac{1}{R_f} + \frac{1}{R_g} \right)^{-1} + R_h,$$

or the surfaces parallel to the x-direction to be adiabatic, in which case we have

$$R_{tot,2} = \left(\frac{1}{R_e/2 + R_f + R_h/2} + \frac{1}{R_e/2 + R_g + R_h/2} \right)^{-1}.$$

Subsequently, bounds for q_x are provided by

$$q_{x,1} = \frac{T_1 - T_2}{R_{tot,1}} \quad \text{and} \quad q_{x,2} = \frac{T_1 - T_2}{R_{tot,2}}.$$

Example 4.2:

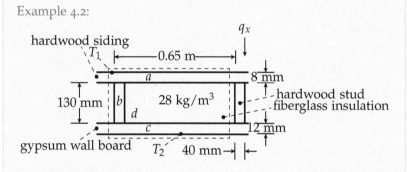

Known: Dimensions and material properties of the composite wall are illustrated, with studs periodically spaced; the wall area is comprised of ten periods.

Find: R_{tot} for the composite wall.

Assumptions: Steady-state, 1-D, constant properties, negligible contact resistance, surfaces normal to heat flux direction are isothermal.

Properties: At $T \approx 300$ K, for the specified materials, we have:

Hardwood siding:	$k_a = 0.092$ W/m·K
Hardwood:	$k_b = 0.159$ W/m·K
Gypsum:	$k_c = 0.166$ W/m·K
Insulation:	$k_d = 0.038$ W/m·K

Analysis: The conductive resistance network in the x-direction between the studs for the one period illustrated is given by where

$$R_a = \frac{L_a}{k_a\, A_a} = \frac{0.008\ \text{m}}{0.092\ \frac{\text{W}}{\text{m}\cdot\text{K}} \times (0.65\ \text{m} \times 2.5\ \text{m})} = 0.0535\ \text{K/W},$$

$$R_b = \frac{L_b}{k_b\, A_b} = \frac{0.13\ \text{m}}{0.159\ \frac{\text{W}}{\text{m}\cdot\text{K}} \times (0.04\ \text{m} \times 2.5\ \text{m})} = 8.176\ \text{K/W},$$

$$R_c = \frac{L_c}{k_c\, A_c} = \frac{0.012\ \text{m}}{0.166\ \frac{\text{W}}{\text{m}\cdot\text{K}} \times (0.65\ \text{m} \times 2.5\ \text{m})} = 0.0445\ \text{K/W},$$

$$R_d = \frac{L_d}{k_d\, A_d} = \frac{0.13\ \text{m}}{0.038\ \frac{\text{W}}{\text{m}\cdot\text{K}} \times (0.61\ \text{m} \times 2.5\ \text{m})} = 2.243\ \text{K/W},$$

and thus

$$R_{tot,1} = R_a + \left(\frac{1}{R_b} + \frac{1}{R_d}\right)^{-1} + R_c = 1.858\ \text{K/W}.$$

Since the 10 areas between the studs are in *parallel*, we have

$$R_{tot} = \left(10 \times \frac{1}{R_{tot,1}}\right)^{-1} = 0.1858\ \text{K/W}.$$

Comments: The result will be different if the surfaces that are parallel to the heat flux are assumed to be adiabatic.

Exercises 4:

1. For most materials, thermal conductivity varies with temperature. Often one assumes a linear relationship $k = k_0\,(1 + a\,T)$. For this linear relationship, evaluate the thermal conductivity at the mean temperature of a material with boundary temperature T_1 and T_2.,

2. Obtain an analytical expression for the temperature distribution $T(x)$ in a plane wall having uniform surface temperatures T_1 and T_2 at x_1 and x_2, respectively, and a thermal conductivity which varies linearly with temperature: $k = k_0\,(1 + a\,T)$, for i) $a > 0$, ii) $a = 0$, and iii) $a < 0$. Verify that for $a > 0$ the temperature profile is concave downward.

3. An industrial oven wall is made up of 25 cm of fireclay brick (inside), 10 cm of kaolin insulating brick, and 20 cm of masonry brick (outside). The inner and outer surface temperatures, T_1 and T_4, are 200°C and 20°C, respectively. Neglecting the resistance of the mortar joints, determine the temperatures T_2 and T_3 at the intermediate insulating brick surfaces.

5 More Steady 1-D Conduction

5.1 Simple Geometries

For 1-D, steady-state, $k = \text{const.}$, $q_g''' = 0$, and $T = T_1$ and $T = T_2$ at $x = x_1$ and $x = x_2 > x_1$ for a plane wall and at $r = r_1 \neq 0$ and $r = r_2 > r_1$ for a cylindrical annulus and spherical shell, we have the relevant equations shown in Table 5.1. In the equations, A is the planar cross-sectional area and L is the length of the cylinder.

Table 5.1: Steady-state 1-D equations.

Quantity	Plane Wall	Cylindrical Annulus	Spherical Shell
$\nabla^2 T =$	$\dfrac{d^2 T}{dx^2} = 0$	$\dfrac{1}{r}\dfrac{d}{dr}\left(r\dfrac{dT}{dr}\right) = 0$	$\dfrac{1}{r^2}\dfrac{d}{dr}\left(r^2\dfrac{dT}{dr}\right) = 0$
$T =$	$T_1 + (T_2 - T_1)\left(\dfrac{x - x_1}{x_2 - x_1}\right)$	$T_1 + (T_2 - T_1)\dfrac{\ln(r/r_1)}{\ln(r_2/r_1)}$	$T_1 + (T_2 - T_1)\dfrac{(1/r - 1/r_1)}{(1/r_2 - 1/r_1)}$
q_x or $q_r =$	$-kA\left(\dfrac{T_2 - T_1}{x_2 - x_1}\right)$	$-k(2\pi L)\dfrac{(T_2 - T_1)}{\ln(r_2/r_1)}$	$k(4\pi)\dfrac{(T_2 - T_1)}{(1/r_2 - 1/r_1)}$
$R_{T,cond} =$	$\dfrac{(x_2 - x_1)}{kA}$	$\dfrac{\ln(r_2/r_1)}{k(2\pi L)}$	$\dfrac{1}{k(4\pi)}\left(\dfrac{1}{r_1} - \dfrac{1}{r_2}\right)$
$R_{T,conv} =$	$\dfrac{1}{hA}$	$\dfrac{1}{h(2\pi r_i L)}$	$\dfrac{1}{h(4\pi r_i^2)}$

5.2 Optimal Conductive Thickness

Note that q_r in cylindrical and spherical coordinates have the potential of yielding an optimal insulation thickness, i.e., one might be able to find an optimal layer thickness such that

$$\frac{dR_{tot}}{dt} = 0.$$

This possibility arises since $R_{T,cond}$ increases with increasing wall thickness, while correspondingly $R_{T,conv}$ decreases with increasing external surface area.

Notes:

- The solutions in cylindirical and spherical coordinates when $r_1 = 0$ are of different forms. They are obtained by requiring that at $r = 0$, $T < \infty$ (i.e., the temperature is bounded).

- For $R_{T,conv}$ in cylindrical and spherical coordinates $i = 1$ or 2 depending on whether the convection is inside or outside the cylindrical tube or spherical shell.

Example 5.1:

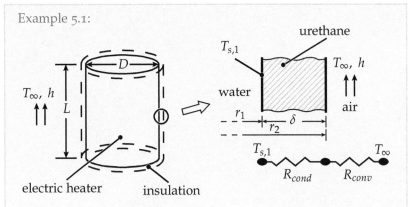

Known: A 100 gallon hot water heater is to maintain water at a temperature of $T_w = 55°C$. The heater is to be insulated by a urethane blanket. The outside air temperature is $T_\infty = 20°C$ and the convection coefficient is 2 W/m²·°C. The unit cost of electric power used to heat the hot water heater is \$0.09/kWhr.

Find: The heater dimensions and insulation thickness for which the annual cost due to heat loss is less than \$50.

Assumptions: 1-D, steady-state, conduction resistance dominated by insulation, the inner surface temperature of the blanket is approximately that of the water ($T_{s,1} = T_w$), constant properties, the water is stagnant, and, for simplicity, we take convective conditions also at the bottom of the heater.

Properties: The thermal conductivity of urethane foam at $T \approx 300$ K is $k = 0.021$ W/m·°C.

Analysis: To minimize the heat loss, the tank dimensions should be such as to minimize the surface area for the given volume of

$$V = 100 \text{ gal} \times 3.79 \times 10^{-3} \text{ m}^3/\text{gal} = 0.379 \text{ m}^3.$$

Thus, with $L = 4V/\pi D^2$ and $A = \pi D L + 2\left(\pi D^2/4\right) = 4V/D + \pi D^2/2$, the tank diameter for which A is an extremum is given by

$$\frac{dA}{dD} = -4\frac{V}{D^2} + \pi D = 0.$$

It follows that

$$D = L = \left(\frac{4V}{\pi}\right)^{1/3}$$

is a minimum since $d^2 A/dD^2 = 8 V/D^3 + \pi > 0$. Now, the total heat loss through the side and ends of the heater are obtained by using the resistances from the table using corresponding relations for a cylindrical annulus and plane wall in series and is given by

$$q = \frac{T_{s,1} - T_\infty}{\dfrac{\ln(r_2/r_1)}{2\pi k L} + \dfrac{1}{h\,2\pi r_2 L}} + \frac{2\,(T_{s,1} - T_\infty)}{\dfrac{\delta}{k\,(\pi D^2/4)} + \dfrac{1}{h\,(\pi D^2/4)}},$$

where $r_1 = D/2$ and $r_2 = r_1 + \delta$. For a fixed insulation thickness δ, the annual energy loss is subsequently given by

$$Q_{annual} = (365 \text{ days})\,(24 \text{ hr/day})\,q$$

and the annual cost due to heat loss is

$$C = (\$0.09/\text{kWhr})\,Q_{annual}.$$

Now the procedure is iterative. With the assumption of a δ, q, Q_{annual}, and C can be computed. If C is greater than \$50, we increase δ and if it is less than \$50 we decrease δ. The iteration is stopped when C is sufficiently close to \$50. To make this concrete, let's take $\delta = 25$ mm. Then we find

$$q = \frac{55 - 20}{\dfrac{\ln(0.417/0.392)}{2\pi\,(0.021)\,(0.784)} + \dfrac{1}{(2)\,2\pi\,(0.417)\,(0.784)}} + \frac{2\,(55-20)}{\dfrac{0.025}{(0.021)\,\pi\,(0.784)^2/4} + \dfrac{1}{(2)\,\pi\,(0.784)^2/4}}\ \text{W}$$

$$= 61.6 \text{ W}$$

Subsequently, $Q_{annual} = 540$ kWhr, and $C = \$48.6$.

Comments: Cylindrical hot water heaters of aspect ratio $L/D = 1$ are seldom used because of floor space constraints. It can easily be shown using the above equations that the annual cost for choosing $L/D = 2$ is only slightly larger than \$50, thus providing little justification for using the optimal heater dimensions.

Exercises 5:

1. Determine an expression for the heat loss from an insulated thick-walled pipe. The inside pipe radius is r_1, the outside pipe radius (and inside insulation radius) is r_2, and the outside insulation radius is r_3. The temperatures corresponding to the three radii are T_1, T_2, and T_3, respectively.

2. Derive an expression for the steady state overall heat transfer co-efficient U for a long pipe for which the convection heat transfer coefficients per unit length inside and outside the pipe are $\bar{h}_i$ and $\bar{h}_o$, respectively, and the fluid temperatures inside and outside the pipe are T_i and T_o, respectively. The pipe's inner and outer radii are r_1 and r_2, respectively, and the corresponding temperatures at those surfaces are T_1 and T_2.

3. Derive expressions for the heat transfer rate and thermal resistance in the spherical shell $r_1 \leq r \leq r_2$.

6 Heat Sources

We consider 1-D steady-state problems with heat sources.

6.1 Plane Wall

For the plane wall illustrated in Fig. 6.1, assume $k = $ const. and $q_g''' = $ const. The governing equation becomes

$$\frac{d^2T}{dx^2} + \frac{q_g'''}{k} = 0,$$

and we take the boundary conditions

$$T(-L) = T_{s,1} \quad \text{and} \quad T(L) = T_{s,2}.$$

By integrating twice, we find the general solution

$$T(x) = -\frac{q_g'''}{2k} x^2 + C_1 x + C_2.$$

Applying the boundary conditions we have that

$$C_1 = \frac{T_{s,2} - T_{s,1}}{2L} \quad \text{and} \quad C_2 = \frac{T_{s,2} + T_{s,1}}{2} + \frac{q_g''' L^2}{2k},$$

so that

$$T(x) = \frac{T_{s,2} + T_{s,1}}{2} + \frac{T_{s,2} - T_{s,1}}{2} \left(\frac{x}{L}\right) + \frac{q_g''' L^2}{2k}\left[1 - \left(\frac{x}{L}\right)^2\right]. \tag{6.1}$$

If we have convection boundaries, the surface energy balances at $x = -L$ and $x = L$, illustrated in Fig. 6.2, give

$$-k\left.\frac{dT}{dx}\right|_{-L} = h_1 (T_{\infty,1} - T_{s,1})$$

and

$$-k\left.\frac{dT}{dx}\right|_{L} = h_2 (T_{s,2} - T_{\infty,2}).$$

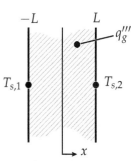

Figure 6.1: Plane wall with heat source.

Notes:

- Thermal resistances cannot be used when $q_g''' \neq 0$ since then $q_x \neq$ const.

- The location where the temperature is a maximum is found by taking $dT/dx = 0$, from which we get that $x^* = C_1 k/q_g'''$, and there the temperature is $T^* = C_1^2 k/2 q_g''' + C_2$.

- $x^* = 0$ only when $T_{s,1} = T_{s,2} = T_s$, so that $T^* = C_2$.

- x^* is an adiabatic surface.

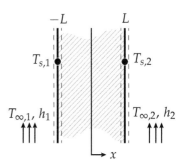

Figure 6.2: Surface energy balances.

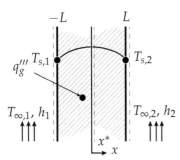

Figure 6.3: Volume energy balances.

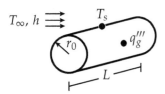

Figure 6.4: Cylindrical wire.

Notes:

- The logarithm term does not disappear in a cylindrical tube.

- In solid cylinders $r^* = 0$ and $T^* = C_2$.

- If a wire of radius r_o and length L conducts electricity, then the energy rate generated within the wire is $\dot{E}_g = I^2 R_e$ (W), where I is the current and R_e is the electrical resistance. Then $q_g''' = \dot{E}_g / (\pi r_o^2 L) = I^2 R_e / (\pi r_o^2 L)$ or $q_g' = \pi r_o^2 q_g''' = I^2 R_e / L$.

If we take the energy balances between $x = -L$ and $x = x^*$, and between $x = x^*$ and $x = L$, as illustrated in Fig. 6.3, we obtain

$$q_g''' \left(x^* - (-L)\right) A = h_1 A \left(T_{\infty,1} - T_{s,1}\right) \tag{6.2}$$

and

$$q_g''' \left(L - x^*\right) = h_2 A \left(T_{s,2} - T_{\infty,2}\right), \tag{6.3}$$

which provide equations for $T_{s,1}$ and $T_{s,2}$ in terms of other given quantities.

6.2   Cylindrical Wire

The 1-D steady-state differential equation for the cylindrical wire illustrated in Fig. 6.4, in which heat is generated within the wire, is given by

$$\frac{1}{r}\frac{d}{dr}\left(r\frac{dT}{dr}\right) + \frac{q_g'''}{k} = 0.$$

Initially, we take the following boundary conditions:

$$T(r_o) = T_s \quad \text{and} \quad T(0) < \infty.$$

The general solution is given by

$$T(r) = -\frac{q_g'''}{4k}r^2 + C_1 \ln r + C_2,$$

and applying boundary conditions we find that

$$C_1 = 0 \quad \text{and} \quad C_2 = T_s + \frac{q_g''' r_o^2}{4k}.$$

Subsequently, the specific solution is given by

given Surface Temp $$\boxed{T(r) = T_s + \frac{q_g'''}{4k}\left(r_o^2 - r^2\right).} \tag{6.4}$$

If we have a convection boundary at $r = r_o$, the overall energy balance gives

$$q_g'''\left(\pi r_o^2 L\right) = h\left(2\pi r_o L\right)\left(T_s - T_\infty\right)$$

or

$$\boxed{T_s = T_\infty + \frac{q_g''' r_o}{2h}.} \tag{6.5}$$

Note that by using the surface energy balance at $r = r_o$,

$$-k\left.\frac{dT}{dr}\right|_{r=ro} = h\left(T_s - T_\infty\right),$$

and using the solution (6.4), we also recover (6.5).

Example 6.1:

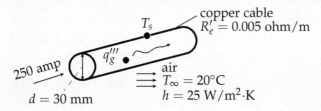

Known: Current flows through a copper cable exposed to air, as illustrated.

Find: The temperatures $T_0 = T(0)$ and $T_s = T(r_0)$.

Assumptions: 1-D, steady-state, constant properties, and $q_g''' = $ const.

Properties: The thermal conductivity of copper at $T \approx 300$ K is $k = 401$ W/m·K.

Analysis: From (6.5),

$$T_s = T_\infty + \frac{q_g''' \, r_0}{2h},$$

but

$$q_g''' = \frac{q_g'}{A} = \frac{I^2 R_e'}{\pi r_o^2} = \frac{(250 \, \text{amp})^2 \, (0.005 \, \text{ohm/m})}{\pi \, (0.015 \, \text{m})^2} = 4.42 \times 10^5 \, \text{W/m}^3,$$

so

$$T_s = 20°\text{C} + \frac{(4.42 \times 10^5 \, \text{W/m}^3) \, (0.015 \, \text{m})}{2 \, (25 \, \text{W/m}^2 \cdot \text{K})} = 152.6°\text{C}.$$

Also from (6.4) we have

$$T_0 = T_s + \frac{q_g''' \, r_o^2}{4k},$$

so

$$T_0 = 152.6°\text{C} + \frac{(4.42 \times 10^5 \, \text{W/m}^3) \, (0.015 \, \text{m})^2}{4 \, (401 \, \text{W/m} \cdot \text{K})} = 152.7°\text{C}.$$

Comments: i) Because of the high thermal conductivity of copper, we see, by comparing T_0 and T_s, that T is nearly uniform; ii) T is primarily controlled by *convection* through T_s.

Exercises 6:

1. Consider a large 5 cm thick brass plate ($k = 111$ W/m·°C) in which

heat is generated uniformly at a rate of 2×10^5 W/m^3. One side of the plate is insulated while the other side is exposed to an environment at $T_\infty = 25°$C with a heat transfer coefficient of $h = 44$ W/m$^2 \cdot °$C. Explain where in the plate the highest and the lowest temperatures will occur, and determine their values.

2. Consider a large plane wall of thickness L. The wall surface at $x = 0$ is insulated, while the surface at $x = L$ is maintained at a temperature of T_s. The thermal conductivity of the wall is k, and heat is generated in the wall at a rate of $q_g''' = q_0''' e^{-0.5 x/L}$ where $q_0''' =$ const. Assuming steady 1-D heat transfer, (i) express the differential equation and the boundary conditions for heat conduction through the wall, (ii) obtain a relation for the variation of temperature in the wall by solving the differential equation, and (iii) determine the temperature of the insulated surface of the wall.

3. Consider a long resistance wire of radius $r_1 = 0.2$ cm and thermal conductivity $k_w = 15$ W/m·°C in which heat is generated uniformly as a result of resistance heating at a constant rate of $q_g''' = 50$ W/cm^3. The wire is embedded in a 0.5 cm thick layer of ceramic whose thermal conductivity is $k_c = 1.2$ W/m·°C. If the outer surface temperature of the ceramic layer is measured to be $T_s = 45°$C, determine the temperatures at the center of the resistance wire and the interface of the wire and the ceramic layer under steady conditions.

7 Fins

Fins are metallic structures usually designed to enhance heat transfer by increasing the surface area exposed to convection. Various designs are used, several of which are illustrated in Fig. 7.1.

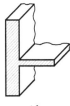  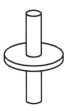 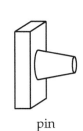

Figure 7.1: Types of fins.

| uniform | non-uniform | annular | pin |
| cross-section | cross-section | | |

To obtain the equation for the steady-state temperature distribution in a fin, it is usually assumed that the temperature is uniform on any cross-section (1-D) and there is no heat generation within the fin. Now we examine the fin differential element as illustrated in Fig. 7.2. In this case the energy balance gives

$$0 = \dot{E}_{in} - \dot{E}_{out} \qquad \text{or} \qquad 0 = q_x - (q_{x+dx} + q_{conv}).$$

But since

$$q_{x+dx} = q_x + \left.\frac{dq_x}{dx}\right|_x dx + \mathrm{O}\left(dx^2\right),$$

we then have that

$$q_{conv} + \left.\frac{dq_x}{dx}\right|_x dx + \mathrm{O}\left(dx^2\right) = 0. \qquad (7.1)$$

Now, using Fourier's law,

$$q_x = -k\,A_c\,(x)\,\frac{dT}{dx},$$

and Newton's law of cooling,

$$q_{conv} = h\,dA_s\,(x)\,(T - T_\infty),$$

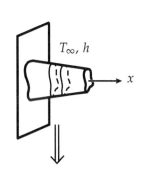

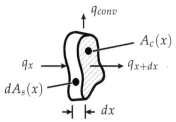

Figure 7.2: Fin and differential element.

where $A_c(x)$ and $dA_s(x)$ are the cross-sectional and differential surface areas, respectively, substituting these expressions into (7.1), dividing by dx, and taking the limit $dx \to 0$, we obtain

$$h \frac{dA_s(x)}{dx}(T - T_\infty) - \frac{d}{dx}\left(k A_c(x) \frac{dT}{dx}\right) = 0. \qquad (7.2)$$

By defining $\theta \equiv (T - T_\infty)$, we can rewrite (7.2) as

$$\frac{d}{dx}\left(k A_c(x)\frac{d\theta}{dx}\right) - h\frac{dA_s(x)}{dx}\theta = 0. \qquad (7.3)$$

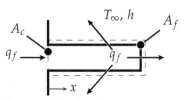

Figure 7.3: Fin of uniform cross-section.

For a fin of uniform cross-section, illustrated in Fig. 7.3, we have that $A_c(x) = $ const. and $dA_s(x) = P\,dx$, where P is the constant cross-sectional perimeter. Furthermore, if we assume that $k = $ const. and $h = $ const., (7.3) simplifies to

$$\frac{d^2\theta}{dx^2} - m^2\,\theta = 0, \qquad (7.4)$$

where we have defined the constant *fin parameter*

$$m^2 = \frac{h\,P}{k\,A_c}.$$

The general solution of (7.4) is given by

$$\theta(x) = C_1\,e^{mx} + C_2\,e^{-mx}. \qquad (7.5)$$

The *fin heat transfer rate* is then given by

$$q_f = -k\,A_c\left.\frac{dT}{dx}\right|_{x=0} = -k\,A_c\left.\frac{d\theta}{dx}\right|_{x=0}.$$

We should note that alternatively we could also compute it from

$$q_f = \int_{A_f} h\,[T(x) - T_\infty]\,dA = h\int_{A_f}\theta(x)\,dA,$$

where A_f is the fin heat transfer surface. In either case, we obtain

$$q_f = k\,A_c\,m\,(C_2 - C_1). \qquad (7.6)$$

To obtain a specific solution we need two boundary conditions. One is always that the temperature at $x = 0$ corresponds to the fin's base temperature, i.e., $T(0) = T_b$ or

$$\theta(0) = T(0) - T_\infty = T_b - T_\infty = \theta_b.$$

Use of this boundary condition results in the following relation between C_1 and C_2:

$$\theta_b = C_1 + C_2. \qquad (7.7)$$

Generally, one of the following four conditions can be applied to the end of a fin of length L:

i) convection heat transfer

$$-k \left.\frac{d\theta}{dx}\right|_{x=L} = h\,\theta\,(L)\,; \qquad (7.8)$$

ii) adiabatic

$$\left.\frac{d\theta}{dx}\right|_{x=L} = 0\,; \qquad (7.9)$$

ii) isothermal

$$\theta\,(L) = \theta_L\,; \qquad (7.10)$$

iv) infinite length

$$\lim_{L\to\infty} \theta\,(L) = 0. \qquad (7.11)$$

If we use the convection heat transfer end condition (7.8), we obtain

$$\left(m + \frac{h}{k}\right) C_1\, e^{mL} - \left(m - \frac{h}{k}\right) C_2\, e^{-mL} = 0,$$

which, with (7.7), gives us that

$$C_1 = \frac{\theta_b}{2}\, \frac{(1 - h/mk)\, e^{-mL}}{\cosh mL + (h/mk)\,\sinh mL}, \qquad (7.12)$$

$$C_2 = \frac{\theta_b}{2}\, \frac{(1 + h/mk)\, e^{mL}}{\cosh mL + (h/mk)\,\sinh mL}, \qquad (7.13)$$

and, subsequently, the solution (7.5) becomes

$$\frac{\theta(x)}{\theta_b} = \frac{\cosh m\,(L - x) + (h/mk)\,\sinh m\,(L - x)}{\cosh mL + (h/mk)\,\sinh mL}. \qquad (7.14)$$

In writing the solution in the above form, we have used the following trigonometric identities:

$$\cosh x = \frac{1}{2}\,(e^x + e^{-x}), \quad \sinh x = \frac{1}{2}\,(e^x - e^{-x}), \quad \tanh x = \frac{\sinh x}{\cosh x}.$$

The fin heat transfer rate (7.6) then becomes

$$q_f = M\, \frac{\sinh mL + (h/mk)\,\cosh mL}{\cosh mL + (h/mk)\,\sinh mL}, \qquad (7.15)$$

where we have introduced a second constant fin parameter:

$$M = k\,A_c\,m\,\theta_b = \sqrt{h\,k\,P\,A_c}\,\theta_b. \qquad (7.16)$$

We note that if we take $h \to 0$ in (7.8), we obtain the condition (7.9), and so using this limit in (7.14) and (7.15), we obtain

$$\frac{\theta(x)}{\theta_b} = \frac{\cosh m\,(L - x)}{\cosh mL} \quad \text{and} \quad q_f = M\,\tanh mL. \qquad (7.17)$$

In addition, taking the limit $L \to \infty$ and, subsequently, letting $k \to 0$ in (7.8), we obtain the condition (7.11), and so using these limits in (7.14) and (7.15), we obtain

$$\frac{\theta(x)}{\theta_b} = e^{-mx} \quad \text{and} \quad q_f = M. \tag{7.18}$$

These results can be obtained much more easily by noting from (7.12) and (7.13) that $C_1 = 0$ and $C_2 = \theta_b$, so that (7.5) and (7.6) result in (7.18).

The solutions corresponding to the isothermal condition (7.10) can be easily shown to be

$$\frac{\theta(x)}{\theta_b} = \frac{(\theta_L/\theta_b) \sinh mx + \sinh m\,(L - x)}{\sinh mL} \quad \text{and}$$

$$q_f = M \frac{\cosh mL - \theta_L/\theta_b}{\sinh mL}. \tag{7.19}$$

Note that the solution for the infinite length fin (7.18) can also be obtained as a limit of this solution by taking $L \to \infty$ and subsequently $\theta_L = 0$.

To assess the benefit of a fin, there are various engineering measures that one can use. One is the *fin effectiveness*:

$$\epsilon_f = \frac{\text{fin heat transfer rate}}{\text{heat transfer rate without the fin}} = \frac{q_f}{h\,A_b\,\theta_b} \tag{7.20}$$

or

$$\epsilon_f = \sqrt{\frac{k\,P}{h\,A_b}\,\frac{C_2 - C_1}{\theta_b}}, \tag{7.21}$$

where $A_b = A_c(0)$. For an infinitely long fin $\epsilon_f = \sqrt{k\,P/h\,A_b}$. Another measure is the *fin resistance*:

$$R_f = \frac{\theta_b}{q_f}. \tag{7.22}$$

Note that the resistance without the fin is $R_b = 1/h\,A_b$ so that we can also write the fin effectiveness as

$$\epsilon_f = \frac{R_b}{R_f}. \tag{7.23}$$

One can also define a *fin efficiency* from

$$\eta_f = \frac{\text{fin heat transfer rate}}{\text{maximum fin heat transfer rate}} = \frac{q_f}{q_{max}} \tag{7.24}$$

or

$$\eta_f = \frac{k\,A_b m}{h\,A_f}\,\frac{C_2 - C_1}{\theta_b}, \tag{7.25}$$

where it is clear that the maximum would be achieved if the complete fin were at the temperature of the fin's base θ_b.

The corresponding fin efficiency for circular fins as a function of fin parameters can be computed analogously and is provided here in Fig. 7.4.

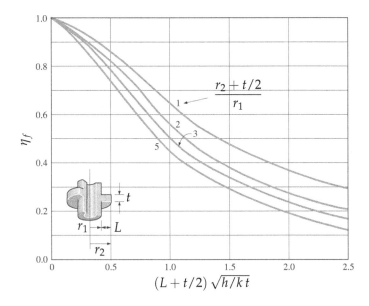

Figure 7.4: Efficiency of circular fins.

Lastly, we note that typically in a design we use a periodic array of fins, so it is important to compute the *overall fin efficiency* over one period. This is given by

$$\eta_o = \frac{\text{total fin heat transfer rate}}{\text{maximum total fin heat transfer rate}} = \frac{q_t}{h\,A_t\,\theta_b}, \quad (7.26)$$

where A_t is the total surface area, which for one fin period is given by $A_t = A_b + A_f$, as indicated in Fig. 7.5. Now it is clear that $q_t = q_b + q_f = h\,A_b\,\theta_b + \eta_f\,q_{max}$, so using the definition (7.25) we can write

$$q_t = h\left(A_t - A_f\right)\theta_b + \eta_f\,h\,A_f\,\theta_b = h\,A_t\left[1 - \frac{A_f}{A_t}\left(1 - \eta_f\right)\right]\theta_b.$$

Thus, it is clear that the overall efficiency is given by

$$\eta_o = 1 - \frac{A_f}{A_t}\left(1 - \eta_f\right). \quad (7.27)$$

Note that the procedure for computing the total heat transfer rate from an array of periodic fins is obtained by first computing the fin efficiency for one fin from (7.25), from which we can compute the overall fin efficiency from (7.27). The total heat transfer rate over one period is then obtained from (7.26). This result would be multiplied by the number of periods to obtain the overall fin heat transfer rate.

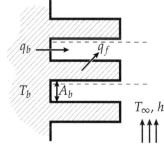

Figure 7.5: Array of fins of uniform cross-section.

Example 7.1:

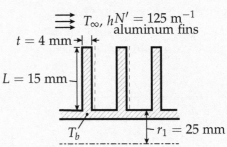

$$T_\infty, hN' = 125 \text{ m}^{-1}$$
aluminum fins
$t = 4$ mm
$L = 15$ mm
T_b
$r_1 = 25$ mm

Known: Dimensions and temperature conditions for aluminum fins on a tube that is exposed to air with $T_b = 200°C$, $T_\infty = 20°C$, and $h = 40$ W/m²·°C as shown.

Find: Fin efficiency, fin effectiveness, and rate of heat transfer per unit length of the tube.

Assumptions: Steady state, one-dimensional radial conduction in fins, constant properties, uniform convection coefficient.

Properties: The thermal conductivity of aluminum is approximately $k = 240$ W/m·°C.

Analysis: The fin parameters are

$$\frac{(r_2 + t/2)}{r_1} = \frac{0.04 \text{ m} + 0.002 \text{ m}}{0.025 \text{ m}} = 1.68,$$

$$(L + t/2)\sqrt{h/kt} = (0.015 \text{ m} + 0.002 \text{ m}) \times$$
$$\sqrt{40 \text{ W/m}^2 \cdot°C / (240 \text{ W/m} \cdot°C)(0.004 \text{ m})}$$
$$= 0.11,$$

$$A_f = 2\pi\left(r_2^2 - r_1^2\right) + 2\pi r_2 t$$
$$= 2\pi\left(0.04^2 - 0.025^2\right) \text{ m}^2 + 2\pi(0.04 \text{ m})(0.004 \text{ m})$$
$$= 7.13 \times 10^{-3} \text{ m}^2,$$
$$A_b = 2\pi r_1 t = 2\pi(0.025 \text{ m})(0.004 \text{ m})$$
$$= 6.28 \times 10^{-4} \text{ m}^2.$$

From Fig. 7.4 we see that $\eta_f = 0.97$; thus, using (7.24), we obtain

$$q_f = \eta_f q_{max} = \eta_f h A_f \theta_b$$
$$= (0.97)\left(40 \text{ W/m}^2 \cdot°C\right)\left(7.13 \times 10^{-3} \text{ m}^2\right)(180°C)$$
$$= 50 \text{ W}.$$

Then, from (7.20), the fin effectiveness is

$$\epsilon_f = \frac{q_f}{h\,A_b\,\theta_b} = \frac{50\text{ W}}{\left(40\,\text{W/m}^2 \cdot{}^\circ\text{C}\right)(6.28 \times 10^{-4}\,\text{m}^2)(180^\circ\text{C})} = 11.06.$$

Lastly, the rate of heat transfer per unit length of the tube is

$$
\begin{aligned}
q' &= N'\,q_f + h\,(1 - N'\,t)\,(2\,\pi\,r_1)\,\theta_b \\
&= (125\,1/\text{m})\,(50\text{ W}) + \\
&\quad \left(40\,\text{W/m}^2 \cdot{}^\circ\text{C}\right)[1 - (125\,1/\text{m})\,(0.004\text{ m})] \times \\
&\quad 2\,\pi\,(0.025\text{ m})\,180^\circ\text{C} \\
&= (6250 + 565)\text{ W/m} = 6.825\text{ kW/m}.
\end{aligned}
$$

Comments: Note the dominant contribution made by the fins to the total heat transfer.

Exercises 7:

1. A thin fin of length L has its two ends attached to two parallel walls which have temperatures T_1 and T_2. The fin loses heat by convection to the ambient air at T_∞. Obtain an analytical expression for the 1=D temperature distribution along the length of the fin and find the heat transfer rate.

2. A thin brass pipe, 3 cm in outside diameter, carries hot water at 85°C. It is proposed to place 0.8 mm thick straight circular fins on the pipe to cool it. The fins are 8 cm in diameter and are spaced 2 cm apart. It is determined that h will equal 20 $\text{W/m}^2\cdot{}^\circ\text{C}$ on the pipe and 15 $\text{W/m}^2\cdot{}^\circ\text{C}$ on the fins, when they have been added. If $T_\infty = 22^\circ\text{C}$, compute the heat loss per meter of pipe before and after the fins are added.

3. A transformer generating 400 W of heat, with its casing, may be modeled as a vertical cylinder, 0.3 m diameter by 0.4 m high. Cooling is only from the vertical sides by natural convection of the air at $T_\infty = 20^\circ\text{C}$ with a heat transfer coefficient of $h = 5.6\ \text{W/m}^2\cdot{}^\circ\text{C}$. i) What is the temperature of the surface of the casing? To improve the cooling, longitudinal aluminum fins (with $k = 200\ \text{W/m}\cdot{}^\circ\text{C}$), 1 mm thick and 10 mm long, with a 6 mm pitch, are added to the outside of the casing. Assuming h is unchanged: ii) what is the fin efficiency? iii) what is the new casing surface temperature?

8 Steady-state 2-D Conduction

The general steady-state form of the equation of heat conduction given by the partial differential equation (3.3) is

$$\nabla \cdot (k \nabla T) + q_g''' = 0.$$

We will assume that the thermal conductivity is constant and no heat is generated within the material, in which case the equation reduces to Laplace's equation which we write explicitly in the 2-D Cartesian coordinate form:

$$\nabla^2 T = 0 \qquad \text{or} \qquad \frac{\partial^2 T}{\partial x^2} + \frac{\partial^2 T}{\partial y^2} = 0. \tag{8.1}$$

To fully define a problem, we need to describe the geometry of the material and provide appropriate boundary conditions. In the 2-D Cartesian case, a simple geometry is a rectangular domain with two boundary conditions in each of the x and y coordinate directions. Two general approaches are used to solve multi-dimensional steady-state heat conduction problems:

i) separation of variables — provides exact solutions, but is limited to linear problems defined on simple geometries; and

ii) numerical methods — provides approximate but accurate solutions for linear and nonlinear problems defined on simple or complex geometries.

While numerical methods provide general and effective means for solving fairly general problems, they will not be discussed in the present text. The reader is encouraged to learn about such methods as they find utility no only in heat transfer, but in all branches of engineering and science. Here we will focus on the use of separation of variables. Indeed, we will outline the procedure through an example.

8.1 Separation of Variables

We first recall a few mathematical facts which are essential in the application of the separation of variables procedure.

An infinite sequence of basis functions $\{\varphi_n(x)\}$ is said to be *orthogonal* in the domain $a \le x \le b$ with weight $w(x)$ if

$$\int_a^b \varphi_m(x)\,\varphi_n(x)\,w(x)\,dx = C(n)\,\delta_{mn},$$

where $C(n)$ is a constant that depends on n and

$$\delta_{mn} = \begin{cases} 1, & m = n \\ 0, & m \neq n \end{cases}$$

is the Kronecker delta symbol. A function $f(x)$ may be expressed by an infinite series of orthogonal functions. Specifically, $\{\varphi_n(x)\} = \{1, \cos x, \sin x, \cos n x, \sin n x, \ldots\}$, $a = -L$ and $b = L$ with weight $w(x) = 1$ provides the Fourier series representation

$$f(x) = \frac{a_0}{2} + \sum_{n=1}^{\infty} \left(a_n \cos \frac{n \pi x}{L} + b_n \sin \frac{n \pi x}{L} \right), \tag{8.2}$$

where

$$a_n = \frac{1}{L} \int_{-L}^{L} f(x) \cos \frac{n \pi x}{L}\,dx, \quad n = 0, 1, 2, \ldots, \tag{8.3}$$

and

$$b_n = \frac{1}{L} \int_{-L}^{L} f(x) \sin \frac{n \pi x}{L}\,dx, \quad n = 1, 2, \ldots. \tag{8.4}$$

Note that

$$\int_{-L}^{L} \cos \frac{m \pi x}{L} \cos \frac{n \pi x}{L}\,dx = L\,\delta_{mn}, \tag{8.5}$$

$$\int_{-L}^{L} \sin \frac{m \pi x}{L} \sin \frac{n \pi x}{L}\,dx = L\,\delta_{mn}, \tag{8.6}$$

$$\int_{-L}^{L} \cos \frac{m \pi x}{L} \sin \frac{n \pi x}{L}\,dx = 0. \tag{8.7}$$

Example 8.1:

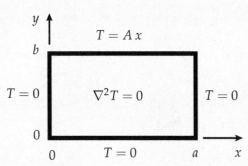

Known: We would like to solve the problem illustrated above.

Find: The temperature $T(x, y)$.

Assumptions: This heat conduction problem assumes 2-D, steady-state, constant properties, and $q_g''' = 0$.

Properties: No properties are required.

Analysis: We assume that the solution is separable,

$$T\left(x,y\right) = X\left(x\right) Y\left(y\right),$$

and substitute this assumption into (8.1) to obtain

$$X''(x)\,Y(y) + X(x)\,Y''(y) = 0.$$

Note that we are using prime superscripts to denote both the derivatives of X with respect to x and the derivatives of Y with respect to y; hopefully this does not lead to confusion since the functional dependences of $X(x)$ and $Y(y)$ are obvious. Now separating the variables which depend on x and y to different sides of the equation, we realize that the only way that a function of x is equal to a function of y is if both functions are equal to a constant:

$$\frac{X''(x)}{X(x)} = -\frac{Y''(y)}{Y(y)} = -\lambda^2.$$

Note that, without loss of generality, we have selected the separation constant to be negative; it can be shown that positive or zero values of the separation constant do not lead to acceptable solutions. Subsequently, the partial differential equation (8.1) is reduced to the following two ordinary differential equations with corresponding general solutions:

$$X''(x) + \lambda^2 X(x) = 0 \quad \rightarrow \quad X\left(x\right) = C_1 \cos \lambda\, x + C_2 \sin \lambda\, x,$$

$$Y''(y) - \lambda^2 Y(y) = 0 \quad \rightarrow \quad Y\left(y\right) = C_3 \cosh \lambda\, y + C_4 \sinh \lambda\, y.$$

The procedure continues by reducing and applying boundary conditions in the coordinate direction for which such conditions are homogeneous. In this case we see that both conditions in the x direction are homogeneous, thus we have that

$$T\left(0,y\right) = X\left(0\right) Y\left(y\right) = 0 \quad \rightarrow \quad X\left(0\right) = 0,$$
$$T\left(a,y\right) = X\left(a\right) Y\left(y\right) = 0 \quad \rightarrow \quad X\left(a\right) = 0.$$

The homogeneous boundary condition in the y direction results in

$$T\left(x,0\right) = X\left(x\right) Y\left(0\right) = 0 \quad \rightarrow \quad Y\left(0\right) = 0.$$

Now

$$X(0) = 0 \quad \rightarrow \quad C_1 = 0,$$

$$X(a) = 0 = C_2 \sin \lambda a \quad \rightarrow \quad \lambda_n = \frac{n\pi}{a} \quad n = 1, 2, \ldots$$

so that

$$X_n(x) = C_n \sin \frac{n\pi x}{a}.$$

Furthermore, we have

$$Y(0) = 0 \quad \rightarrow \quad C_3 = 0,$$

so that

$$Y_n(y) = D_n \sinh \frac{n\pi y}{a}$$

and thus

$$T(x,y) = \sum_{n=1}^{\infty} B_n \sin \frac{n\pi x}{a} \sinh \frac{n\pi y}{a}.$$

Lastly, using the non-homogeneous boundary condition,

$$T(x,b) = Ax = \sum_{n=1}^{\infty} B_n \sin \frac{n\pi x}{a} \sinh \frac{n\pi b}{a},$$

multiplying both sides by $\sin(m\pi x)/a$, and integrating from 0 to a, we have

$$\int_0^a (Ax) \sin \frac{m\pi x}{a} \, dx = \sum_{n=1}^{\infty} B_n \sinh \frac{n\pi b}{a} \int_0^a \sin \frac{n\pi x}{a} \sin \frac{m\pi x}{a} \, dx.$$

Subsequently, using the orthogonality of the basis, we have that

$$\int_0^a (Ax) \sin \frac{m\pi x}{a} \, dx = B_m \sinh \frac{m\pi b}{a} \int_0^a \left(\sin \frac{m\pi x}{a} \right)^2 dx$$

or

$$\frac{A a^2}{m\pi} (-1)^{m+1} = B_m \sinh \frac{m\pi b}{a} \left(\frac{a}{2} \right),$$

so

$$B_n = \frac{2 A a (-1)^{n+1}}{n\pi \sinh \frac{n\pi b}{a}}$$

and

$$T(x,y) = \frac{2Aa}{\pi} \sum_{n=1}^{\infty} \frac{(-1)^{n+1}}{n} \sin \left(\frac{n\pi x}{a} \right) \frac{\sinh(n\pi y/a)}{\sinh(n\pi b/a)}.$$

Comments: i) It may be necessary to transform the dependent variable so as to obtain homogeneous boundary conditions in one coordinate direction; ii) the separated problem with all homogeneous boundary conditions should be solved first — this problem gives rise to the eigenvalues; iii) the integer $n = 0$ would not be acceptable since it would lead to a trivial solution of the problem; iv) always apply the non-homogeneous boundary conditions after the separated dependent variables are recombined into the original dependent variable; v) to use the orthogonality properties (8.5)–(8.7) directly, it may be convenient if one first takes

$$z = 2x - a \quad \text{or} \quad x = \frac{z + a}{2}$$

so that

$$\int_0^a f(x)\, dx \rightarrow \frac{1}{2} \int_{-a}^a f(z)\, dz.$$

Exercises 8:

1. Verify that the separation constant must be negative.

2. Example 8.1 is modified so that the temperature along the $y = b$ boundary is given by the arbitrary function $f(x)$. Find the temperature distribution within the region. What is the solution for the special case $f(x) = A = \text{const.}$?

3. Since equation (8.1) is linear, use the principle of superposition to solve the problem in Example 8.1 with boundary conditions $T(0, y) = T_1$, $T(a, y) = T_2$, $T(x, 0) = T_3$, and $T(x, b) = T_4$, where T_i, $i = 1, \ldots, 4$ are constants.

9 Transient 0-D Conduction

9.1 Lumped Capacitance Approximation

Let's consider the transient thermal response of the body illustrated in Fig. 9.1. We will assume that the body does not generate heat, $q_g''' = 0$ (this assumption can be relaxed). The unsteady temperature of the body is then described by Eq. (3.3) with the body having some initial temperature that is assumed larger than that of the surrounding fluid, $T_i > T_\infty$, both assumed constant, and with convective boundary conditions, as indicated in the illustration. In the lumped capacitance method, we assume that the temperature of the body is spatially uniform at any instant of time. Clearly, this is a good approximation when

$$\nabla T \ll 1 \quad \text{or} \quad k \to \infty. \tag{9.1}$$

An energy balance over the body now immediately results in

$$q_{st} = -q_{out} \quad \text{or} \quad \rho V c_p \frac{dT}{dt} = -h A_s (T - T_\infty),$$

where $T(t)$ is the instantaneous temperature of the body, and $T(0) = T_i$. Let

$$\theta \equiv T - T_\infty \quad \text{and} \quad \boxed{\tau_t \equiv \frac{\rho V c_p}{h A_s}}, \tag{9.2}$$

where τ_t is the *thermal time constant*.

Now, the problem can be rewritten as

$$\frac{d\theta}{dt} + \frac{\theta}{\tau_t} = 0, \quad \theta(0) = \theta_i = T_i - T_\infty \tag{9.3}$$

with the solution given by

$$\frac{\theta}{\theta_i} = \frac{T - T_\infty}{T_i - T_\infty} = e^{-t/\tau_t} \tag{9.4}$$

and qualitatively illustrated in Fig. 9.2. Note that $\theta \to 0$ (or $T \to T_\infty$) as $t \to \infty$.

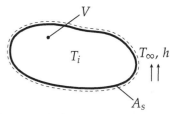

Figure 9.1: Body.

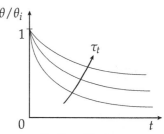

Figure 9.2: Cooling of body.

Note:

- We can write $\tau_t = R_t C_t$, where $R_t = 1/h A_s$ and $C_t = \rho V c_p$ are the *thermal resistance* and *capacitance*, respectively, which combined make up the *lumped thermal capacitance*. The problem can then be represented by the electrical circuit shown in Fig. 9.3.

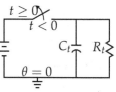

Figure 9.3: Lumped capacitance RC circuit.

9.2   Energy Transfer

The total energy change in the body at time t is clearly equal to the convected energy gained or lost, $Q = -\Delta E_{st}$. To see this, consider

$$-\Delta E_{st} = -\int_0^t \dot{E}_{st}(t)\, dt = -\left[E_{st}(t) - E_{st}(0)\right]$$
$$= -\rho\, c_p \int_V \left[T(\mathbf{x}, t) - T_i\right] dV, \qquad (9.5)$$

where we have assumed that ρ and c_p are constant. Now, within the lumped capacitance approximation we have that $T(\mathbf{x}, t) = T(t)$. Thus,

$$-\Delta E_{st} = -\rho\, V\, c_p\, (T - T_i)$$
$$= \rho\, V\, c_p\, \left[(T_i - T_\infty) - (T - T_\infty)\right]$$
$$= \rho\, V\, c_p\, \theta_i \left(1 - \frac{\theta}{\theta_i}\right)$$
$$= \rho\, V\, c_p\, \theta_i \left(1 - e^{-t/\tau_t}\right).$$

Note:

- If we take $Q_0 = \rho\, V\, c_p\, \theta_i$, which represents the initial energy stored in the body, then we can also write $Q/Q_0 = 1 - e^{-t/\tau_t}$.

On the other hand, the energy convected from the body to the fluid is given by

$$Q = -\int_0^t q_{conv}\, dt = -h\, A_s \int_0^t (T - T_\infty)\, dt = -h\, A_s \int_0^t \theta\, dt.$$

Using the solution (9.4), we readily see that

$$Q = \rho\, V\, c_p\, \theta_i \left(1 - e^{-t/\tau_t}\right), \qquad (9.6)$$

and thus $Q = -\Delta E_{st}$.

9.3   Validity of Lumped Capacitance Approximation

Let us examine the surface energy balance of the plane body illustrated in Fig. 9.4:

$$-k\, A\, \frac{dT}{dx}\bigg|_{x=L} = h\, A\, (T_{s,2} - T_\infty).$$

Assuming no energy sources, the temperature distribution within the body is linear and thus we have

$$-k\, A\, \frac{T_{s,2} - T_{s,1}}{L} = h\, A\, (T_{s,2} - T_\infty)$$

or

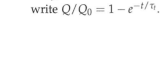
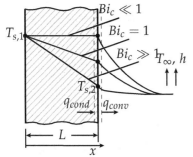

Figure 9.4: Temperature distributions.

$$\frac{T_{s,1} - T_{s,2}}{T_{s,2} - T_\infty} = \frac{h\, L}{k} = \frac{L/k\, A}{1/h\, A} = \frac{R_{cond}}{R_{conv}} = Bi_c$$

where Bi_c is the Biot number which is equal to the temperature drop by conduction divided by the temperature drop by convection, or analogously the conduction resistance divided by the convection resistance. Now, since the lumped capacitance approximation requires that (9.1) be satisfied, we subsequently must have that $Bi_c \ll 1$. Typically $Bi_c \lesssim 0.1$ is sufficiently small to allow the use of the approximation.

More generally, we will define the *lumped capacitance Biot number* as

$$Bi_c = \frac{h L_c}{k},$$ (9.7)

where the lumped capacitance characteristic length is given by

$$L_c = \frac{V}{A_s},$$ (9.8)

and V and A_s are the volume and the surface area of an arbitrary body. If we define the non-dimensional time

$$t^* = \frac{\alpha t}{L_c^2}, \qquad \alpha = \frac{k}{\rho c_p}$$ (9.9)

which is also called the *Fourier modulus*, then

$$\frac{t}{\tau_t} = Bi_c \, t^*$$ (9.10)

and subsequently we can write the solution as

$$\frac{\theta}{\theta_i} = e^{-Bi_c \, t^*}.$$ (9.11)

Characteristic lengths for a plane wall, a cylindrical section, and a sphere are provided in Fig. 9.5.

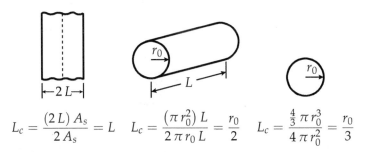

$$L_c = \frac{(2 L) A_s}{2 A_s} = L \qquad L_c = \frac{(\pi r_0^2) L}{2 \pi r_0 L} = \frac{r_0}{2} \qquad L_c = \frac{\frac{4}{3} \pi r_0^3}{4 \pi r_0^2} = \frac{r_0}{3}$$

Figure 9.5: Lumped capacitance characteristic lengths.

9.4 Lumped Capacitance Approximation Revisited

We will re-examine the lumped capacitance approximation using a more general approach. Starting from Eq. (3.3), we wish to obtain an equation describing the *spatially averaged temperature* of the arbitrary body illustrated in Fig. 9.1. Thus we write

$$\int_V \left[\rho c_p \frac{\partial T}{\partial t} - \nabla \cdot (k \nabla T) - q_g''' \right] dV = 0.$$

We now assume that ρ, c_p and V are constant (these assumptions can be relaxed) and use the divergence theorem to rewrite the above equation as

$$\rho\, c_p \frac{d}{dt} \int_V T\, dV = \int_{A_s} k\, \nabla T \cdot \mathbf{n}\, dA_s + \int_V q_g''' \, dV,$$

where $\mathbf{n}$ is the body's surface area normal vector. Subsequently, using the convection boundary condition on A_s,

$$-k\, \nabla T \cdot \mathbf{n} = h\, (T - T_\infty),$$

assuming that h is constant, $T_\infty = T_\infty(t)$, and defining volume and surface averages as

$$\overline{f} = \frac{1}{V} \int_V f\, dV \qquad \text{and} \qquad \overline{\overline{g}} = \frac{1}{A_s} \int_{A_s} g\, dA_s,$$

we arrive at the average equation for the body's temperature:

$$\rho\, V\, c_p \frac{d\overline{T}}{dt} = -h\, A_s \left(\overline{\overline{T}} - T_\infty \right) + V\overline{q}_g'''.$$

It is not necessary for q_g''' to be uniform in a body; all that is required is the volume averaged heat generation within the body. Clearly, if the body's temperature T is uniform in space, then $T = \overline{T} = \overline{\overline{T}}$ and we recover the standard lumped capacitance approximation. However, in cases where the temperature distribution in the body is not uniform, it may be possible to relate the average surface temperature to the body's average temperature, in which case, the above equation represents a *generalized lumped capacitance* equation.

Example 9.1:

Known: A pure copper sphere of diameter $d = 12.7$ mm, initially at a temperature of $T_i = 66°C$, is exposed to an air stream having a temperature of $T_\infty = 27°C$. The temperature of the sphere after 69 s is measure to be $55°C$.

Find: The convection heat transfer coefficient, h, between the sphere and the air stream.

Assumptions: The temperature of the sphere is spatially uniform so that the lumped capacitance analysis can be used (this can be verified after obtaining h) and the properties are constant.

Properties: The density, specific heat capacity, and thermal conductivity of pure copper are $\rho = 8960 \text{ kg/m}^3$, $c_p = 385 \text{ J/kg·°C}$, and $k = 401 \text{ W/m·°C}$.

Analysis: The temperature history is given by Eq. (9.4), so

$$\frac{\theta(t)}{\theta_i} = \frac{(55-27)°\text{C}}{(66-27)°\text{C}} = 0.718 = \exp\left(-\frac{69\,\text{s}}{\tau_t}\right),$$

and thus $\tau_t = 208$ s. Subsequently, using Eq. (9.2), we obtain

$$h = \frac{\rho V c_p}{\tau_t A_s} = \frac{(8960\,\text{kg/m}^3)(\pi\,0.0127^3/6\,\text{m}^3)(385\,\text{J/kg}\cdot°\text{C})}{(208\,\text{s})(\pi\,0.0127^2\text{m}^2)}$$

$$= 35.1\,\text{W/m}^2\cdot°\text{C}.$$

Comments: The lumped capacitance analysis is applicable since (see Eq. (9.7))

$$Bi_c = \frac{h\,(d/6)}{k} = \frac{(35.1\,\text{W/m}^2\cdot°\text{C})(0.0127/6\,\text{m})}{401\,\text{W/m}\cdot°\text{C}} = 1.85\times 10^{-4},$$

which is much less than 0.1.

Exercises 9:

1. A thermocouple is being used to measure the temperature of a stream of air with $h = 74.17 \text{ W/m}^2\cdot°\text{C}$. The temperature of the air suddenly changes from 20°C to 100°C. If the thermocouple junction can be modeled as a 3 mm diameter sphere (with properties $\rho = 8600 \text{ kg/m}^3$, $c_p = 400 \text{ J/kg·°C}$, and $k = 30 \text{ W/m·°C}$) with negligible conduction down the wires, how long will it take for the measured temperature to reach i) 90°C and ii) 99°C? Show that the lumped capacitance approximation is justified.

2. Determine the time constant for a spherically shaped, copper-constantan thermocouple at an average temperature of 20°C, exposed to a convective environment where $h = 110 \text{ W/m}^2\cdot°\text{C}$, for a bead diameter of i) 0.125 mm and ii) 0.25 mm.

3. A body of known volume, surface area, and temperature T_i is suddenly immersed in a bath whose temperature is rising as $T_{bath} = T_i + (T_0 - T_i)e^{t/\tau}$, where T_0 is a constant. If h is known, $\tau = 10\rho c_p V/h A_s$, t is measured from the time of immersion, and the Biot number of the body is small, find the temperature response of the body. Plot it and the bath temperature against time up to $t = 2\tau$.

10 Transient 1-D Conduction

Assuming 1-D, constant properties, and no heat generation, from (3.6) we have

$$\frac{\partial T}{\partial t} = \frac{\alpha}{r^n} \frac{\partial}{\partial r}\left(r^n \frac{\partial T}{\partial r}\right), \quad n = 0,\ 1,\ 2, \tag{10.1}$$

where $n = 0$ for Cartesian coordinates with $r \rightarrow x$, $n = 1$ for cylindrical coordinates, and $n = 2$ for spherical coordinates, and with initial and boundary conditions

$$T(r,0) = T_i, \quad \left.\frac{\partial T}{\partial r}\right|_{r=0} < \infty, \quad -k \left.\frac{\partial T}{\partial r}\right|_{r=r_0} = h\left[T(r_0,t) - T_\infty\right]. \tag{10.2}$$

For a plane layer ($n = 0$) such that $-L \le r \le L$, the condition at $r = 0$ is replaced by the symmetry condition $\partial T/\partial r = 0$ and $r_0 = L$. We now note that the solution for a chosen n must be a function of the independent variables r and t, and all parameters appearing in the problem:

$$T = T(r, t; T_i, T_\infty, r_0, k, \alpha, h). \tag{10.3}$$

10.1 Non-dimensionalization

It is useful to non-dimensionalize the problem to reduce the number of parameters which the solution depends on. Recalling that $\theta = T - T_\infty$, we take

$$\theta^* \equiv \frac{\theta}{\theta_i} = \frac{T - T_\infty}{T_i - T_\infty}, \quad r^* \equiv \frac{r}{r_0}, \quad t^* \equiv \frac{\alpha t}{r_0^2}. \tag{10.4}$$

With these normalizations, the differential equation (10.1) and initial and boundary conditions (10.2) become

$$\frac{\partial \theta^*}{\partial t^*} = \frac{1}{r^{*n}} \frac{\partial}{\partial r^*}\left(r^{*n} \frac{\partial \theta^*}{\partial r^*}\right), \quad n = 0,\ 1,\ 2, \tag{10.5}$$

$$\theta^*(r^*,0) = 1, \quad \left.\frac{\partial \theta^*}{\partial r^*}\right|_{r^*=0} < \infty, \quad \left.\frac{\partial \theta^*}{\partial r^*}\right|_{r^*=1} = -Bi\,\theta^*(1,t^*), \tag{10.6}$$

Notes:

- Taking $h = 0$ would provide the adiabatic boundary condition $\partial T/\partial r = 0$ at $r = r_0$.

- Taking $k = 0$ would provide the isothermal boundary condition $T(r_0,t) = T_\infty$ at $r = r_0$.

Notes:

- The dimensionless time, t^*, is also referred to as the Fourier modulus, *Fo*.

- Taking $Bi = 0$ would provide the adiabatic boundary condition $\partial \theta^*/\partial r^* = 0$ at $r^* = 1$.

- Taking $Bi \rightarrow \infty$ would provide the isothermal boundary condition $\theta^*(1,t^*) = 0$ at $r^* = 1$.

where

$$\theta^* (1,t) = \frac{T (r_0,t) - T_\infty}{T_i - T_\infty},$$ (10.7)

and

$$Bi = \frac{h \, r_0}{k}.$$ (10.8)

For a plane layer ($n = 0$), the condition at $r^* = 0$ is replaced by the symmetry condition $\partial \theta^* / \partial r^* = 0$. Now note that the dimensionless solution corresponding to (10.3), in addition to the dimensionless independent variables, depends only on the Biot number:

$$\theta^* = \theta^* (r^*, t^*; Bi).$$ (10.9)

Notes:

• Note the different length scale in the Biot number, Bi, than in lumped capacitance method with Bi_c.

10.2 Total Energy Transferred up to Time t

We recall from Eq. (9.5) that given the solution $T(r,t)$ we can compute the energy transferred by a body from

$$\frac{Q}{Q_{max}} = \frac{1}{V} \int \left(\frac{T_i - T}{T_i - T_\infty} \right) dV,$$ (10.10)

where

$$Q = \rho \, c_p \int_V [T_i - T (r,t)] \, dV \quad \text{and} \quad Q_{max} = \rho \, c_p \, V \, (T_i - T_\infty). \quad (10.11)$$

Non-dimensionalizing the above expression, we see that

$$Q^* = \frac{Q}{Q_{max}} = \frac{1}{V} \int \frac{(T_i - T_\infty) - [T (r,t) - T_\infty]}{T_i - T_\infty} \, dV,$$

or

$$Q^* = \frac{1}{V^*} \int_{V^*} (1 - \theta^*) \, dV^*.$$ (10.12)

10.3 Separation of Variables

Suppressing the dependence on the Biot number, we assume a solution of the form $\theta^* (r^*, t^*) = R (r^*) \, \tau (t^*)$ and substitute it into Eq. (10.5):

$$R \tau' = \frac{\tau}{r^{*n}} \frac{\partial}{\partial r^*} (r^{*n} R') = \frac{\tau}{r^{*n}} \left[n \, r^{*n-1} R' + r^{*n} R'' \right].$$

Primes denote derivatives of the new dependent variables with respect to the corresponding independent variables. Separating such dependences, and introducing a negative separation constant, we have

$$\frac{\tau'}{\tau} = \frac{n}{r^*} \frac{R'}{R} + \frac{R''}{R} = -\lambda^2.$$

Notes:

• It can be shown that only a negative separation constant leads to an acceptable solution.

Subsequently, we see that

$$\tau' + \lambda^2 \tau = 0, \tag{10.13}$$

with general solution

$$\tau(t^*) = C\,e^{-\lambda^2 t^*}, \tag{10.14}$$

and

$$R'' + \frac{n}{r^*} R' + \lambda^2 R = 0, \tag{10.15}$$

Note:

- The boundedness condition $\partial \theta^* / \partial r^* |_{r^*=0} < \infty$ in this case reduces to the symmetry condition $\partial \theta^* / \partial r^* |_{r^*=0} = 0$ or $R'(0) = 0$.

satisfying the boundary conditions

$$R'(0) = 0, \quad R'(1) + Bi\,R(1) = 0. \tag{10.16}$$

The problem for $R(r)$ corresponds to a *Sturm-Liouville* problem whose solutions for $n = 0, 1$, and 2 satisfying the inhomogeneous initial condition

$$\theta^*(r^*, 0) = 1 \tag{10.17}$$

are given by

10.3.1   *Plane Wall:*

Note:

- For $t^* \gtrsim 0.2$, the first term in this infinite series, as well as in those given below, is sufficient. See Table 10.1 for specific values of λ_1 and C_1.

- When $t^* \lesssim 0.2$ the solutions are also displayed in graphical forms called Heisler charts.

$$\theta^* = \sum_{n=1}^{\infty} C_n \exp\left(-\lambda_n^2 t^*\right) \cos\left(\lambda_n x^*\right), \tag{10.18}$$

where

$$\lambda_n \tan \lambda_n = Bi, \quad \text{and} \quad C_n = \frac{4 \sin \lambda_n}{2\lambda_n + \sin\left(2\lambda_n\right)}. \tag{10.19}$$

For $t^* \gtrsim 0.2$,

$$\theta^* = \theta_0^* \cos\left(\lambda_1 x^*\right), \quad \theta_0^* = C_1 \exp\left(-\lambda_1^2 t^*\right), \quad Q^* = 1 - \frac{\sin \lambda_1}{\lambda_1}\theta_0^*. \tag{10.20}$$

10.3.2   *Infinite Cylinder:*

Note:

- J_0 and J_1 are Bessel functions of the first kind of order 0 and 1, respectively. Their values are given in Table 10.2.

$$\theta^* = \sum_{n=1}^{\infty} C_n \exp\left(-\lambda_n^2 t^*\right) J_0\left(\lambda_n r^*\right), \tag{10.21}$$

where

$$\lambda_n \frac{J_1(\lambda_n)}{J_0(\lambda_n)} = Bi, \quad \text{and} \quad C_n = \frac{2}{\lambda_n} \frac{J_1(\lambda_n)}{J_0^2(\lambda_n) + J_1^2(\lambda_n)}. \tag{10.22}$$

For $t^* \gtrsim 0.2$,

$$\theta^* = \theta_0^* J_0\left(\lambda_1 r^*\right), \quad \theta_0^* = C_1 \exp\left(-\lambda_1^2 t^*\right), \quad Q^* = 1 - \frac{2 J_1(\lambda_1)}{\lambda_1}\theta_0^*. \tag{10.23}$$

Bi	Plane Wall λ_1	C_1	Cylinder λ_1	C_1	Sphere λ_1	C_1
0.01	0.0998	1.0017	0.1412	1.0025	0.1730	1.0030
0.02	0.1410	1.0033	0.1995	1.0050	0.2445	1.0060
0.04	0.1987	1.0066	0.2814	1.0099	0.3450	1.0120
0.06	0.2425	1.0098	0.3438	1.0148	0.4217	1.0179
0.08	0.2791	1.0130	0.3960	1.0197	0.4860	1.0239
0.1	0.3111	1.0161	0.4417	1.0246	0.5423	1.0298
0.2	0.4328	1.0311	0.6170	1.0483	0.7593	1.0592
0.3	0.5218	1.0450	0.7465	1.0712	0.9208	1.0880
0.4	0.5932	1.0580	0.8516	1.0931	1.0528	1.1164
0.5	0.6533	1.0701	0.9408	1.1143	1.1656	1.1441
0.6	0.7051	1.0814	1.0184	1.1345	1.2644	1.1713
0.7	0.7506	1.0918	1.0873	1.1539	1.3525	1.1978
0.8	0.7910	1.1016	1.1490	1.1724	1.4320	1.2236
0.9	0.8274	1.1107	1.2048	1.1902	1.5044	1.2488
1.0	0.8603	1.1191	1.2558	1.2071	1.5708	1.2732
2.0	1.0769	1.1785	1.5995	1.3384	2.0288	1.4793
3.0	1.1925	1.2102	1.7887	1.4191	2.2889	1.6227
4.0	1.2646	1.2287	1.9081	1.4698	2.4556	1.7202
5.0	1.3138	1.2403	1.9898	1.5029	2.5704	1.7870
6.0	1.3496	1.2479	2.0490	1.5253	2.6537	1.8338
7.0	1.3766	1.2532	2.0937	1.5411	2.7165	1.8673
8.0	1.3978	1.2570	2.1286	1.5526	2.7654	1.8920
9.0	1.4149	1.2598	2.1566	1.5611	2.8044	1.9106
10.0	1.4289	1.2620	2.1795	1.5677	2.8363	1.9249
20.0	1.4961	1.2699	2.2880	1.5919	2.9857	1.9781
30.0	1.5202	1.2717	2.3261	1.5973	3.0372	1.9898
40.0	1.5325	1.2723	2.3455	1.5993	3.0632	1.9942
50.0	1.5400	1.2727	2.3572	1.6002	3.0788	1.9962
100.0	1.5552	1.2731	2.3809	1.6015	3.1102	1.9990
∞	1.5708	1.2732	2.4048	1.6021	3.1416	2.0000

Table 10.1: Quantities used in the one-term approximate solution of transient 1-D heat conduction in plane walls, cylinders, and spheres.

Table 10.2: Zeroth- and first-order Bessel functions of the first kind.

η	$J_0(\eta)$	$J_1(\eta)$
0.0	1.0000	0.0000
0.1	0.9975	0.0499
0.2	0.9900	0.0995
0.3	0.9776	0.1483
0.4	0.9604	0.1960
0.5	0.9385	0.2423
0.6	0.9120	0.2867
0.7	0.8812	0.3290
0.8	0.8463	0.3688
0.9	0.8075	0.4059
1.0	0.7652	0.4400
1.1	0.7196	0.4709
1.2	0.6711	0.4983
1.3	0.6201	0.5220
1.4	0.5669	0.5419
1.5	0.5118	0.5579
1.6	0.4554	0.5699
1.7	0.3980	0.5778
1.8	0.3400	0.5815
1.9	0.2818	0.5812
2.0	0.2239	0.5767
2.1	0.1666	0.5683
2.2	0.1104	0.5560
2.3	0.0555	0.5399
2.4	0.0025	0.5202
2.6	0.0968	0.4708
2.8	0.1850	0.4097
3.0	0.2601	0..3391
3.2	0.3202	0..2613

10.3.3   Sphere:

$$\theta^* = \sum_{n=1}^{\infty} C_n \exp\left(-\lambda_n^2\, t^*\right) \frac{\sin\left(\lambda_n\, r^*\right)}{\lambda_n\, r^*}, \tag{10.24}$$

where

$$1 - \lambda_n \cot \lambda_n = Bi, \quad \text{and} \quad C_n = \frac{4\left(\sin \lambda_n - \lambda_n \cos \lambda_n\right)}{2\,\lambda_n - \sin\left(2\,\lambda_n\right)}. \tag{10.25}$$

For $t^* \gtrsim 0.2$,

$$\theta^* = \theta_0^* \frac{\sin\left(\lambda_1\, r^*\right)}{\lambda_1\, r^*}, \quad \theta_0^* = C_1 \exp\left(-\lambda_1^2\, t^*\right),$$

$$Q^* = 1 - 3\,\frac{\left(\sin \lambda_1 - \lambda_1 \cos \lambda_1\right)}{\lambda_1^3}\,\theta_0^*. \tag{10.26}$$

10.4   Semi-infinite Region

We would like to examine the unsteady 1-D solution in a semi-infinite region:

$$\frac{\partial T}{\partial t} = \alpha\,\frac{\partial^2 T}{\partial x^2},$$

with initial and boundary condition

$$T\left(x,0\right) = T_i \quad \text{and} \quad T\left(\infty, t\right) = T_i.$$

The last boundary condition is provided at the surface of the semi-infinite region, $x = 0$. We consider three choices for this condition:

(a) $T\left(0, t\right) = T_0$,

(b) $-k\,\dfrac{\partial T}{\partial x}\bigg|_{x=0} = q_0''$,

(c) $-k\,\dfrac{\partial T}{\partial x}\bigg|_{x=0} = h\left(T_\infty - T\left(0, t\right)\right)$

where T_0, q_0'', and T_∞ are prescribed constant quantities. The separation of variables technique does not work in any of the above cases. Nevertheless, such problems can be tackled by using similarity arguments or by the Laplace transform method. We will discuss in detail case (a), but corresponding solutions to cases (b) and (c) are given as well.

The solution through similarity arguments proceeds as follows. We first introduce a dimensionless temperature,

$$\theta^* = \frac{\theta}{\theta_0} = \frac{T - T_i}{T_0 - T_i}, \tag{10.27}$$

TRANSIENT 1-D CONDUCTION 57

so that the equation, and initial and boundary conditions become:

$$\frac{\partial \theta^*}{\partial t} = \alpha \frac{\partial^2 \theta^*}{\partial x^2} \qquad (10.28)$$

$$\theta^*(x,0) = 0, \qquad \theta^*(0,t) = 1, \quad \text{and} \quad \theta^*(\infty,t) = 0. \qquad (10.29)$$

Since the initial and boundary conditions contain only pure numbers, the solution of the differential equation has to be of the form $\theta^* = \theta^*(x,t;\alpha)$. However, since θ^* is a dimensionless function, the quantities x, t and α must always appear in a dimensionless combination. The only dimensionless combination of these three quantities are $x/\sqrt{\alpha t}$ or powers or multiples thereof. We therefore conclude that

$$\theta^* = \theta^*(\eta), \qquad \text{where} \qquad \eta = \frac{x}{\sqrt{4\alpha t}}. \qquad (10.30)$$

The "4" is included so that the final result will look neater; of course we know this only after solving the problem without it. The form of the solution in Eq. (10.30) is possible essentially because there is no characteristic length or time scale in the physical system.

We now convert the derivatives in x and t in the differential equation (10.28) into derivatives with respect to the new variable η:

$$\frac{\partial \theta^*}{\partial t} = \frac{d\theta^*}{d\eta}\frac{\partial \eta}{\partial t} = -\frac{1}{2}\frac{\eta}{t}\frac{d\theta^*}{d\eta},$$

$$\frac{\partial \theta^*}{\partial x} = \frac{d\theta^*}{d\eta}\frac{\partial \eta}{\partial x} = \frac{1}{\sqrt{4\alpha t}}\frac{d\theta^*}{d\eta} \quad \text{and} \quad \frac{\partial^2 \theta^*}{\partial x^2} = \frac{1}{4\alpha t}\frac{d^2\theta^*}{d\eta^2}.$$

Substituting these expressions into (10.28) and (10.29), we obtain the following boundary value problem:

$$\frac{d^2\theta^*}{d\eta^2} + 2\eta\frac{d\theta^*}{d\eta} = 0 \qquad \text{and} \qquad \theta^*(0) = 1, \quad \theta^*(\infty) = 0. \qquad (10.31)$$

If we now let $\phi = d\theta^*/d\eta$, we obtain a simple first-order equation for ϕ whose general solution is given by

$$\phi = \frac{d\theta^*}{d\eta} = c_1 e^{-\eta^2}. \qquad (10.32)$$

A second integration gives

$$\theta^* = c_1 \int_0^\eta e^{-\bar{\eta}^2} d\bar{\eta} + c_2. \qquad (10.33)$$

Application of the two boundary conditions, makes it possible to evaluate the two constants, and thus obtain

$$\theta^* = 1 - \frac{\int_0^\eta e^{-\bar{\eta}^2} d\bar{\eta}}{\int_0^\infty e^{-\bar{\eta}^2} d\bar{\eta}} = 1 - \frac{2}{\sqrt{\pi}}\int_0^\eta e^{-\bar{\eta}^2} d\bar{\eta}$$

or

$$\text{for } T(0,t) = T_0$$

$$\theta^* = 1 - \operatorname{erf} \eta = \operatorname{erfc} \eta. \qquad (10.34)$$

The function erf η expressed by the integral in the above expression is called the *error function*. It is a special function that is well-known and usually represented in table form or as a graph. The related function erfc η is called the *complementary error function*.

The second approach to solve (10.28)-(10.29) is to use the Laplace transform approach. In this case, defining the Laplace transform of θ^* by

$$\theta^* (x,t) \to \Theta (x,s) = \int_0^\infty \theta (x,t) e^{-st} dt, \quad Re(s) > C > 0,$$

the problem becomes

$$\frac{d^2 \Theta}{d x^2} - \frac{s}{\alpha} \Theta = 0, \quad \Theta (0,s) = \frac{1}{s}, \quad \Theta (\infty,s) = 0$$

whose general solution is given by

$$\Theta (x,s) = C_1 e^{\sqrt{s/\alpha}\,x} + C_2 e^{-\sqrt{s/\alpha}\,x}.$$

Applying the boundary conditions, we obtain C_1 and C_2,

$$\Theta (\infty,s) = 0 = C_1, \qquad \Theta (0,s) = \frac{1}{s} = C_2,$$

and subsequently can write the solution of the transformed problem:

$$\Theta (x,s) = \frac{1}{s} e^{-\sqrt{s/\alpha}\,x}$$

Now, the inverse Laplace transform is defined by

$$\Theta (x,s) \to \theta^* (x,t) = \frac{1}{2\pi i} \int_{\gamma - i\infty}^{\gamma + i\infty} \Theta (x,s) e^{st} ds, \quad \gamma > C > 0,$$

where $i = \sqrt{-1}$ denotes the imaginary number. Subsequently, we have

$$\theta^* (x,t) = \int_0^t \frac{x e^{-\frac{x^2}{4\alpha\tau}}}{2 \sqrt{\pi \alpha}\,\tau^{3/2}} d\tau$$

and if we let

$$\eta = \frac{x}{2 \sqrt{\alpha\tau}},$$

then we obtain

$$\theta^* (x,t) = \frac{2}{\sqrt{\pi}} \int_\eta^\infty e^{-\bar{\eta}^2} d\bar{\eta} = \operatorname{erfc}(\eta),$$

which is the same solution (10.34) obtained through similarity arguments.

We note that the solution in terms of the original variables is given by

$$\frac{T - T_i}{T_0 - T_i} = 1 - \text{erf}\left(\frac{x}{\sqrt{4\,\alpha\,t}}\right) = \text{erfc}\left(\frac{x}{\sqrt{4\,\alpha\,t}}\right). \qquad (10.35) \quad A$$

Using this solution, it is straightforward to also show that the heat flux at the surface is given by

$$q''(0,t) = -k\left.\frac{\partial T}{\partial x}\right|_{x=0} = \frac{k\,(T_0 - T_i)}{\sqrt{\pi\,\alpha\,t}}.$$

The corresponding solution for case (b) is

$$T - T_i = \frac{2\,q_0''\,(\alpha\,t/\pi)^{1/2}}{k}\,e^{-x^2/4\alpha t} - \frac{q_0''\,x}{k}\,\text{erfc}\left(\frac{x}{2\sqrt{\alpha\,t}}\right) \qquad (10.36) \quad B$$

and the surface temperature is

$$T(0,t) = T_i + \frac{2\,q_0''\,(\alpha\,t/\pi)^{1/2}}{k}. \qquad (10.37)$$

Lastly, the solution for case (c) is

$$\frac{T - T_i}{T_\infty - T_i} = \text{erfc}\left(\frac{x}{2\sqrt{\alpha\,t}}\right) - e^{\left(h x/k + h^2\,\alpha\,t/k^2\right)}\,\text{erfc}\left(\frac{x}{2\sqrt{\alpha\,t}} + \frac{h\sqrt{\alpha\,t}}{k}\right)$$
$$(10.38) \quad C$$

and the heat flux at the surface is given by

$$q''(0,t) = -k\left.\frac{\partial T}{\partial x}\right|_{x=0} = h\,(T_\infty - T(0,t)). \qquad (10.39)$$

Note:

- Note that when $h \to \infty$ and $T_\infty = T_0$ we recover the solution of case (a).

Example 10.1:

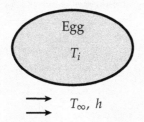

Egg

T_i

T_∞, h

Known: An egg with initial temperature of 5°C is dropped into boiling water at 100°C. The convection heat transfer coefficient is $h = 1000$ W/m²·°C.

Find: How long it takes for the center of the egg to reach 75°C.

Assumptions: The egg is approximated by a spherical shape having 5 cm diameter and does not crack in the water, 1-D conduction, the egg has the same properties as water, the properties are constant, and $t \gtrsim 0.2$ (this assumption can be verified after obtaining the solution).

Properties: The density, specific heat capacity, and thermal conductivity of water at the average temperature of $(5+75)°C/2 = 40°C$ are $\rho = 992.2 \text{ kg/m}^3$, $c_p = 4182 \text{ J/kg·°C}$, and $k = 0.631 \text{ W/m·°C}$. Subsequently, the thermal diffusivity is $\alpha = k/\rho c_p = 1.52 \times 10^{-7}$ m^2/s.

Analysis: The Biot number is

$$Bi = \frac{h\, r_0}{k} = \frac{(1000 \text{ W/m}^2 \cdot° \text{C})(0.025 \text{ m})}{0.631 \text{ W/m} \cdot° \text{C}} = 39.6.$$

From Table 10.1 we have the following leading coefficients for a sphere:

$$\lambda_1 = 3.063 \quad \text{and} \quad C_1 = 1.994.$$

Thus, from Eq. (10.26), we have

$$\theta_0^* = \frac{T(0, t^*) - T_\infty}{T_i - T_\infty} = C_1 \exp\left(-\lambda_1^2 t^*\right)$$

or

$$\frac{75 - 100}{5 - 100} = 1.994 \exp\left(-3.063^2\, t^*\right),$$

and solving for the dimensionless time, we obtain

$$t^* = 0.216,$$

which is greater than 0.2, and thus the one term solution can be used to good accuracy. Then, the cooking time is determined from Eq. (10.4):

$$t = \frac{r_0^2\, t^*}{\alpha} = \frac{(0.025 \text{ m})^2 (0.216)}{1.52 \times 10^{-7} \text{ m}^2/\text{s}} = 888\,\text{s} \approx 14.8\,\text{min}.$$

Comments: The lumped capacitance analysis is not applicable in the problem since (see Eq. (9.7))

$$Bi_c = \frac{h\,(r_0/3)}{k} = \frac{1}{3}\,Bi = 13.2,$$

which is much bigger than 0.1.

Exercises 10:

1. At what minimal depth should a water pipe be buried in soil initially at 20°C if the surface temperature drops to $-15°C$ for 30 days? The soil's thermal diffusivity is $1.394 \times 10^{-7} \text{ m}^2/\text{s}$.

2. A long, 6.50 cm diameter, solid cylinder is made of Cr-Ni steel. It is initially at a uniform temperature $T_i = 150°C$. It is suddenly exposed to a convective environment at $T_\infty = 50°C$, and the surface convective heat transfer coefficient is $h = 285$ W/m²·K. Calculate the temperature at (a) the axis of the cylinder and (b) at a 2.5 cm radial distance, after 5 minutes of exposure to the cooling flow. (c) Determine the total energy transferred from the cylinder per centimeter of length during the first 5 minutes of cooling. (Take $\rho = 7817$ kg/m³, $c_p = 460$ J/kg·K, and $k = 16.3$ W/m·K.)

3. Citrus fruits are very susceptible to cold weather, and extended exposure to subfreezing temperatures can destroy them. Consider an 8 cm diameter orange that is initially at 15°C. A cold front moves in one night, and the ambient temperature suddenly drops to $-6°C$, with a heat transfer coefficient of 15 W/m²·°C. Using the properties of water for the orange and assuming the ambient conditions to remain constant for 4 h before the cold front moves out, determine if any part of the orange will freeze that night.

11 Transient 2-D and 3-D Conduction

11.1 Multi-dimensional Systems

The transient 1-D solutions presented in the previous lecture can be used to determine the transient temperature distribution and heat transfer in 2-D and 3-D transient heat conduction problems with geometries such as a short cylinder, a rectangular bar, a semi-infinite cylinder or plate, a rectangular prism, or a semi-infinite rectangular bar. To construct such solutions a superposition approach, called the *product solution*, is used provided that all surfaces of the 2-D or 3-D solid are subjected to the same boundary condition, the same heat transfer coefficient h, the properties are constant, and the body involves no heat generation. In this case, the governing equation is

$$\frac{\partial T}{\partial t} = \alpha \, \nabla^2 \, T. \qquad (11.1)$$

The solution for multi-dimensional geometries is expressed as the product of the solutions of one-dimensional geometries whose intersection is the multi-dimensional geometry.

To illustrate how a product solution is obtained, we consider the case of determining the temperature distribution in a 2-D rectangular bar. In this case, the temperature is given by the solution of the equation

$$\frac{\partial T}{\partial t} = \alpha \left(\frac{\partial^2 T}{\partial x^2} + \frac{\partial^2 T}{\partial y^2} \right). \qquad (11.2)$$

Assuming separation of variables, we take

$$T(x, y, t) = T_1(x, t) \cdot T_2(y, t). \qquad (11.3)$$

Now, substituting (11.3) into (11.2), separating terms involving T_1 and T_2 into the two sides of the equation, we obtain

$$\frac{1}{T_1} \left(\frac{\partial T_1}{\partial t} - \alpha \frac{\partial^2 T_1}{\partial x^2} \right) = -\frac{1}{T_2} \left(\frac{\partial T_2}{\partial t} - \alpha \frac{\partial^2 T_2}{\partial y^2} \right) = F(t). \qquad (11.4)$$

We note that since $T_1(x, t)$ and $T_2(y, t)$ depend on x and y respectively, the separation function F can be at most a function of t. Furthermore, if the initial condition is constant and we have no heat generation, we must have that $F(t) = 0$. Using this fact, we then have the following equations:

$$\frac{\partial T_1}{\partial t} - \alpha \frac{\partial^2 T_1}{\partial x^2} = 0 \quad \text{and} \quad \frac{\partial T_2}{\partial t} - \alpha \frac{\partial^2 T_2}{\partial y^2} = 0. \qquad (11.5)$$

Thus, the two-dimensional unsteady heat conduction problem with constant initial conditions and given boundary conditions is reduced to two unsteady one-dimensional heat conduction problems with the same constant initial conditions and with identical boundary conditions.

More generally, the solution for a multi-dimensional geometry is the product of solutions of one-dimensional geometries whose intersection corresponds to the multi-dimensional body. To eliminate confusion in applications of the unsteady one-dimensional solutions, we relabel them as follows:

Table 11.1: Dimensionless transient 1-D conduction solutions.

$$S(x^*, t^*) = \left. \frac{T(x, t) - T_\infty}{T_i - T_\infty} \right|_{\text{semi-infinite solid}}$$

erfc soln

$$P(x^*, t^*) = \left. \frac{T(x, t) - T_\infty}{T_i - T_\infty} \right|_{\text{plane wall}}$$

Sin(x) Soln

$$C(r^*, t^*) = \left. \frac{T(r, t) - T_\infty}{T_i - T_\infty} \right|_{\text{infinite cylinder}}$$

bessel func soln

A specific form of the product solution can also be used to determine the total transient heat transfer to or from a multi-dimensional geometry by using the one-dimensional values. The transient heat transfer for an n-D geometry formed by the intersection of n 1-D geometries is

$$Q^*_{n-D} = \frac{Q}{Q_{\max}} = \sum_{i=1}^{n} Q^*_i \prod_{j=1}^{i-1} \left(1 - Q^*_j\right), \qquad (11.6)$$

where $Q_{\max}$ is the maximum heat transferred (see Eq. (10.11)), and Q^*_i is an appropriate 1-D dimensionless actual heat transferred.

Example 11.1:

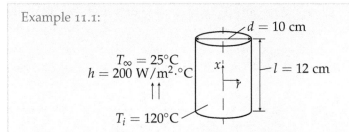

$$T_\infty = 25°C$$
$$h = 200 \text{ W/m}^2\cdot°C$$
$$T_i = 120°C$$
$$d = 10 \text{ cm}$$
$$l = 12 \text{ cm}$$

Known: A copper cylinder of diameter $d = 10$ cm and height $l = 12$ cm is initially at a uniform temperature $T_i = 120°C$. The cylinder is sitting in atmospheric air at 25°C, where heat is transferred by convection with a heat transfer coefficient of $h = 200$ W/m²·°C.

Find: The temperatures at the center of the cylinder and the center of the top surface of the cylinder 5 min after the start of cooling. In addition, determine the total heat transfer from the cylinder.

Assumptions: Heat conduction is two-dimensional with temperature varying in the axial and radial directions $T = T(r, x, t)$:

$$\frac{\partial T}{\partial t} = \alpha \left[\frac{1}{r} \frac{\partial}{\partial r} \left(r \frac{\partial T}{\partial r} \right) + \frac{\partial^2 T}{\partial x^2} \right];$$

the thermal properties are constant.

Properties: The density, specific heat capacity, and thermal conductivity of copper at $T = 25°C$ are $\rho = 8960$ kg/m³, $c_p = 385$ J/kg·°C, and $k = 401$ W/m·°C; the thermal diffusivity of copper is then $\alpha = k/\rho c_p = 1.162 \times 10^{-4}$ m²/s.

Analysis: The cylinder can be formed by the intersection of an infinite cylinder of radius $r_0 = 5$ cm and a plane wall with $L = 6$ cm, that is $\theta^* (r^*, x^*, t^*) = C (r^*, t^*) \cdot P (x^*, t^*)$, as indicated below:

$$C(r^*, t^*) \cdot P(x^*, t^*) = C(r^*, t^*) \times P(x^*, t^*)$$

Now, for the plane wall, we have

$$Bi = \frac{h\,L}{k} = \frac{(200 \text{ W/m}^2 \cdot°\text{C})(0.06\,\text{m})}{401 \text{ W/m} \cdot°\text{C}} = 2.99 \times 10^{-2},$$

$$t^* = \frac{\alpha t}{L^2} = \frac{(1.162 \times 10^{-4}\,\mathrm{m^2/s})(300\,\mathrm{s})}{(0.06\,\mathrm{m})^2} = 9.68,$$

and since $t^* \gtrsim 0.2$, from Table 10.1 and Eq. (10.20), we have that the dimensionless temperature at the center is

$$P(0, t^*) = 0.76.$$

Similarly, for the infinite cylinder, we have

$$Bi = \frac{h\,r_0}{k} = \frac{(200\,\mathrm{W/m^2 \cdot {}^\circ C})(0.05\,\mathrm{m})}{401\,\mathrm{W/m \cdot {}^\circ C}} = 2.49 \times 10^{-2},$$

$$t^* = \frac{\alpha t}{r_0^2} = \frac{(1.162 \times 10^{-4}\,\mathrm{m^2/s})(300\,\mathrm{s})}{(0.05\,\mathrm{m})^2} = 13.94,$$

and since $t^* \gtrsim 0.2$, from Table 10.1 and Eq. (10.23), we have that the dimensionless temperature at the center is

$$C(0, t^*) = 0.051.$$

Therefore, the temperature at the center of the finite cylinder is

$$\theta^*(0,0,t^*) = \frac{T(0,0,t) - T_\infty}{T_i - T_\infty} = C(0,t^*) \cdot P(0,t^*)$$

$$= (0.051)(0.76) = 0.39,$$

0.039? *(handwritten)*

or

$$T(0,0,t) = T_\infty + \theta^*(0,0,t^*)\,(T_i - T_\infty)$$

$$= 25^\circ C + 0.39\,(120 - 25)^\circ\,C = 61.8^\circ C.$$

Note that the center of the cylinder is also the center of both the infinite cylinder and the plane wall.

The center of the top surface of the cylinder is still at the center of the infinite cylinder ($r = 0$), but at the outer surface of the plane wall ($x = L$). Therefore, we first need to find the surface temperature of the wall. Noting that $x = L = 0.06$ m,

$$Bi = \frac{h\,L}{k} = \frac{(200\,\mathrm{W/m^2 \cdot {}^\circ C})(0.06\,\mathrm{m})}{401\,\mathrm{W/m \cdot {}^\circ C}} = 2.99 \times 10^{-2},$$

$$x^* = \frac{x}{L} = \frac{0.06\,\mathrm{m}}{0.06\,\mathrm{m}} = 1,$$

so that from Eq. (10.20), we have that

$$\frac{P(1, t^*)}{P(0, t^*)} = 0.986.$$

Then,

$$P(1, t^*) = \frac{P(1, t^*)}{P(0, t^*)} \cdot P(0, t^*) = (0.986)(0.76) = 0.75.$$

Therefore,

$$\theta^*(0, 1, t^*) = \frac{T(0, x, t) - T_\infty}{T_i - T_\infty} = C(0, t^*) \cdot P(1, t^*)$$

$$= (0.51)(0.75) = 0.38,$$

and

$$T(0, x, t) = T_\infty + \theta^*(0, 1, t^*)(T_i - T_\infty)$$
$$= 25^\circ C + 0.38(120 - 25)^\circ C = 61.3^\circ C.$$

which is the temperature at the center of the top surface of the cylinder, and it is slightly cooler than at the center of the cylinder.

Now, to determine the total heat transfer from the cylinder, we first calculate its volume,

$$V = \pi r_0^2 l = \pi (0.05\,\text{m})^2 (0.12\,\text{m}) = 9.42 \times 10^{-4}\,\text{m}^3,$$

and then determine the maximum heat that can be transferred from the cylinder, which is the sensible energy content of the cylinder relative to its environment:

$$Q_{\max} = \rho\, c_p\, V\, (T_i - T_\infty)$$
$$= (8960\,\text{kg/m}^3)(0.385\,\text{kJ/kg} \cdot^\circ C)(9.42 \times 10^{-4}\,\text{m}^3) \times$$
$$(120 - 25)^\circ C$$
$$= 308.7\,\text{kJ}.$$

Then, we determine the dimensionless heat transfer ratios for both geometries. For the plane wall, from Eq. (10.20) we have

$$Q^*_{\text{plane wall}} = 0.244.$$

Similarly, for the cylinder, from Eq. (10.23) we have

$$Q^*_{\text{infinite cylinder}} = 0.493.$$

Lastly, the heat transfer ratio for the finite cylinder is, from Eq. (11.6),

$$Q^* = Q_1^* + Q_2^* (1 - Q_1^*) = 0.244 + 0.493(1 - 0.244) = 0.617,$$

where, in this case, we have taken $Q_1^* = Q_{\text{plane wall}}^*$ and $Q_2^* = Q_{\text{infinite cylinder}}^*$. Therefore, the total heat transfer from the cylinder during the first 5 min of cooling is

$$Q = Q^* Q_{\max} = 0.617(308.7 \, \text{kJ}) = 190 \, \text{kJ}.$$

Comments: Since the Biot numbers for the plane wall and infinite cylinder were both much smaller than 0.1, we could have deduced that the temperatures in the middle of the cylinder and the top surface where essentially the same and approximately equal to that obtained through the lumped capacitance approximation; more accurate results can be obtained by using properties at the approximate average temperature of 70°C.

Exercises 11:

1. Consider a cubic block whose sides are 5 cm long and a cylindrical block whose height and diameter are also 5 cm. Both blocks are initially at 20°C and are made of granite ($k = 2.5 \, \text{W/m·°C}$ and $\alpha = 1.15 \times 10^{-6} \, \text{m}^2/\text{s}$). Now both blocks are exposed to hot gases at 500°C in a furnace on all of their surfaces with a heat transfer coefficient of 40 $\text{W/m}^2 \cdot °\text{C}$. Determine the center temperature of each geometry after 10, 20, and 60 min.

2. A thermocouple is inserted into the midpoint of a hot dog that is 12.5 cm long and 2.2 cm diameter and another thermocouple just under the skin. Initially both thermocouples read 20°C. The hot dog is dropped into boiling water at 100°C. Exactly 2 min after the hot dog was dropped into the boiling water, the center and the surface temperatures were recorded to be 62°C and 94°C, respectively. The density and specific heat of the hot dog can be taken to be 980 kg/m^3 and 3900 J/kg·°C, respectively. Determine (a) the thermal diffusivity and thermal conductivity of the hot dog, and (b) the convection heat transfer coefficient.

3. A 20 cm long 15 cm diameter cylindrical aluminum block ($\rho = 2702 \, \text{kg/m}^3$, $c_p = 0.896 \, \text{kJ/kg·°C}$, $k = 236 \, \text{W/m·°C}$) is initially at a uniform temperature of 20°C. The block is to be heated in a furnace at 1200°C until its center temperature rises to 300°C. If the heat transfer coefficient on all surfaces of the block is 80 $\text{W/m}^2 \cdot °\text{C}$, determine how long the block should be kept in the furnace. Also, determine the amount of heat transfer from the aluminum block if it is allowed to cool in the room until its temperature drops to 20°C throughout.

Part III

Convection

12 Basic Concepts

12.1 Average Convection Coefficient

Recall that

$$q'' = h(T_s - T_\infty),$$

where the convection heat transfer coefficient h is a function of the properties of the fluid, the surface area, the surface geometry and characteristics, and the flow conditions, as indicated in Fig. 12.1. The total heat transfer rate is equal to

$$q = \int_{A_s} q''\, dA = \int_{A_s} h(T_s - T_\infty)\, dA = (T_s - T_\infty) \int_{A_s} h\, dA,$$

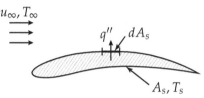

Figure 12.1: Convection heat transfer from a surface.

where we have assumed that T_s is constant. The average convection coefficient is defined as

$$\bar{h} \equiv \frac{1}{A_s} \int_{A_s} h\, dA, \qquad (12.1)$$

or in 1-D, as illustrated in Fig. 12.2,

$$\bar{h} = \frac{1}{L} \int_0^L h\, dx. \qquad (12.2)$$

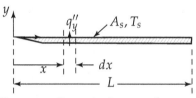

Figure 12.2: Convection heat transfer from a plate.

Therefore, we can write

$$q = \bar{h} A_s (T_s - T_\infty). \qquad (12.3)$$

12.2 Boundary Layers

Velocity and thermal boundary layers are illustrated in Fig. 12.3.

Velocity — As indicated in Fig. 12.4, the velocity at a wall's surface is

$$u(x,0) = 0, \quad x \geq 0,$$

and we have a shear of fluid in the boundary layer. The *surface shear stress* is defined as

$$\tau_s \equiv \mu \left. \frac{\partial u}{\partial y} \right|_{y=0}, \qquad (12.4)$$

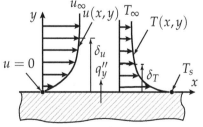

Figure 12.3: Velocity and temperature profiles.

where μ is a fluid property, the dynamic viscosity (N·s/m^2). Now from the velocity field, we define the *velocity boundary layer thickness* by

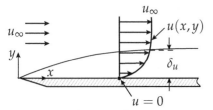

Figure 12.4: Velocity profile.

$$\delta_u(x): \quad \frac{u(x, \delta_u)}{u_\infty} = 0.99, \tag{12.5}$$

the *friction coefficient* as

$$c_f(x) \equiv \frac{\tau_s(x)}{\rho\, u_\infty^2/2}, \tag{12.6}$$

and the *drag coefficient* by

$$c_D \equiv \frac{F_D}{A_s\, \rho\, u_\infty^2/2}, \tag{12.7}$$

where A_s is the surface area, and the *drag force* is given by

$$F_D = \int_{A_s} \tau_s\, dA. \tag{12.8}$$

Note that

$$c_D = \frac{1}{A_s} \int_{A_s} c_f\, dA. \tag{12.9}$$

Also note that τ_s is a function of x, it decreases as $\delta_u(x)$ increases, and

$$\lim_{x \to 0+} \tau_s(x) = +\infty \tag{12.10}$$

so that the leading edge $x = 0$ is a singular point. The qualitative behavior is illustrated in Fig. 12.6.

Temperature — As indicated in Fig. 12.5, we define the *temperature boundary layer thickness* by

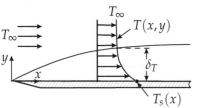

Figure 12.5: Temperature profile.

$$\delta_T(x): \quad \frac{T_s - T(x, \delta_T)}{T_s - T_\infty} \equiv 0.99. \tag{12.11}$$

Since $u = 0$ at the wall, the heat flux at the surface is

$$q_s'' = -k \left.\frac{\partial T}{\partial y}\right|_{y=0}, \tag{12.12}$$

where the thermal conductivity k (W/m·K) is a fluid property. Therefore we can write

$$h(x) = \frac{q_s''(x)}{T_s - T_\infty} = \frac{-k\, \partial T/\partial y|_{y=0}}{T_s - T_\infty}. \tag{12.13}$$

Note that q_s'' is a function of x, it decreases as $\delta_T(x)$ increases, and

$$\lim_{x \to 0+} q_s''(x) = +\infty \tag{12.14}$$

so that the leading edge at $x = 0$ is a singular point. The qualitative behavior is illustrated in Fig. 12.6.

Note:

- To find h we need to know the behavior of T near the surface, which of course is affected by the behavior of u near the surface!

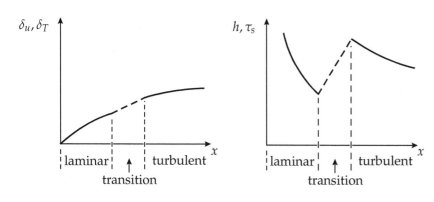

Figure 12.6: Qualitative behaviors of laminar to turbulent behaviors of (δ_u, δ_T) and (h, τ_s).

12.3   Laminar and Turbulent Flow

Generally, the flow is characterized by the *local Reynolds number*

$$Re_x = \frac{\rho\, u_\infty x}{\mu} = \frac{u_\infty x}{\nu}, \tag{12.15}$$

where $\nu = \mu/\rho$ is the kinematic viscosity (m^2/s). In addition, the flow also depends on the *Prandtl number*,

$$Pr = \frac{\nu}{\alpha}, \tag{12.16}$$

whose values for air and water are approximately given by 0.7 and 7, respectively. The transition region from laminar to turbulent flow, illustrated in Fig. 12.7, is often idealized so that it occurs at a single point x_c. Subsequently, we typically characterize the transition point by the *critical Reynolds number*, Re_c. For a flat plate we use

$$Re_c = \frac{u_\infty x_c}{\nu} = 5 \times 10^5. \tag{12.17}$$

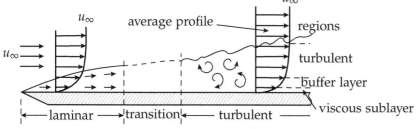

Figure 12.7: Laminar and turbulent flow.

> **Example 12.1:**
> Experimental results for the local heat transfer coefficient for flow over a flat plate were found to fit the relation $h_x(x) = c\,x^{-0.1}$ where c is a constant and x is the distance from the leading edge of the plate.

Known: Variation of the local heat transfer coefficient, $h_x(x)$.

Find: The ratio of the average heat transfer coefficient $\bar{h}(x)$ to the local value $h_x(x)$.

Analysis: From Eq. (12.2) the average convection heat transfer coefficient over the region from 0 to x is

$$\bar{h}_x(x) = \frac{1}{x}\int_0^x h_x(x)\,dx = \frac{c}{x}\int_0^x x^{-0.1}\,dx = 1.11\,c\,x^{-0.1},$$

so

$$\frac{\bar{h}_x(x)}{h_x(x)} = 1.11.$$

Comments: As the boundary layer thickness increases, since both the local and average coefficients decrease, the average coefficient up to x will always be greater than the local value at x.

Exercises 12:

1. For an airflow over a flat plate of length L, transition occurs at $x_c = L/2$ based on the critical Reynolds number Re_c. In the laminar and turbulent regions, the local convection coefficients are, respectively,

$$h_{lam}(x) = c_{lam}x^{-0.5} \quad\text{and}\quad h_{turb}(x) = c_{turb}x^{-0.2}.$$

   i) Determine the air velocity. ii) Develop an expression for the average convection coefficient as a function of distance from the leading edge up to x_c. iii) Develop an expression for the average convection coefficient as a function of distance from x_c up to L. Plot the local and average convection coefficients as a function of x for $0 < x \leq L$.

2. For an airflow over a heated surface, the boundary layer temperature distribution is approximates as

$$\frac{T - T_s}{T_\infty - T_s} = 1 - \exp\left(-Pr\,\frac{u_\infty y}{\nu}\right),$$

   where y is the distance normal to the surface and Pr is the Prandtl number. What is the surface heat flux?

3. Consider steady, laminar, two-dimensional flow over an isothermal plate, with constant properties and a Prandtl number of unity. Does the wall shear stress increase, decrease, or remain constant with distance from the leading edge? Is it correct to say that both the average friction and heat transfer coefficients depend on the Reynolds number only?

13 Fundamental Equations

13.1 General Equations

We will assume, as is done quite often, that $q_g''' = 0$. In such case, the general compressible *Navier-Stokes-Fourier equations* are given by

mass conservation:

$$\dot{\rho} + \rho \nabla \cdot v = 0, \tag{13.1}$$

linear momentum balance:

$$\rho \dot{v} = -\nabla p + \nabla \cdot \tau + \rho g, \tag{13.2}$$

with *shear stress tensor* components (assuming Stokes' hypothesis)

$$\tau_{ij} = \mu \left(\frac{\partial v_i}{\partial x_j} + \frac{\partial v_j}{\partial x_i} \right) - \frac{2}{3} \mu \, \delta_{ij} \frac{\partial v_k}{\partial x_k}, \tag{13.3}$$

energy conservation:

$$\rho \dot{h} = \dot{p} - \nabla \cdot q + \Phi, \tag{13.4}$$

with *heat flux* components and *viscous dissipation* given by

$$q_i = -k \frac{\partial T}{\partial x_i} \quad \text{and} \quad \Phi = \tau_{ij} \frac{\partial v_i}{\partial x_j}, \tag{13.5}$$

and the *material derivative* is given by

$$\dot{f} = \frac{\partial f}{\partial t} + v \cdot \nabla f. \tag{13.6}$$

Note:

- In the equations, we have introduced the velocity vector v, the pressure p, the gravitational vector g, the enthalpy h, and the shear viscosity μ.

- The Kronecker delta δ_{ij} is equal to 1 if $i = j$ and 0 if $i \neq j$.

Additionally we have to introduce *equations of state* $\rho = \rho(p, T)$ and $h = h(p, T)$, and equations for the *transport properties* $\mu = \mu(p, T)$ and $k = k(p, T)$ (from equilibrium thermodynamics).

13.2   Boussinesq Approximation

If we expand the thermal equation of state about a constant reference density ρ_0 at pressure p_0 and temperature T_0, we have

$$\rho = \rho_0 \left[1 - \beta_0 \left(T - T_0 \right) + \kappa_0 \left(p - p_0 \right) + \cdots \right], \tag{13.7}$$

where

$$\beta_0 = -\frac{1}{\rho_0} \left. \frac{\partial \rho}{\partial T} \right|_{p_0, T_0} \quad \left(\text{K}^{-1} \right) \quad \text{and} \quad \kappa_0 = \frac{1}{\rho_0} \left. \frac{\partial \rho}{\partial p} \right|_{p_0, T_0} \quad \left(\text{Pa}^{-1} \right) \tag{13.8}$$

Note:

- For an ideal gas, $\rho = p/RT$, where R is the gas constant, it is easy to see that $\beta_0 = 1/T_0$ and $\kappa_0 = 1/p_0$.

are the *coefficients of volume expansion* and *isothermal compressibility*, respectively. Furthermore, we assume that the fluid is calorically perfect so that

$$dh = c_p \, dT \quad \text{with} \quad c_p = c_{p0} = \text{const.}, \tag{13.9}$$

and the transport properties are constant,

$$\mu = \mu_0 = \text{const.} \quad \text{and} \quad k = k_0 = \text{const.} \tag{13.10}$$

Note:

- The isothermal compressibility coefficient κ_0 is typically very small for fluids under convective conditions.

Lastly, we assume that $(\rho - \rho_0)/\rho_0 \ll 1$. In such case it is reasonable to take $\rho = \rho_0$ for all terms in equations (13.1)–(13.5) with the exception of the buoyancy term $\rho \, g$ in (13.2) where, to retain such term to leading order, we take $\rho = \rho_0 \left[1 - \beta_0 \left(T - T_0 \right) \right]$. If we subsequently decompose the pressure into hydrostatic and hydrodynamic components, $p = P_h + P$, and note that $\nabla P_h = \rho_0 \, g$, then we obtain the *Boussinesq equations* as

$$\nabla \cdot \boldsymbol{v} = 0, \tag{13.11}$$

Note:

- When buoyancy is absent, we note one-way coupling between the momentum and energy equations. Solve for momentum first, than we can obtain τ_s, e.g. $\tau_s = \mu_0 \left. \left(\partial u / \partial y \right) \right|_{y=0}$, and then using v solve the energy equation for T. Subsequently, we obtain q_s'', e.g. $q_s'' = -k_0 \left. \left(\partial T / \partial y \right) \right|_{y=0}$, and ultimately $h = q_s'' / \left(T_s - T_\infty \right)$. When buoyancy is present, we have two-way coupling between linear momentum and energy.

$$\dot{\boldsymbol{v}} = -\frac{1}{\rho_0} \nabla P + \nu_0 \nabla^2 \boldsymbol{v} - \beta_0 \left(T - T_0 \right) \boldsymbol{g}, \tag{13.12}$$

$$\dot{T} = \alpha_0 \nabla^2 T + \frac{1}{\rho_0 \, c_{p0}} \Phi, \tag{13.13}$$

where

$$\nu_0 = \frac{\mu_0}{\rho_0} \quad \text{and} \quad \alpha_0 = \frac{k_0}{\rho_0 \, c_{p0}}$$

are the *kinematic viscosity* and the *thermal diffusivity*, respectively, and they both have units of m^2/s. The viscous dissipation Φ, given by

$$\Phi = \mu_0 \left\{ 2 \left[\left(\frac{\partial u}{\partial x} \right)^2 + \left(\frac{\partial v}{\partial y} \right)^2 + \left(\frac{\partial w}{\partial z} \right)^2 \right] + \left(\frac{\partial u}{\partial y} + \frac{\partial v}{\partial x} \right)^2 + \right.$$
$$\left. \left(\frac{\partial v}{\partial z} + \frac{\partial w}{\partial y} \right)^2 + \left(\frac{\partial w}{\partial x} + \frac{\partial u}{\partial z} \right)^2 \right\}, \tag{13.14}$$

can be neglected in most cases. Without the buoyancy and viscous dissipation terms, (13.11)-(13.13) also correspond to the incompressible equations.

13.3   Boundary Layer Approximation

We limit our discussion to two dimensional flows in Cartesian coordinates and ignore the buoyancy term in the linear momentum equation and the viscous dissipation in the energy equation. Extension to three dimensions and incorporation of the buoyancy term and viscous dissipation are easily done afterwards. Futhermore, from now on, we drop the zero subscripts to simplify notations. Thus, we start by writing the explicit forms of such equations:

$$\frac{\partial u}{\partial x} + \frac{\partial v}{\partial y} = 0, \tag{13.15}$$

$$\frac{\partial u}{\partial t} + u \frac{\partial u}{\partial x} + v \frac{\partial u}{\partial y} = -\frac{1}{\rho} \frac{\partial P}{\partial x} + \nu \left(\frac{\partial^2 u}{\partial x^2} + \frac{\partial^2 u}{\partial y^2} \right), \tag{13.16}$$

$$\frac{\partial v}{\partial t} + u \frac{\partial v}{\partial x} + v \frac{\partial v}{\partial y} = -\frac{1}{\rho} \frac{\partial P}{\partial y} + \nu \left(\frac{\partial^2 v}{\partial x^2} + \frac{\partial^2 v}{\partial y^2} \right), \tag{13.17}$$

$$\frac{\partial T}{\partial t} + u \frac{\partial T}{\partial x} + v \frac{\partial T}{\partial y} = \alpha \left(\frac{\partial^2 T}{\partial x^2} + \frac{\partial^2 T}{\partial y^2} \right). \tag{13.18}$$

We now recognize the following scales present in the linear momentum and energy equations:

t-scale: $x/u_\infty \sim O(1)$.

x-length scale: $x \sim O(1)$;

y-length scale: $\delta_u \sim \sqrt{\nu}$;

u-scale: $u_\infty \sim O(1)$;

P-scale: $P_\infty \sim O(1)$;

T-scale: $T_\infty \sim O(1)$;

The characteristic of a boundary layer is such that $\delta_u/x \ll 1$, so that from the mass balance equation (13.15) we see that $v \sim (\delta_u/x)u_\infty$. Subsequently, we write symbolically the separate terms of the components of the linear momentum equation as

x-momentum:

$$\frac{u_\infty^2}{x} + \frac{u_\infty^2}{x} + \left(\frac{\delta_u u_\infty}{x} \right) \frac{u_\infty}{\delta_u} = -\frac{P_\infty}{x} + \delta_u^2 \left(\frac{u_\infty}{x^2} + \frac{u_\infty}{\delta_u^2} \right)$$

y-momentum:

$$\frac{u_\infty}{x} \left(\frac{\delta_u u_\infty}{x} \right) + \frac{u_\infty}{x} \left(\frac{\delta_u u_\infty}{x} \right) + \left(\frac{\delta_u u_\infty}{x} \right)^2 \frac{1}{\delta_u} = -\frac{P_\infty}{\delta_u} +$$
$$\delta_u^2 \left[\left(\frac{\delta_u u_\infty}{x} \right) \frac{1}{x^2} + \left(\frac{\delta_u u_\infty}{x} \right) \frac{1}{\delta_u^2} \right].$$

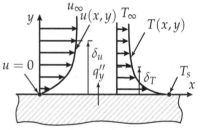

Figure 13.1: Velocity and temperature boundary layers on a flat surface.

Note:

- The corresponding scaling relation between the momentum boundary layer thickness δ_u and the kinematic viscosity ν is necessitated to have the leading viscous term balance with convective terms in the x-momentum equation, where it is found that $\delta_u \sim \sqrt{\nu x/u_\infty}$.

By examining the magnitudes of terms in the y-momentum equation, (13.17) effectively becomes $\partial P/\partial y = 0$ or $P = P(x) = P_\infty(x)$. The x-momentum equation (13.16), considering the magnitudes of the different terms, subsequently becomes

$$\frac{\partial u}{\partial t} + u\frac{\partial u}{\partial x} + v\frac{\partial u}{\partial y} = -\frac{1}{\rho}\frac{dP_\infty}{dx} + \nu\frac{\partial^2 u}{\partial y^2}. \tag{13.19}$$

Now, from the energy equation, we write symbolically

$$\left(\frac{u_\infty}{x}\right)T_\infty + \left(\frac{u_\infty}{x}\right)T_\infty + \left(\frac{\delta_u u_\infty}{x}\right)\frac{T_\infty}{\delta_u} = \frac{\delta_u^2}{Pr}\left(\frac{T_\infty}{x^2} + \frac{T_\infty}{\delta_u^2}\right). \tag{13.20}$$

We note that for $Pr = O(1)$, $\delta_T \sim \delta_u$. Subsequently, considering the above orders of magnitude, the energy equations (13.18) can be rewritten as

$$\frac{\partial T}{\partial t} + u\frac{\partial T}{\partial x} + v\frac{\partial T}{\partial y} = \alpha\frac{\partial^2 T}{\partial y^2}. \tag{13.21}$$

Regarding the viscous dissipation (13.14), in two dimensional flow it is given by

$$\frac{1}{\rho}\Phi = \nu\left\{2\left[\left(\frac{\partial u}{\partial x}\right)^2 + \left(\frac{\partial v}{\partial y}\right)^2\right] + \left(\frac{\partial u}{\partial y} + \frac{\partial v}{\partial x}\right)^2\right\}. \tag{13.22}$$

Using the above scalings, we symbolically write

$$\frac{1}{\rho}\Phi = \delta_u^2\left\{2\left[\left(\frac{u_\infty}{x}\right)^2 + \left(\frac{\delta_u u_\infty}{x\,\delta_u}\right)^2\right] + \left(\frac{u_\infty}{\delta_u} + \frac{\delta_u u_\infty}{x^2}\right)^2\right\} \tag{13.23}$$

Subsequently, we see that to leading order, in the boundary layer approximation we have that

$$\Phi = \mu\left(\frac{\partial u}{\partial y}\right)^2. \tag{13.24}$$

Note:

- We note that in most convective conditions the viscous dissipation can be neglected. It only becomes important when the viscosity of the fluid is large. In such case, the buoyancy terms is then quite often negligible.

In summary, the two dimensional *boundary layer equations* in Cartesian coordinates are:

$$\frac{\partial u}{\partial x} + \frac{\partial v}{\partial y} = 0, \tag{13.25}$$

$$\frac{\partial u}{\partial t} + u\frac{\partial u}{\partial x} + v\frac{\partial u}{\partial y} = -\frac{1}{\rho}\frac{dP_\infty}{dx} + \nu\frac{\partial^2 u}{\partial y^2} + \beta g\,(T - T_s), \tag{13.26}$$

$$\frac{\partial T}{\partial t} + u\frac{\partial T}{\partial x} + v\frac{\partial T}{\partial y} = \alpha\frac{\partial^2 T}{\partial y^2} + \frac{\nu}{c_p}\left(\frac{\partial u}{\partial y}\right)^2, \tag{13.27}$$

where we have now re-introduced the buoyancy term in the relevant case where $g = (-1,0)g$ and have taken the reference temperature (see (13.12)) to correspond to the surface temperature. Typical boundary conditions are

$$v\,(x,0) = 0, \quad T\,(x,0) = T_s, \quad u\,(x,\infty) = u_\infty, \quad T\,(x,\infty) = T_\infty. \tag{13.28}$$

Example 13.1:

Known: The flow of oil in a journal bearing can be approximated as parallel flow between two large plates with one plate moving and the other stationary. Such flows are known as Couette flow. Consider two large isothermal plates at temperature of T_0 separated by a distance L by oil film. The upper plate moves at a constant velocity U, while the lower plate is stationary.

Find: (a) Obtain relations for the velocity and temperature distributions in the oil. (b) Determine the maximum temperature in the oil and the heat flux from the oil to each plate.

Assumptions: Steady operating conditions exist; oil is an incompressible substance with constant properties; body forces such as gravity are negligible; the plates are large so that there is no variation in the transverse direction.

Properties: All properties are evaluated at T_0.

Analysis: (a) We take the x-axis to be the flow direction, and y to be the normal direction. This is parallel flow between two plates, and thus $v = 0$. Then the continuity equation (13.25) reduces to

$$\frac{\partial u}{\partial x} + \frac{\partial v}{\partial y} = 0 \quad \longrightarrow \quad \frac{\partial u}{\partial x} = 0 \quad \longrightarrow \quad u = u(y).$$

Therefore, the x-component of velocity does not change in the flow direction. Noting that $u = u(y)$, $v = 0$, and $dP_\infty/dx = 0$ (flow is maintained by the motion of the upper plate rather than the pressure gradient), the x-momentum equation (13.26) reduces to

$$u\frac{\partial u}{\partial x} + v\frac{\partial u}{\partial y} = \nu\frac{\partial^2 u}{\partial y^2} \quad \longrightarrow \quad \frac{d^2 u}{dy^2} = 0.$$

Integrating it twice gives

$$u(y) = c_1 y + c_2.$$

The fluid velocities at the plate surfaces must be equal to the velocities of the plates because of the no-slip condition. Therefore, the boundary conditions are $u(0) = 0$ and $u(L) = U$. Applying them gives the velocity distribution:

$$u(y) = \frac{y}{L} U.$$

Frictional heating due to viscous dissipation is significant since oil typically has a high viscosity and a journal bearing would create a large plate velocity. The plates are isothermal and there is no change in the flow direction, and thus the temperature depends on y only, $T = T(y)$. Then the energy equation with dissipation (13.27) reduces to

$$0 = k \frac{\partial^2 T}{\partial y^2} + \mu \left(\frac{\partial u}{\partial y} \right)^2 \quad \longrightarrow \quad k \frac{d^2 T}{dy^2} = -\mu \left(\frac{U}{L} \right)^2,$$

since $\partial u / \partial y = U/L$. Dividing both sides by k and integrating twice gives

$$T(y) = -\frac{\mu}{2k} \left(\frac{y}{L} U \right)^2 + c_3 y + c_4.$$

Applying the boundary conditions $T(0) = T_0$ and $T(L) = T_0$ gives the temperature distribution to be

$$T(y) = T_0 + \frac{\mu U^2}{2k} \left(\frac{y}{L} - \frac{y^2}{L^2} \right).$$

(b) The temperature gradient is determined by differentiating $T(y)$ with respect to y,

$$\frac{dT}{dy} = \frac{\mu U^2}{2kL} \left(1 - 2\frac{y}{L} \right).$$

The location of maximum temperature is determined by setting $dT/dy = 0$ and solving for y,

$$\frac{dT}{dy} = \frac{\mu U^2}{2kL} \left(1 - 2\frac{y}{L} \right) = 0 \quad \longrightarrow \quad y = \frac{L}{2}.$$

Therefore, maximum temperature will occur at mid-plane, which is not surprising since both plates are maintained at the same temperature. The maximum temperature is the value of temperature at $y = L/2$,

$$T_{\max} = T \left(\frac{L}{2} \right) = T_0 + \frac{\mu U^2}{2k} \left(\frac{L/2}{L} - \frac{(L/2)^2}{L^2} \right) = T_0 + \frac{\mu U^2}{8k}.$$

Heat flux at the plates is determined from the definition:

$$q_0'' = -k \left. \frac{dT}{dy} \right|_{y=0} = -k \frac{\mu U^2}{2kL} (1 - 0) = -\frac{\mu U^2}{2L}$$

and

$$q_L'' = -k \left. \frac{dT}{dy} \right|_{y=L} = -k \frac{\mu U^2}{2kL} (1 - 2) = \frac{\mu U^2}{2L} = -q_0''.$$

Therefore, heat fluxes at the two plates are equal in magnitude but opposite in sign.

Comments: A temperature rise confirms that viscous dissipation is significant. The heat flux is equivalent to the rate of mechanical energy dissipation. Therefore, mechanical energy is being converted to thermal energy to overcome friction in the oil. Calculations are done using oil properties at T_0. Knowing the strong dependence of viscosity on temperature, properties should be evaluated at the average temperature to improve accuracy.

Exercises 13:

1. Using, what is called, the von Karman integral technique, the following integral equation for the boundary layer thickness is obtained:

$$\nu \left.\frac{\partial u}{\partial y}\right|_{y=0} = \frac{d}{dx}\left[\int_0^\delta (u_\infty - u)\,u\,dy\right].$$

Assuming a velocity profile of the form

$$\frac{u}{u_\infty} = c_0 + c_1\frac{y}{\delta} + c_2\left(\frac{y}{\delta}\right)^2 + c_3\left(\frac{y}{\delta}\right)^3$$

within a boundary layer, evaluate the constants subject to the boundary conditions

$$u = \frac{\partial^2 u}{\partial y^2} = 0 \text{ at } y = 0 \quad \text{and} \quad u = u_\infty, \frac{\partial u}{\partial y} = 0 \text{ at } y = \delta.$$

Using the resulting profile in the integral equation, determine the boundary layer thickness and the average friction coefficient for laminar flow over a flat plate of length L.

2. Consider the flow of oil between two large parallel isothermal plates separated by a distance L. The upper plate is moving at a constant velocity of U and maintained at temperature T_0 while the lower plate is stationary and insulated. By simplifying and solving the continuity, momentum, and energy equations (13.25)-(13.27) (ignoring buoyancy), obtain relations for the maximum temperature of oil, the location where it occurs, and heat flux at the upper plate.

3. Reconsider Exercise 2. Using the results of this exercise, obtain a relation for the volumetric heat generation rate q_g''' of the oil. Then express the convection problem as an equivalent conduction problem in the oil layer. Verify your model by solving the conduction problem and obtaining a relation for the maximum temperature, which should be identical to the one obtained in the convection analysis.

14 Dimensionless Equations

14.1 Non-dimensionalization and Similarity

We assume that u_∞, T_∞, and T_s are constant and dP_∞/dx is given. Then, we normalize the dependent and independent variables as follows (star quantities are dimensionless):

$$x = L x^*, \quad v = u_\infty v^*, \quad t = (L/u_\infty) t^*,$$

$$P_\infty = \left(\rho u_\infty^2 \right) P_\infty^*, \quad T - T_s = (T_\infty - T_s) T^*, \qquad (14.1)$$

where L is the length of a plate. Substituting the above relations into the boundary layer equations (13.25)-(13.27) we obtain

$$\frac{\partial u^*}{\partial x^*} + \frac{\partial v^*}{\partial y^*} = 0, \qquad (14.2)$$

$$\overset{0}{\cancel{\frac{\partial u^*}{\partial t^*}}} + u^* \frac{\partial u^*}{\partial x^*} + v^* \frac{\partial u^*}{\partial y^*} = -\frac{dP_\infty^*}{dx^*} + \frac{1}{Re_L} \frac{\partial^2 u^*}{\partial y^{*2}} + \frac{Gr_L}{Re_L^2} T^*, \qquad (14.3)$$

$$\overset{0}{\cancel{\frac{\partial T^*}{\partial t^*}}} + u^* \frac{\partial T^*}{\partial x^*} + v^* \frac{\partial T^*}{\partial y^*} = \frac{1}{Pe_L} \frac{\partial^2 T^*}{\partial y^{*2}} + \frac{Ec}{Re_L} \left(\frac{\partial u^*}{\partial y^*} \right)^2, \qquad (14.4)$$

We consider steady state so that the time dependent terms drop out. Also, substituting (14.1) into boundary conditions (13.28), we have

$$v^* (x^*, 0) = 0, \quad T^* (x^*, 0) = 0, \quad u^* (x^*, \infty) = 1, \quad T^* (x^*, \infty) = 1. \quad (14.5)$$

Above, we have introduced the *Reynolds number*, Re_L, the *Grashof number*, Gr_L, the *Prandtl number*, Pr, the *Péclet number*, Pe_L, and the *Eckert number*, Ec, defined as follows:

$$Re_L = \frac{u_\infty L}{\nu}, \quad Gr_L = \frac{\beta g (T_\infty - T_s) L^3}{\nu^2}, \quad Pr = \frac{\nu}{\alpha},$$

$$Pe_L = Re_L \, Pr = \frac{u_\infty L}{\alpha}, \quad Ec = \frac{u_\infty^2}{c_p (T_\infty - T_s)}. \quad (14.6)$$

Note:

- From now, relevant dimensionless parameters will be denoted by the subscript L indicating the length scale being used in the respective definitions.

If buoyancy and viscous dissipation are not important ($Gr_L = Ec = 0$), as is the case in most forced convection problems, then

$$u^* = u^* \left(x^*, y^*; Re_L, \frac{dP_\infty^*}{dx^*} \right) \qquad (14.7)$$

and

$$T^* = T^* \left(x^*, y^*; Re_L, Pr, \frac{dP_\infty^*}{dx^*} \right). \qquad (14.8)$$

In addition, the shear stress and friction coefficient equations (12.4) and (12.6) can be rewritten as

$$\tau_s = \mu \left. \frac{\partial u}{\partial y} \right|_{y=0} = \left(\frac{\mu u_\infty}{L} \right) \left. \frac{\partial u^*}{\partial y^*} \right|_{y^*=0} \qquad (14.9)$$

and

$$c_f = \frac{\tau_s}{\rho u_\infty^2 / 2} = \frac{2}{Re_L} \left. \frac{\partial u^*}{\partial y^*} \right|_{y^*=0}. \qquad (14.10)$$

Lastly, from a surface energy balance at the plate surface, we can write the convection heat transfer coefficient as

$$h = \frac{-k \left. \frac{\partial T}{\partial y} \right|_{y=0}}{T_s - T_\infty} = \frac{-k (T_\infty - T_s)}{L (T_s - T_\infty)} \left. \frac{\partial T^*}{\partial y^*} \right|_{y^*=0} = \frac{k}{L} \left. \frac{\partial T^*}{\partial y^*} \right|_{y^*=0}, \qquad (14.11)$$

and subsequently we can introduce the *Nusselt number*, Nu_L, and write

$$Nu_L \equiv \frac{hL}{k} = \left. \frac{\partial T^*}{\partial y^*} \right|_{y^*=0}. \qquad (14.12)$$

Note:

- dP_∞^*/dx^* depends largely on the geometry.

Note:

- While the definitions of Nusselt number (14.12) and Biot numbers (9.7) and (10.8) appear to be essentially the same, they are different quantities. The Nusselt number corresponds to the dimensionless form of the convection heat transfer coefficient computed through the dimensionless temperature gradient at the surface. In the definitions of Biot numbers, the convection heat transfer coefficient is a given parameter; they thus provide measures of the different length scales used in their corresponding definitions.

Example 14.1:

Ignoring buoyancy and viscous dissipation, the steady dimensionless boundary layer equations involve three unknown functions, u^*, v^*, and T^*, the two independent variables x^* and y^*, and the two parameters Re_L and Pr. The quantity dP_∞^*/dx^* is determined from free stream conditions and can be treated as a known function of x^*.

Known: For a given geometry, u^* and T^* can be expressed as

$$u^* = u^* (x^*, y^*; Re_L) \qquad (14.13)$$

and

$$T^* = T^* (x^*, y^*; Re_L, Pr). \qquad (14.14)$$

Find: The functional forms of the friction and convection coefficients.

Assumptions: Steady-state conditions; dP_∞^*/dx^* is a known function of x^*; body forces and viscous dissipation are negligible.

Properties: All properties are constant.

Analysis: From Eqs. (14.13), (14.9), and (14.10), given the assumptions, we have that

$$\tau_s = \left(\frac{\mu\, u_\infty}{L}\right) \frac{\partial u^*}{\partial y^*}\bigg|_{y^*=0} = \left(\frac{\mu\, u_\infty}{L}\right) f_1\left(x^*; Re_L\right)$$

and

$$c_f = \frac{2}{Re_L} \frac{\partial u^*}{\partial y^*}\bigg|_{y^*=0} = \frac{2}{Re_L} f_1\left(x^*; Re_L\right) = f_2\left(x^*; Re_L\right).$$

Similarly, From Eqs. (14.14), (14.11), and (14.12) for a given geometry, the convection heat transfer coefficient and Nusselt Number can be expressed as

$$h = \frac{k}{L} \frac{\partial T^*}{\partial y^*}\bigg|_{y^*=0} = \frac{k}{L} g_1\left(x^*; Re_L, Pr\right),$$

and

$$Nu_L \equiv \frac{h\,L}{k} = \frac{\partial T^*}{\partial y^*}\bigg|_{y^*=0} = g_1\left(x^*; Re_L, Pr\right).$$

Comments: The Nusselt number is equivalent to the dimensionless temperature gradient at the surface, and thus it is properly referred to as the dimensionless heat transfer coefficient. Also, the Nusselt number for a given geometry can be expressed in terms of the Reynolds number, the Prandtl number, and the space variable x^*, and such a relation can be used for different fluids flowing at different velocities over similar geometries of different lengths.

Exercises 14:

1. Experimental results for heat transfer over a flat plate were found to be correlated by an expression of the form

$$Nu_x = 0.04\, Re_x^{0.9} Pr^{1/3},$$

where Nu_x is the local value of the Nusselt number at position x measured from the leading edge of the plate. Obtain an expression for the ratio of the average heat transfer coefficient $\bar{h}_x$ to the local coefficient h_x.

2. To assess the efficacy of different liquids for cooling an object of given size and shape by forced convection, it is convenient to intro-

duce a *figure of merit*, F_M, which combines the influence of all pertinent fluid properties on the convection coefficient. If the Nusselt number is governed by an expression of the form, $\overline{Nu}_L \sim Re_L^m Pr^n$, obtain the corresponding relationship between F_M and the fluid properties. For representative values of $m = 0.80$ and $n = 0.33$, calculate values of F_M for air ($k = 0.026$ W/m·K, $v = 1.6 \times 10^{-5}$ m^2/s, $Pr = 0.71$), water ($k = 0.600$ W/m·K, $v = 10^{-6}$ m^2/s, $Pr = 5.0$), and a dielectric liquid ($k = 0.064$ W/m·K, $v = 10^{-6}$ m^2/s, $Pr = 25$). Which fluid is the most effective cooling agent?

3. Experiments have shown that, for airflow at $T_\infty = 35°C$ and $V_1 = 100$ m/s, the rate of heat transfer from a turbine blade of characteristic length $L_1 = 0.15$ m and surface temperature $T_{s,1} = 300°C$ is $q_1 = 1500$ W. What would be the heat transfer rate from a second turbine blade of characteristic length $L_2 = 0.3$ m operating at $T_{s,2} = 400°C$ in airflow of $T_\infty = 35°C$ and $V_2 = 50$ m/s? The surface area of the blade may be assumed to be directly proportional to its characteristic length.

15 Dimensionless Parameters and Reynolds Analogy

15.1   Dimensionless Parameters

Note:

- As Re_L increases, the boundary layer thickness decreases and the flow eventually becomes unstable at some value of Re_L that we call the critical Reynolds number, Re_c.

The dimensionless parameters (14.6) have physical significance. To see this, we rewrite them as follows.

First, we see that the Reynolds number provides a measure of the relative importance of inertial and viscous forces:

$$Re_L = \frac{u_\infty L}{\nu} = \frac{\rho\, u_\infty L}{\mu} = \frac{\rho\, \dfrac{u_\infty^2}{L}}{\mu\, \dfrac{u_\infty}{L^2}} = \frac{\text{inertial force}}{\text{viscous force}}. \tag{15.1}$$

Similarly, the Grashof number provides a measure of the relative importance of the product of the buoyancy and inertial forces to the viscous force squared:

$$Gr_L = \frac{\beta\, g(T_\infty - T_s)L^3}{\nu^2} = \frac{\rho\, \beta\, g(T_\infty - T_s)}{\dfrac{\rho\, \nu^2}{L^3}} =$$

$$\frac{[\rho\, \beta\, g(T_\infty - T_s)] \cdot \left(\rho\, \dfrac{u_\infty^2}{L}\right)}{\left(\mu\, \dfrac{u_\infty}{L^2}\right)^2} = \frac{(\text{buoyancy force}) \cdot (\text{inertial force})}{(\text{viscous force})^2}. \tag{15.2}$$

Note:

- For laminar boundary layers we can write

$$\frac{\delta_u}{\delta_T} \approx Pr^n, \quad n > 0,$$

where $n \approx \frac{1}{2}$ for gases.

The Prandtl number, on the other hand, depends only on the properties of the fluid and measures the relative importance of momentum and energy transports:

$$Pr = \frac{\nu}{\alpha} = \frac{\dfrac{1}{Re_L}}{\dfrac{1}{Pe_L}} = \frac{\text{momentum transport}}{\text{energy transport}}. \tag{15.3}$$

Estimates of Pr for different fluids are given in the following table:

Fluid	Pr	δ_u / δ_T
Gases	$O(1)$	$O(1)$
Liquids	> 1 or $\gg 1$	> 1 or $\gg 1$
Liquid metals	$\ll 1$	$\ll 1$

Table 15.1: Common estimates of Pr and ratio of boundary layer thicknesses.

The Eckert number provides a measure of the relative importance of kinetic and stored energies:

$$Ec = \frac{u_\infty^2}{c_p\,(T_\infty - T_s)} = \frac{\rho\, u_\infty^2}{\rho\, c_p\,(T_\infty - T_s)} = \frac{\text{kinetic energy}}{\text{stored energy}}. \qquad (15.4)$$

Lastly, the Nusselt number indicates the relative measure of heat convection over heat conduction:

$$Nu_L = \frac{h\,L}{k} = \frac{h\,(T_\infty - T_s)}{k\dfrac{(T_\infty - T_s)}{L}} = \frac{\text{heat convection}}{\text{heat conduction}}. \qquad (15.5)$$

15.2 Reynolds Analogy

In the case where buoyancy effects can be ignored and viscous dissipation is not important ($Gr_L = Ec = 0$), if we take

$$\frac{dP_\infty^*}{dx^*} = 0 \qquad \text{and} \qquad Pr = 1, \qquad (15.6)$$

the equations and boundary conditions for u^* and T^* have the same form (see (14.2)-(14.5)) and so their solutions are equivalent. Thus,

$$\frac{\partial u^*}{\partial y^*} = \frac{\partial T^*}{\partial y^*} \qquad (15.7)$$

and particularly at $y^* = 0$, so from (14.10) and (14.12) we see that

$$c_f\, \frac{Re_L}{2} = Nu_L \qquad (15.8)$$

or

$$St \equiv \frac{Nu_L}{Re_L\, Pr} = \frac{c_f}{2}, \quad (\text{since } Pr = 1) \qquad (15.9)$$

where St is the *Stanton number*. This is called the *Reynolds analogy*. The Reynolds analogy has been found to hold true even when $Pr \neq 1$ if it is corrected as

$$\frac{c_f}{2} = St\, Pr^{2/3} \equiv j_H, \quad (0.6 \lesssim Pr \lesssim 60) \qquad (15.10)$$

where j_H is known as the *Colburn factor*. This is called the *modified Reynolds analogy* or *Chilton-Colburn analogy*.

Note:

- In laminar flow $dP_\infty^*/dx^* \approx 0$, but even in turbulent flow equation (15.9) is found to be a good approximation.

Example 15.1:

A flat plate of width W and length L is suspended in a room, and is subjected to air flow parallel to its surfaces along the side of length L. The free stream temperature, pressure and velocity of air are P_∞, T_∞ and u_∞.

Known: Plate size, free stream temperature and velocity, and that the total drag force acting on the plate is F_D.

Find: The average convection heat transfer coefficient for the plate.

Assumptions: Steady-state; edge effects are negligible; body forces and viscous dissipation are negligible.

Properties: The properties of air at P_∞ and T_∞.

Analysis: The flow is along the characteristic length L. Both sides of the plate are exposed to air flow, and thus the total surface area is $A_s = 2WL$. The drag coefficient c_D can be determined from Eq. (12.7),

$$c_D = \frac{F_D}{\rho\, A_s\, u_\infty^2 / 2}.$$

Then the average heat transfer coefficient can be determined from averaging the modified Reynolds analogy (15.10) (using Eq. (12.9)) to be

$$\bar{h} = \frac{c_D}{2}\, \frac{\rho\, u_\infty\, c_p}{Pr^{2/3}}.$$

Comments: This example shows the great utility of momentum-heat transfer analogies in that the convection heat transfer coefficient can be determined from a knowledge of friction coefficient, which is easier to determine.

Exercises 15:

1. What physical processes are represented by the terms of the x-momentum equation (14.3)? By the energy equation (14.4)?

2. Under what conditions may velocity and thermal boundary layers be termed analogous? What is the physical basis of analogous behavior?

3. What important parameters are linked by the Reynolds analogy?

16 Turbulent Boundary Layer

16.1 Description of Turbulence

In the following, we continue to ignore buoyancy effects and viscous dissipation.

When the Reynolds number associated with the flow is larger than the critical Reynolds number, *i.e.*, $Re > Re_c$, we have turbulent flow. Turbulence is a random time-dependent process. This means that we cannot predict instantaneous values of u, v, and T. Due to this random behavior, turbulence increases mixing, and therefore also increases the heat transfer rate.

While local values of quantities are random, we can obtain their time average as indicated in Fig. 16.1. Let $f(x, y, t)$ represent any of our dependent variables u, v, or T. Then we can write such quantity as the sum of the time average plus the instantaneous fluctuation from the average:

$$f(x, y, t) = \overline{f}(x, y) + f'(x, y, t), \qquad (16.1)$$

where, for an arbitrary time t_0, the time average is defined as

$$\overline{f}(x, y) \equiv \lim_{\tau \to \infty} \frac{1}{\tau} \int_{t_0}^{t_0 + \tau} f(x, y, t) \, dt, \qquad \tau \gg t'. \qquad (16.2)$$

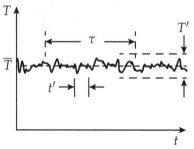

Figure 16.1: Temperature measurement at a point in a turbulent flow.

Note that for statistically steady flow $\overline{f'}(x, y, t) = 0$. Now, using (16.1) for u, v, and T, substituting such expressions in the dimensional boundary layer equations (13.25)-(13.27), and taking the time average of the resulting equations, we obtain the following equations for the (statistically steady) mean flow:

$$\frac{\partial \overline{u}}{\partial x} + \frac{\partial \overline{v}}{\partial y} = 0, \qquad (16.3)$$

$$\rho \left(\overline{u} \frac{\partial \overline{u}}{\partial x} + \overline{v} \frac{\partial \overline{u}}{\partial y} \right) = -\frac{dP_\infty}{dx} + \frac{\partial \tau_{tot}}{\partial y}, \qquad (16.4)$$

$$\rho c_p \left(\overline{u} \frac{\partial \overline{T}}{\partial x} + \overline{v} \frac{\partial \overline{T}}{\partial y} \right) = -\frac{\partial q''_{tot}}{\partial y}, \qquad (16.5)$$

Note:

- In writing equations (16.4) and (16.5), based on the boundary layer assumptions, we have assumed that the streamwise gradient of the product of two fluctuations is much smaller than the transverse gradient of the product of two fluctuations.

- The term $-\rho \overline{u' v'}$ is called the *Reynolds stress*.

where we have defined the total shear stress and heat flux as

$$
\tau_{tot} \equiv \left(\underbrace{\mu \frac{\partial \overline{u}}{\partial y}}_{\text{molecular}} - \underbrace{\rho \overline{u' v'}}_{\text{turbulent}} \right) \quad \text{and} \quad q''_{tot} = - \left(\underbrace{k \frac{\partial \overline{T}}{\partial y}}_{\text{molecular}} - \underbrace{\rho c_p \overline{v' T'}}_{\text{turbulent}} \right).
\tag{16.6}
$$

The additional terms in (16.6) over those of steady laminar boundary layers are due to turbulence. These terms account for turbulent momentum and energy transport. Since we refer to those terms as turbulent transport, in analogy with molecular transport we *assume* that

$$
-\rho \overline{u' v'} = \rho \nu_T \frac{\partial \overline{u}}{\partial y} = \mu_T \frac{\partial \overline{u}}{\partial y} \quad \text{or} \quad -\overline{u' v'} = \nu_T \frac{\partial \overline{u}}{\partial y},
\tag{16.7}
$$

and

$$
-\rho c_p \overline{v' T'} = k_T \frac{\partial \overline{T}}{\partial y} \quad \text{or} \quad -\overline{v' T'} = \alpha_T \frac{\partial \overline{T}}{\partial y}.
\tag{16.8}
$$

Subsequently, we can write

$$
\tau_{tot} = \rho \left(\nu + \nu_T \right) \frac{\partial \overline{u}}{\partial y} = \left(\mu + \mu_T \right) \frac{\partial \overline{u}}{\partial y}
\tag{16.9}
$$

and

$$
q''_{tot} = -\rho c_p \left(\alpha + \alpha_T \right) \frac{\partial \overline{T}}{\partial y} = - \left(k + k_T \right) \frac{\partial \overline{T}}{\partial y}.
\tag{16.10}
$$

We conclude by making the following observations based on the behaviors of the laminar and turbulent boundary layers illustrated in Fig. 16.2:

$$
\left. \frac{\partial \overline{u}}{\partial y} \right|_{y=0,\text{turb}} > \left. \frac{\partial u}{\partial y} \right|_{y=0,\text{lam}} \quad \text{and} \quad \left. \frac{\partial \overline{T}}{\partial y} \right|_{y=0,\text{turb}} > \left. \frac{\partial T}{\partial y} \right|_{y=0,\text{lam}}.
\tag{16.11}
$$

Note:

- ν_T and α_T are *not* fluid properties; they are determined by the flow.

Figure 16.2: Laminar and turbulent boundary layers.

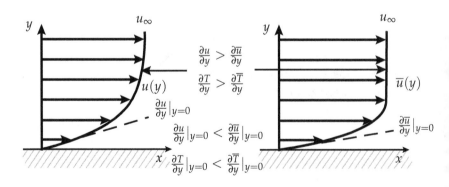

Example 16.1:

A fluid at temperature T_∞ flows at a velocity u_∞ over a flat plate of length L. In the laminar and turbulent regions, experimental measurements show that the local convection coefficients are well described by

$$h_{\text{lam}} = c_{\text{lam}}\, x^{-0.5} \quad \text{and} \quad h_{\text{turb}} = c_{\text{turb}}\, x^{-0.2},$$

where the constants c_{lam} and c_{turb} depend on the fluid temperature.

Known: Fluid flow over a flat plate, expressions for the local convection coefficient from the plate's leading edge x, and velocity and temperature of the fluid.

Find: Determine the average convection coefficient, $\bar{h}$, over the entire plate.

Assumptions: Steady-state; transition occurs at the critical Reynolds number of $Re_c = 5 \times 10^5$.

Properties: The properties of the fluid are evaluated at T_∞.

Analysis: Since the local convection coefficient is highly dependent on whether laminar or turbulent conditions exist, we first determine the location where transition occurs:

$$x_c = \frac{Re_c\, \nu}{u_\infty}.$$

Subsequently,

$$\bar{h} = \frac{1}{L}\int_0^L h\, dx = \frac{1}{L}\left(\int_0^{x_c} h_{\text{lam}}\, dx + \int_{x_c}^L h_{\text{turb}}\, dx\right)$$

or

$$\bar{h} = \frac{1}{L}\left[\frac{c_{\text{lam}}}{0.5}\, x_c^{0.5} + \frac{c_{\text{turb}}}{0.8}\left(x_L^{0.8} - x_c^{0.8}\right)\right].$$

Comments: Careful consideration of the temperature dependence of fluid properties is crucial when performing a convection heat transfer analysis. The largest local convection coefficients occur at the leading edge of the flat plate, where the laminar thermal boundary layer is extremely thin, and just downstream of x_c where the turbulent boundary layer is thinnest.

Exercises 16:

1. Verify Eqs. (16.3)-(16.5) by substituting Eq. (16.1) into the boundary layer Eqs. (13.25)-(13.27) (ignore buoyancy effects and viscous dissipation) and taking the time average (16.2) for which $\overline{f'}(x, y, t) = 0$.

2. The transition (from laminar to turbulent flow) Reynolds number for pipe flow is $Re_c \approx 2300$, whereas for flow over a plate it is $Re_c \approx 2 \times 10^5$. What do you believe to be the reason for this difference?

3. It is known from flow measurements that the transition to turbulence occurs when the Reynolds number based on mean velocity and diameter exceeds 4000 in a certain pipe. Use the fact that the laminar boundary layer on a flat plate grows according to the relation

$$\frac{\delta}{x} = 4.92 \sqrt{\frac{\nu}{u_{max}\, x}}$$

to find an equivalent value for the Reynolds number of transition based on distance from the leading edge of a plate and u_{max}. (Note that $u_{max} = 2\,\bar{u}_{av}$ during laminar flow in a pipe.)

17 External Laminar Flow

In this lecture, we continue to ignore buoyancy effects and viscous dissipation. In such case, and in analogy to (14.6) and (14.12), we define local values of Reynolds and Nusselt numbers as

$$Re_x = \frac{u_\infty x}{\nu} \quad \text{and} \quad Nu_x = \frac{h_x x}{k}, \tag{17.1}$$

where from (14.8) and (14.11) we see that the local convection heat transfer coefficient is given by

$$h_x = h_x\left(x; Re_x, Pr\right) \tag{17.2}$$

since in external flow we typically have that

$$\frac{dP_\infty}{dx} \approx 0. \tag{17.3}$$

Subsequently, it also follows that

$$Nu_x = Nu_x\left(x; Re_x, Pr\right). \tag{17.4}$$

We also define the corresponding average Nusselt number,

$$\overline{Nu}_x = \bar{h}_x\, x/k, \tag{17.5}$$

where the average convection heat transfer coefficient is given by

$$\bar{h}_x = \frac{1}{x} \int_0^x h_{x'}\, dx'. \tag{17.6}$$

It is then subsequently clear that

$$\overline{Nu}_x = \overline{Nu}_x\left(Re_x, Pr\right). \tag{17.7}$$

There are two approaches that one can take to obtain an explicit expression for (17.7): a) experimental, and b) theoretical. We will discuss both approaches, focusing on expressions for a flat plate.

Note:

• If we take $x = L$, we recover the previous definitions of Reynolds and Nusselt numbers.

Note:

• The average Nusselt number over a plate of length L is given by $\overline{Nu}_L = \bar{h}_L\, L/k$, where $\bar{h}_L = \frac{1}{L} \int_0^L h_{x'}\, dx'$, and thus it follows that $\overline{Nu}_L = \overline{Nu}_L\left(Re_L, Pr\right).$

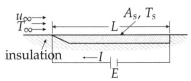

Figure 17.1: Flow over a flat plate.

Note:

- To obtain $\overline{Nu}_L$ we can use k evaluated at the plate's surface temperature, T_s, or at the *film temperature*, $T_f = \frac{1}{2}(T_s + T_\infty)$.

- Re_L is most easily varied by varying u_∞.

17.1 *Experiments*

Using the electrical circuit indicated in Fig. 17.1, in conjunction with a flat plate that is well insulated as indicated in the figure, we can obtain $\overline{h}_L$ from experimental measurements.

Subsequently, we obtain the average Nusselt number over the length of the plate, and we know that it depends only on Re_L and Pr:

$$\overline{Nu}_L = \frac{\overline{h}_L L}{k} = \overline{Nu}_L\left(Re_L, Pr\right). \tag{17.8}$$

We assume the dependence on Re_L and Pr to be in the form of power laws:

$$\overline{Nu}_L = C\, Re_L^m\, Pr^n, \tag{17.9}$$

where C, m and n are constants.

Now, experimentally, for each fixed fluid (*i.e.*, fixed Pr), we obtain a value of $\overline{Nu}_L$ for varying values of Re_L. We subsequently perform a least square fit, and if the behavior follows a power law, then the fit should correspond to a line on a log Re_L vs. log $\overline{Nu}_L$ plot, as indicated in the plot for Pr_1 in Fig. 17.2 (a). By using different fluids having different Prandtl numbers and repeating the procedure outlined above, we are able to generate the plots shown in the figure. Note that we will subsequently average the different values of slopes and intercepts to obtain the average slope m and the average value of the intercept, which depends on averages of C and n for each Pr as indicated by

$$\log \overline{Nu}_L = (\log C + n \log Pr) + m \log Re_L \tag{17.10}$$

Figure 17.2: Plots of experimental data: (a) log $\overline{Nu}_L$ vs. log Re_L for different Pr; (b) log $\overline{Nu}_L$ vs. log Pr for different Re_L.

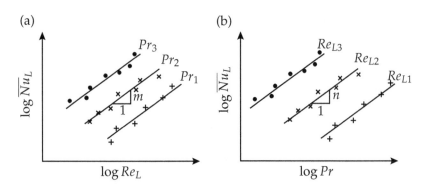

Alternately, for each fixed flow rate (*i.e.*, fixed Re_L), we obtain a value of $\overline{Nu}_L$ for each value of Pr (by varying the fluid). By using different flow rates resulting in different Reynolds numbers, we are able to generate the plots shown in Fig. 17.2 (b). Subsequently, we perform a similar least square averaging procedure to obtain the average value of the slope n and the average value of the intercepts, which in this case depend on C and m for each Re_L as indicated by

$$\log \overline{Nu}_L = (\log C + m \log Re_L) + n \log Pr. \qquad (17.11)$$

Since we have already obtained the average value of m from the analysis of Fig. 17.2 (a), we can now obtain the average value of C, and subsequently have fully obtained experimentally the approximation to equation (17.9).

17.2   Theory

Assuming 2-D, steady, incompressible, laminar flow on a flat plate, ignoring buoyancy and viscous dissipation effects, using constant properties, and taking $dP_\infty/dx = 0$, we have the following system of governing equations (see (13.25)-(13.27)):

$$\frac{\partial u}{\partial x} + \frac{\partial v}{\partial y} = 0, \qquad (17.12)$$

$$u \frac{\partial u}{\partial x} + v \frac{\partial u}{\partial y} = \nu \frac{\partial^2 u}{\partial y^2}, \qquad (17.13)$$

$$u \frac{\partial T}{\partial x} + v \frac{\partial T}{\partial y} = \alpha \frac{\partial^2 T}{\partial y^2}, \qquad (17.14)$$

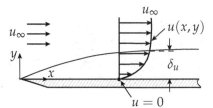

Figure 17.3: Velocity profile.

with boundary conditions (see (13.28))

$$v(x,0) = 0, \quad T(x,0) = T_s, \quad u(x,\infty) = u_\infty, \quad T(x,\infty) = T_\infty. \quad (17.15)$$

See Figs. 17.3 and 17.4.

For 2-D incompressible flow we can always introduce a stream function, ψ, such that the continuity equation (17.12) is automatically satisfied:

$$u = \frac{\partial \psi}{\partial y} \quad \text{and} \quad v = -\frac{\partial \psi}{\partial x}. \qquad (17.16)$$

Now, the basic assumption is that the laminar boundary layer is similar:

$$\frac{u}{u_\infty} = \phi\left(\frac{y}{\delta_u(x)}\right) \quad \text{and} \quad \frac{T - T_s}{T_\infty - T_s} = \theta\left(\frac{y}{\delta_u(x)}\right),$$

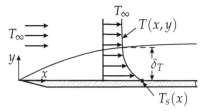

Figure 17.4: Temperature profile.

where we note that ϕ and θ are dimensionless functions of the dimensionless quantity $y/\delta_u(x)$, where $\delta_u(x)$ is given from the scaling arguments in Sec. 13.3:

$$\delta_u(x) \sim \sqrt{\frac{\nu x}{u_\infty}}.$$

Subsequently, we define the new independent (similarity) variable and dependent variables as

$$\eta = y\sqrt{\frac{u_\infty}{\nu x}}, \qquad \psi = u_\infty\sqrt{\frac{\nu x}{u_\infty}}f(\eta), \qquad \frac{T-T_s}{T_\infty-T_s}=\theta(\eta), \quad (17.17)$$

where we use the similarity variable η in lieu of the independent variable y. Now, we have

$$u = \frac{\partial\psi}{\partial y} = \frac{\partial\psi}{\partial\eta}\frac{\partial\eta}{\partial y} = \left(u_\infty\sqrt{\frac{\nu x}{u_\infty}}\frac{df}{d\eta}\right)\left(\sqrt{\frac{u_\infty}{\nu x}}\right) = u_\infty\frac{df}{d\eta}, \quad (17.18)$$

$$v = -\frac{\partial\psi}{\partial x} = -u_\infty\left(\sqrt{\frac{\nu x}{u_\infty}}\frac{df}{d\eta}\frac{\partial\eta}{\partial x}+\frac{1}{2}\sqrt{\frac{\nu}{u_\infty x}}f\right)$$

$$= \frac{1}{2}\sqrt{\frac{u_\infty\nu}{x}}\left(\eta\frac{df}{d\eta}-f\right). \quad (17.19)$$

Similarly,

$$\frac{\partial u}{\partial x} = -\frac{u_\infty}{2x}\eta\frac{d^2f}{d\eta^2}, \quad (17.20)$$

$$\frac{\partial u}{\partial y} = u_\infty\sqrt{\frac{u_\infty}{\nu x}}\frac{d^2f}{d\eta^2}, \quad (17.21)$$

$$\frac{\partial^2 u}{\partial y^2} = \frac{u_\infty^2}{\nu x}\frac{d^3f}{d\eta^3}, \quad (17.22)$$

$$\frac{\partial T}{\partial x} = -\frac{(T_\infty-T_s)}{2x}\eta\frac{d\theta}{d\eta}, \quad (17.23)$$

$$\frac{\partial T}{\partial y} = (T_\infty-T_s)\sqrt{\frac{u_\infty}{\nu x}}\frac{d\theta}{d\eta}, \quad (17.24)$$

$$\frac{\partial^2 T}{\partial y^2} = (T_\infty-T_s)\left(\frac{u_\infty}{\nu x}\right)\frac{d^2\theta}{d\eta^2}. \quad (17.25)$$

Substituting (17.17)-(17.25) into (17.13)-(17.15), we obtain the following system of ordinary differential equations with corresponding boundary conditions:

$$\frac{d^3f}{d\eta^3}+\frac{1}{2}f\frac{d^2f}{d\eta^2}=0, \quad f(0)=\frac{df}{d\eta}\Big|_{\eta=0}=0, \quad \frac{df}{d\eta}\Big|_{\eta\to\infty}=1, \quad (17.26)$$

$$\frac{d^2\theta}{d\eta^2}+\frac{Pr}{2}f\frac{d\theta}{d\eta}=0, \quad \theta(0)=0, \quad \theta(\infty)=1. \quad (17.27)$$

The problem (17.26), called the Blasius problem, is totally decoupled from (17.27) and thus can be solved first. The equation is non-linear and can only be solved approximately. Computed results are given in Table 17.1. Note that

$$\frac{u}{u_\infty}=\frac{df}{d\eta} \quad (17.28)$$

Table 17.1: Similarity solution $f(\eta)$.

η	f	$df/d\eta$	$d^2f/d\eta^2$
0.00	0.0000	0.0000	0.3321
0.25	0.0104	0.0830	0.3319
0.50	0.0415	0.1659	0.3309
0.75	0.0933	0.2483	0.3282
1.00	0.1656	0.3298	0.3230
1.25	0.2580	0.4096	0.3146
1.50	0.3701	0.4868	0.3026
1.75	0.5011	0.5605	0.2866
2.00	0.6500	0.6298	0.2668
2.25	0.8156	0.6936	0.2434
2.50	0.9963	0.7513	0.2174
2.75	1.1906	0.8022	0.1897
3.00	1.3968	0.8460	0.1614
3.25	1.6131	0.8829	0.1337
3.50	1.8377	0.9130	0.1078
3.75	2.0691	0.9370	0.0844
4.00	2.3057	0.9555	0.0642
4.25	2.5464	0.9694	0.0474
4.50	2.7901	0.9795	0.0340
4.75	3.0360	0.9867	0.0236
5.00	3.2833	0.9915	0.0159
5.25	3.5316	0.9948	0.0104
5.50	3.7806	0.9969	0.0066
5.75	4.0300	0.9982	0.0040
6.00	4.2796	0.9990	0.0024
6.25	4.5294	0.9994	0.0014
6.50	4.7793	0.9997	0.0008
6.75	5.0293	0.9998	0.0004
7.00	5.2792	0.9999	0.0002
7.25	5.5292	1.0000	0.0001
7.50	5.7792	1.0000	0.0001
7.75	6.0292	1.0000	0.0000
8.00	6.2792	1.0000	0.0000

and from the table we see that

$$\frac{u}{u_\infty} \approx 0.99 \quad \text{at} \quad \eta \approx 5.0, \tag{17.29}$$

so that

$$\delta_u(x) \approx \frac{5.0}{\sqrt{\frac{u_\infty}{\nu x}}} = \frac{5.0\,x}{\sqrt{Re_x}}. \tag{17.30}$$

We additionally see from Table 17.1 that the local shear stress is given by (see (14.9))

$$\tau_{s,x} = \mu \left.\frac{\partial u}{\partial y}\right|_{y=0} = \mu\, u_\infty \sqrt{\frac{u_\infty}{\nu x}}\, \left.\frac{d^2 f}{d\eta^2}\right|_{\eta=0} = 0.332\, u_\infty \sqrt{\frac{\rho\,\mu\,u_\infty}{x}} \tag{17.31}$$

and the local friction coefficient by (see (14.10))

$$c_{f,x} = \frac{\tau_{s,x}}{\rho\, u_\infty^2/2} = 0.664\, Re_x^{-1/2}. \tag{17.32}$$

Now, from (14.11), it follows that the local convection heat transfer coefficient is given by

$$h_x = \frac{q_s''}{T_s - T_\infty} = -\frac{T_\infty - T_s}{T_s - T_\infty} k \left.\frac{\partial\theta}{\partial y}\right|_{y=0} = k \left(\frac{u_\infty}{\nu x}\right)^{1/2} \left.\frac{d\theta}{d\eta}\right|_{\eta=0}. \tag{17.33}$$

Using the solution of (17.26), problem (17.27) is solved for different Prandtl numbers. After many calculations, we find values of $d\theta/d\eta|_{\eta=0}$ for the range of Prandtl numbers; such values are given in Table 17.2. In the table we also show the quantity $0.332\, Pr^{1/3}$ which most resources recommend as an approximation for the following range of Prandtl numbers:

$$\left.\frac{d\theta}{d\eta}\right|_{\eta=0} \approx 0.332\, Pr^{1/3}, \quad 0.6 \lesssim Pr \lesssim 60. \tag{17.34}$$

From (17.33) and (17.34), we obtain the local Nusselt number:

$$Nu_x = \frac{h_x\, x}{k} \approx 0.332\, Re_x^{1/2}\, Pr^{1/3}, \quad 0.6 \lesssim Pr \lesssim 60. \tag{17.35}$$

Clearly, more accurate values of Nu_x can be obtained by using values of $d\theta/dx|_{\eta=0}$ in Table 17.2.

From solutions of (17.26), we can also obtain the thermal boundary layer thickness for different values of Prandtl number. The thermal boundary layer thickness relative to the momentum boundary layer thickness is given in Fig. 17.5 as a function of $Pr^{-1/3}$. The behavior makes sense physically, since the Prandtl number is the ratio of the kinematic viscosity to the thermal diffusivity, and the larger the thermal diffusivity, the thicker the corresponding thermal boundary layer

Table 17.2: Surface temperature slope.

Pr	$d\theta/d\eta\|_{\eta=0}$	$0.3321\, Pr^{1/3}$
0.2	0.1852	0.1942
0.3	0.2149	0.2223
0.4	0.2390	0.2447
0.5	0.2593	0.2636
0.6	0.2770	0.2801
0.7	0.2927	0.2949
0.8	0.3069	0.3083
0.9	0.3200	0.3206
1.0	0.3321	0.3321
1.1	0.3433	0.3428
1.2	0.3539	0.3529
1.3	0.3639	0.3625
1.4	0.3733	0.3715
1.5	0.3823	0.3802
1.6	0.3909	0.3884
1.7	0.3991	0.3964
1.8	0.4069	0.4040
1.9	0.4145	0.4113
2.0	0.4217	0.4184
4.0	0.5199	0.5272
6.0	0.3860	0.6035
8.0	0.0498	0.6642
10	0.0027	0.7155
12	0.0001	0.7603
14	0.0000	0.8004
16	0.0000	0.8368
18	0.0000	0.8703
20	0.0000	0.9015
25	0.0000	0.9711
30	0.0000	1.0319
35	0.0000	1.0863
40	0.0000	1.1358
45	0.0000	1.1812
50	0.0000	1.2235
55	0.0000	1.2630
60	0.0000	1.3001

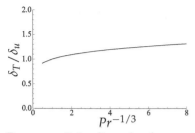

Figure 17.5: Ratio of boundary layer thicknesses.

relative to the momentum boundary layer. We see that the approximation

$$\frac{\delta_T}{\delta_u} \approx Pr^{-1/3} \tag{17.36}$$

is reasonable for the range of Prandtl numbers shown in the figure.

Lastly, averaging the local shear stress and convection heat transfer coefficient,

$$\overline{\tau}_{s,x} = \frac{1}{x} \int_0^x \tau_{s,x'} \, dx' \quad \text{and} \quad \overline{h}_x = \frac{1}{x} \int_0^x h_{x'} \, dx', \tag{17.37}$$

we obtain the average friction coefficient and Nusselt number:

$$\overline{c}_{f,x} = 1.328 \, Re_x^{-1/2} \quad \text{and} \quad \overline{Nu}_x \approx 0.664 \, Re_x^{1/2} \, Pr^{1/3}, \quad 0.6 \lesssim Pr \lesssim 60. \tag{17.38}$$

Again, more accurate values of the average Nusselt number can be obtained using values from Table 17.2. Note that

$$\overline{c}_{f,x} = 2 \, c_{f,x} \quad \text{and} \quad \overline{Nu}_x = 2 \, Nu_x. \tag{17.39}$$

Example 17.1:

A strut of characteristic length L_1 is exposed to hydrogen flowing at $P_{\infty,1}$, $V_{\infty,1}$, and $T_{\infty,1}$. Of interest is the value of the average heat transfer coefficient $\overline{h}_1$, when the surface temperature is $T_{s,1}$. Rather than conducting expensive experiments involving hydrogen, an engineer proposes to take advantage of similarity by performing wind tunnel experiments using air at pressure $P_{\infty,2}$ with $T_{\infty,2}$. A geometrically similar strut of characteristic length L_2 and perimeter $\mathcal{P}_2$ is placed in the wind tunnel. Measurements reveal a surface temperature of $T_{s,2}$ when the heat loss per unit length is q_2'. Determine the required air velocity, $V_{\infty,2}$, in the wind tunnel experiment and the average convective heat transfer coefficient, $\overline{h}_1$, in the hydrogen.

Known: Flow across the strut. Hydrogen pressure, velocity, and temperature. Air temperature and pressure, as well as heat loss per unit length. Surface temperatures of the strut in hydrogen and in air.

Find: Air velocity and average convective heat transfer coefficient for the strut in hydrogen.

Assumptions: Steady-state; $dP_\infty/dx = 0$; body forces and viscous dissipation are negligible; ideal gas behavior; constant properties.

Properties: Since properties are constant, from the ideal gas law $\rho = P/RT$ and since $\nu = \mu/\rho$, we find that

$$\frac{\nu_1}{\nu_2} = \frac{\mu_1 \, T_{\infty,1} \, P_{\infty,2}}{\mu_2 \, T_{\infty,2} \, P_{\infty,1}}.$$

It is also noted that $Pr_1 \approx Pr_2$. $Pr\ air\ vs\ Pr\ hydrogen$?

Analysis: From (17.8) we know that

$$\overline{Nu}_1 = \frac{\overline{h}_1 L_1}{k_1} = \overline{Nu}_1\,(Re_{L1}, Pr_1) \text{ and } \overline{Nu}_2 = \frac{\overline{h}_2 L_2}{k_2} = \overline{Nu}_2\,(Re_{L2}, Pr_2).$$

If we take $Pr_1 = Pr_2$, similarity exists if $Re_{L1} = Re_{L2}$ in which case $\overline{Nu}_1 = \overline{Nu}_2$. Equating Reynolds numbers, we have

$$V_{\infty,2} = \frac{Re_{L2}\,\nu_2}{L_2} = \frac{Re_{L1}\,\nu_2}{L_2} = \frac{V_{\infty,1}\,L_1\,\nu_2}{\nu_1\,L_2}.$$

Now equating Nusselt numbers and incorporating Newton's law of cooling, we obtain

$$\overline{h}_1 = \overline{h}_2 \frac{L_2\,k_1}{L_1\,k_2} = \frac{q_2'}{P_2\,(T_{s,2} - T_{\infty,2})} \frac{L_2\,k_1}{L_1\,k_2}.$$

Comments: Experiments involving pressurized hydrogen can be expensive. The fluid properties should be evaluated at the arithmetic mean of the free stream and surface temperatures.

Exercises 17:

1. A thermal sensor is to be located 2 m from the leading edge of a flat plate along which 10°C glycerine ($\nu = 2.79 \times 10^{-3}$ m^2/s) flows at 19 m/s. The pressure is atmospheric. In order to calibrate the sensor the velocity components, u and v, must be known. At $y = 4.5$ cm determine the velocity components.

2. Air at 27°C blows over a flat surface with a sharp leading edge at 1.5 m/s. Find the boundary layer thickness 1/2 m from the leading edge. Check the boundary layer assumption that $u \gg v$ at the trailing edge.

3. Calculate the average shear stress and the overall friction coefficient for the surface in Exercise 2 if its total length is $L = 1/2$ m. Compare $\overline{\tau}_{s,x}$ with $\tau_{s,x}$ at the trailing edge. At what point on the surface does $\tau_{s,x} = \overline{\tau}_{s,x}$? Finally, estimate what fraction of the surface can legitimately be analyzed using boundary layer theory.

18 External Turbulent Flow

18.1 Turbulent Flow

From experiments of turbulent flow on a flat plate, we find that the local friction coefficient and momentum boundary layer thickness are approximately given by

$$c_{f,x} \approx 0.0592 \, Re_x^{-1/5}, \quad \delta_u \approx 0.37 \, x \, Re_x^{-1/5}, \quad 5 \times 10^5 < Re_x \lesssim 10^8. \quad (18.1)$$

Note that we have assumed that the transition from laminar to turbulent flow occurs at the critical Reynolds number of $Re_c = 5 \times 10^5$ (see (12.17)). It should be observed that the turbulent momentum boundary layer thickness varies much more rapidly than the laminar one (see (17.30)), since

$$\delta_{u,lam} \propto x^{1/2} \quad \text{and} \quad \delta_{u,turb} \propto x^{4/5}, \quad (18.2)$$

and that in turbulent flow $\delta_{u,turb} \approx \delta_{T,turb}$ because molecular effects are negligible. Lastly, it is also found that the local Nusselt number is approximately given by

$$Nu_x \approx 0.0296 \, Re_x^{4/5} \, Pr^{1/3}, \quad 0.6 < Pr < 60 \quad (18.3)$$

Note that in this case it does not make any sense to obtain $\overline{Nu_x}$ since we always have a laminar region from the plate's leading edge up to the critical point x_c.

18.2 Mixed Boundary Layer

To compute $\bar{c}_{f,L}$ and $\overline{Nu_L}$ for a flat plate of length L, in general we must add the contributions of both the laminar and turbulent regions:

$$\bar{c}_{f,L} = \frac{1}{L} \left(\int_0^{x_c} c_{f,x,lam} \, dx + \int_{x_c}^{L} c_{f,x,turb} \, dx \right) \quad (18.4)$$

and

$$\bar{h}_L = \frac{1}{L} \left(\int_0^{x_c} h_{x,lam} \, dx + \int_{x_c}^{L} h_{x,turb} \, dx \right). \quad (18.5)$$

Subsequently, we have that

$$\bar{c}_{f,L} \approx \frac{0.074}{Re_L^{1/5}} - \frac{2A}{Re_L} \quad \text{and} \quad \overline{Nu}_L \approx \left(0.037\, Re_L^{4/5} - A\right) Pr^{1/3}$$

$$\text{for} \quad Re_x \lesssim 10^8 \quad \text{and} \quad 0.6 < Pr < 60, \quad (18.6)$$

where

$$A = 0.037\, Re_c^{4/5} - 0.664\, Re_c^{1/2}. \qquad (18.7)$$

For $Re_c = 5 \times 10^5$, we have that $A = 871$. Note that if the plate is not sufficiently long, then it is possible that $x_c > L$ and thus no turbulent region exists. Alternately, when $L \gg x_c$, then

$$2A \ll Re_L \quad \text{and} \quad A \ll 0.037\, Re_L^{4/5} \qquad (18.8)$$

in which case

$$\bar{c}_{f,L} \approx 0.074\, Re_L^{-1/5} \quad \text{and} \quad \overline{Nu}_L \approx 0.037\, Re_L^{4/5} Pr^{1/3}. \qquad (18.9)$$

Example 18.1:

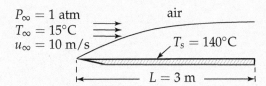

$P_\infty = 1$ atm
$T_\infty = 15°C$
$u_\infty = 10$ m/s
air
$T_s = 140°C$
$L = 3$ m

Known: Air at prescribed thermodynamic conditions flows at a certain speed above a finite flat plate that has a prescribed surface temperature.

Find: i) The average heat transfer coefficient over the plate; ii) the local convection heat transfer coefficient at the midpoint of the plate; iii) sketch the variation of heat flux along the plate.

Assumptions: Uniform surface temperature, $Re_c = 5 \times 10^5$.

Properties: For air at $P_\infty = 1$ atm and $T_f = (T_s + T_\infty)/2 \approx 350$ K: $\nu = 20.92 \times 10^{-6}$ m^2/s, $k = 0.03$ W/m·K, $Pr = 0.7$.

Analysis:

i) We examine first whether the boundary layer is laminar or mixed by computing Re_L:

$$Re_L = \frac{u_\infty L}{\nu} = \frac{10\,\text{m/s} \times 3\,\text{m}}{20.92 \times 10^{-6}\,\text{m}^2/\text{s}} = 1.434 \times 10^6.$$

Since $Re_L > Re_c$ we have a mixed boundary layer. Hence, from

(18.6) and (18.7), we have

$$\bar{h}_L = \frac{k}{L}\left(0.037\,Re_L^{4/5} - 871\right)Pr^{1/3}$$

$$= \frac{0.03\,\text{W/m}\cdot\text{K}}{3\,\text{m}}\left[0.037\left(1.434\times10^6\right)^{4/5} - 871\right](0.7)^{1/3}$$

$$= 1.99\,\text{W/m}^2\cdot\text{K}.$$

ii) To obtain the local heat transfer coefficient at the midpoint we have to first determine where the transition critical point is located:

$$x_c = L\left(\frac{Re_c}{Re_L}\right) = 3\,\text{m}\left(\frac{5\times10^5}{1.434\times10^6}\right) = 1.046\,\text{m}.$$

We thus see that the plate midpoint $x = 1.5\,\text{m}$ is in the turbulent boundary layer. So, using (18.3) and noting that $Re_{x=L/2} = Re_L/2$, we have

$$h_x = \frac{k}{x}\left(0.0296\,Re_x^{4/5}\,Pr^{1/3}\right)$$

$$= \frac{0.03\,\text{W/m}\cdot\text{K}}{1.5\,\text{m}}\left[0.0296\left(0.717\times10^6\right)^{4/5}(0.7)^{1/3}\right]$$

$$= 25.4\,\text{W/m}^2\cdot\text{K}.$$

iii) Since $q_x'' = h_x\,(T_s - T_\infty)$, it follows that local heat flux will vary with x as h_x. Subsequently, from (17.35) and (18.3), we have

$$h_{x,lam} = 0.332\,\frac{k}{x}\,Re_x^{1/2}\,Pr^{1/3}, \quad h_{x,turb} = 0.0296\,\frac{k}{x}\,Re_x^{4/5}\,Pr^{1/3},$$

and thus the variation of q_x'' with x is as sketched.

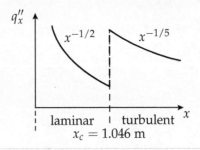

Exercises 18:

1. Oil at 40°C flows at 0.8 m/s over a 1 m long plate. The surface temperature of the plate is 80°C. Find the average heat transfer coefficient and the total heat transferred to the oil if the plate is 0.7 m

wide. Properties of the oil at 60°C are: $\rho = 880$ kg/m^3, $\mu = 0.20$ kg/m·s, $c_p = 1900$ J/kg·K, and $k = 0.14$ W/m·K.

2. Air at $P_\infty = 83.4$ kPa and $T_\infty = 20°C$ flows with a velocity of 8 m/s over a 1.5 m×6 m flat plate whose temperature is $T_s = 140°C$. Determine the rate of heat transfer from the plate if the air flows parallel to the (a) 6 m side and (b) the 1.5 m side. The properties of air at 1 atm and $T_f = (T_s + T_\infty)/2 = 80°C$ are: $\nu = 2.097 \times 10^{-5}$ m^2/s, $k = 0.02953$ W/m·K, $Pr = 0.7154$.

3. The weight of a thin flat plate 50 cm×50 cm in size is balanced by a counterweight that has a mass of 2 kg. Now a fan is turned on, and air at 1 atm and 25°C flows downward over both surfaces of the plate with a freestream velocity of 10 m/s. Determine the mass of the counterweight that needs to be added in order to balance the plate in this case.

19 External Flow – Miscellaneous Topics

19.1 Plate with Constant Heat Flux Surface

If $q_s'' = $ const. is prescribed on the plate surface, then the local surface temperature is found from

$$T_s(x) = T_\infty + \frac{q_s''}{h_x},\qquad (19.1)$$

where the local convection heat transfer coefficient h_x is obtained from the following corresponding correlations:

$$Nu_{x,lam} = 0.453\,Re_x^{1/2}\,Pr^{1/3} \text{ and } Nu_{x,turb} = 0.0308\,Re_x^{4/5}\,Pr^{1/3}. \quad (19.2)$$

19.2 Plate with Unheated Starting Length

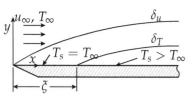

Figure 19.1: Flow over a flat plate with unheated starting length.

If the flat plate is unheated for the starting length $0 \le x \le \xi$, as illustrated in Fig. 19.1, then the correlations for the local Nusselt numbers for $x > \xi$ are modified as follows:

$$Nu_{x,lam} = \frac{Nu_{x,lam}\big|_{\xi=0}}{\left[1 - (\xi/x)^{3/4}\right]^{1/3}} \text{ and } Nu_{x,turb} = \frac{Nu_{x,turb}\big|_{\xi=0}}{\left[1 - (\xi/x)^{9/10}\right]^{1/9}}.$$

$$(19.3)$$

19.3 Dependence on Pressure

Assuming the fluid is an ideal gas satisfying $P = \rho R T$, the kinematic viscosity ν is affected through the density since $\nu = \mu/\rho$. Thus, we see that

$$\frac{\nu_2}{\nu_1} = \frac{\mu_2/\rho_2}{\mu_1/\rho_1} = \frac{\rho_1}{\rho_2} = \left(\frac{P_1/R\,T_1}{P_2/R\,T_2}\right) = \left(\frac{P_1}{P_2}\right),$$

since $T_1 = T_2$ and the dynamic viscosity μ is mainly only a function of temperature. Thus,

$$\nu_2 = \left(\frac{P_1}{P_2}\right)\nu_1.$$

If we take the value of pressure at state "1" to correspond to 1 atm, then

$$\nu_2 = \frac{\nu_1|_{P_1=1\,\text{atm}}}{P_2}, \qquad (19.4)$$

where it is understood that P_2 is given in units of atm.

Analogously, the pressure effect on the thermal diffusivity is given by

$$\alpha_2 = \frac{\alpha_1|_{P_1=1\,\text{atm}}}{P_2}. \qquad (19.5)$$

Note:

- The effect of pressure enters in all quantities that make use of the kinematic viscosity ν and thermal diffusivity α, such as the Reynolds and Péclet numbers.

- The Prandtl number is not affected by pressure variation since the density entering ν and α cancel and μ, k, and c_p depend mostly on temperature: $Pr = \frac{\nu}{\alpha} = \frac{\mu/\rho}{k/\rho\,c_p} = \frac{\mu\,c_p}{k}$.

19.4   Cross Flow Over Circular Cylinder

For cross flow over a circular cylinder of diameter D, the Reynolds number is defined as

$$Re_D = \frac{u_\infty D}{\nu}. \qquad (19.6)$$

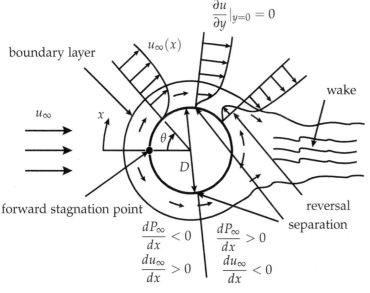

Figure 19.2: Cylinder in cross flow.

For such geometry, flow separation followed by flow reversal occurs. The separation occurs at an angle of the cylinder θ_s measured from the cylinder's stagnation point, as illustrated in Fig. 19.2. For $Re_D \lesssim 2 \times 10^5$, separation occurs at $\theta_s \approx 80°$, after which the flow transitions from laminar to turbulent. If $Re_D \gtrsim 2 \times 10^5$, flow separation occurs at $\theta_s \approx 140°$, long after the flow has transitioned and become turbulent.

Figure 19.3: Drag coefficients for smooth circular cylinder in cross flow, and for a sphere.

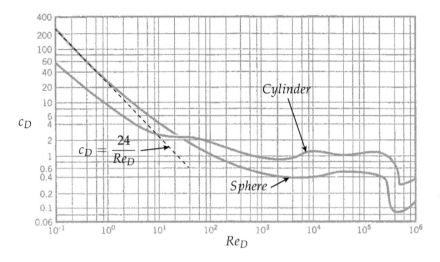

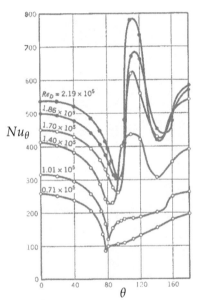

Figure 19.4: Local Nusselt number for circular cylinder in cross flow.

Table 19.1: Constants for correlation (19.8).

Re_D	C	m
0.4-4	0.989	0.330
4-40	0.911	0.385
40-4 × 10³	0.683	0.466
4 × 10³-4 × 10⁴	0.193	0.618
4 × 10⁴-4 × 10⁵	0.027	0.805

The drag coefficient (see (12.7)) for this flow is given by

$$c_D = \frac{F_D}{A_f \rho u_\infty^2/2},\qquad(19.7)$$

where F_D is the drag force, which is the sum of the friction drag and the form (or pressure) drag due to the wake, and A_f is the cylinder's frontal area. The value of C_D is given in Fig. 19.3. In Fig. 19.4 we have the local Nusselt number, Nu_D, as a function of the angle around the cylinder, θ. Note the separation and transition points. Several correlations exist for the average Nusselt number. One of the simplest is given by

$$\overline{Nu}_D = \frac{\overline{h}D}{k} = C\,Re_D^m\,Pr^{1/3},\qquad Pr \gtrsim 0.7,\qquad(19.8)$$

with C and m given in Table 19.1 as functions of Re_D. This correlation is also used for cross flow of gases over non-circular cylinders with approximate values of C and m and particular characteristic length scales D shown in Table 19.2.

More accurate correlations for cross-flow over a circular cylinder are those of Zukauskas,

$$\overline{Nu}_D = C\,Re_D^m\,Pr^n\left(\frac{Pr_\infty}{Pr_s}\right)^{1/4},\quad 0.7 \lesssim Pr \lesssim 500,\ 1 \lesssim Re_D \lesssim 10^6,\qquad(19.9)$$

with Pr_∞ and Pr_s evaluated at T_∞ and T_s, respectively, n equal to 0.37 for $Pr \le 10$ and 0.36 for $Pr > 10$, and C and m given in Table 19.3, and

Table 19.2: Constants for correlation (19.8) for non-circular cylinders.

Geometry	Re_D	C	m
$u_\infty \rightarrow$ ◇ D	$6 \times 10^3 - 6 \times 10^4$	0.304	0.59
$u_\infty \rightarrow$ ▢ D	$5 \times 10^3 - 6 \times 10^4$	0.158	0.66
$u_\infty \rightarrow$ ⬡ D	$5.2 \times 10^3 - 2.04 \times 10^4$ $2.04 \times 10^4 - 1.05 \times 10^5$	0.164 0.039	0.638 0.78
$u_\infty \rightarrow$ ⬡ D	$4.5 \times 10^3 - 9.07 \times 10^4$	0.150	0.638
$u_\infty \rightarrow$ ▯ D	Front: $10^4 - 5 \times 10^4$ Back: $7 \times 10^3 - 8 \times 10^4$	0.667 0.191	0.500 0.667

Churchill and Bernstein,

$$\overline{Nu}_D = 0.3 + \frac{0.62\, Re_D^{1/2}\, Pr^{1/3}}{[1 + (0.4/Pr)^{2/3}]^{1/4}} \left[1 + \left(\frac{Re_D}{2.82 \times 10^5}\right)^{5/8}\right]^{4/5},$$

$$Re_D Pr \gtrsim 0.2. \quad (19.10)$$

For all the correlations given above, unless stated otherwise, all properties are evaluated at the film temperature T_f.

Table 19.3: Constants for correlation (19.9).

Re_D	C	m
1-40	0.75	0.4
40-10^3	0.51	0.5
10^3-2×10^5	0.26	0.6
2×10^5-10^6	0.076	0.7

19.5   Flow Over Sphere

For flow past a sphere, the drag coefficient (see (12.7)) for this flow is given in Fig. 19.3. In laminar flow, $c_D = 24/Re_D$, as indicated in the figure. The average Nusselt number correlation, due to Whitaker, is given by

$$\overline{Nu}_D = 2 + \left(0.4\, Re_D^{1/2} + 0.06\, Re_D^{2/3}\right) Pr^{0.4} \left(\frac{\mu_\infty}{\mu_s}\right)^{1/4},$$

$$3.5 \lesssim Re_D \lesssim 7.6 \times 10^4, \quad 0.71 \lesssim Pr \lesssim 380, \quad 1.0 \lesssim \left(\frac{\mu_\infty}{\mu_s}\right) \lesssim 3.2, \quad (19.11)$$

where μ_∞ and μ_s are evaluated at T_∞ and T_s, respectively, and all other properties are evaluated at T_∞.

19.5.1   Freely falling liquid drop

The average Nusselt number correlation for a freely falling drop under gravity is given by

$$\overline{Nu}_D = 2 + 0.6\, Re_D^{1/2}\, Pr^{1/3} \left[25 \left(\frac{x}{D}\right)^{-0.7}\right], \quad (19.12)$$

where x is the distance measured from the release point. In this correlation, all properties are evaluated at T_∞. The term in brackets in (19.12) is due to oscillation and distortion of the liquid drop.

Example 19.1:

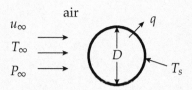

Known: Air at $T_\infty = 25°C$ and $P_\infty = 1$ atm flows with a velocity of $u_\infty = 0.5$ m/s over a 50 W light bulb of diameter $D = 0.05$ m and surface temperature of $T_s = 140°$ C.

Find: Heat loss by convection.

Assumptions: Steady state conditions, uniform surface temperature, and light bulb can be approximated by a sphere.

Properties: For air at $P_\infty = 1$ atm and $T_\infty = 25°C$: $\nu = 15.71 \times 10^{-6}$ m^2/s, $k = 0.0261$ W/m·K, $Pr = 0.71$, $\mu = 183.6 \times 10^{-7}$ N·s/m^2, while at $P_\infty = 1$ atm and $T_s = 140°C$: $\mu = 235.5 \times 10^{-7}$ N·s/m^2.

Analysis: The heat loss by convection is given by

$$q = \bar{h} A \left(T_s - T_\infty\right) = \bar{h} \left(\pi D^2\right) \left(T_s - T_\infty\right),$$

where $\bar{h}$ is estimated from the Whitaker correlation (19.11) with

$$Re_D = \frac{u_\infty D}{\nu} = \frac{0.05 \text{ m/s} \times 0.05 \text{ m}}{15.71 \times 10^{-6} \text{ m}^2/\text{s}} = 1591.$$

Thus,

$$\bar{h} = \frac{0.0261 \, \frac{\text{W}}{\text{m} \cdot \text{K}}}{0.05 \text{ m}} \left\{ 2 + \left[0.4 \, (1591)^{1/2} + \right. \right.$$
$$\left. \left. 0.06 \, (1591)^{2/3} \right] (0.71)^{0.4} \left(\frac{183.6}{235.5} \right)^{1/4} \right\}$$
$$= 11.4 \text{ W/m}^2 \cdot \text{K}.$$

Subsequently,

$$q = \left(11.4 \, \frac{\text{W}}{\text{m}^2 \cdot \text{K}} \right) \pi \, (0.05 \text{ m})^2 \, (140 - 25)° \text{C} = 10.3 \text{ W}.$$

Comments: i) The light bulb also loses heat by radiation to the surroundings, and by conduction through the socket; the correlation has been used outside its range of validity since $\mu_\infty / \mu_s < 1$.

Exercises 19:

1. A long 8 cm diameter steam pipe whose external surface temperature is 90°C passes through some open area that is not protected against the winds. Determine the rate of heat loss from the pipe per unit length when the air is at 1 atm pressure and 7°C and the wind is blowing across the pipe at a velocity of 50 km/h.

2. A pin fin of 10 mm diameter dissipates 30 W by forced convection to air in cross flow with a Reynolds number of 4000. If the diameter of the fin is doubled and all other conditions remain the same, estimate the fin heat rate. Assume the pin to be infinitely long.

3. Water droplets at 87°C in a cooling tower have an average diameter of 0.15 cm. The air stream, which moves at a velocity of 0.9 m/s relative to the water drops, is at 17°C. Determine the heat transfer coefficient from water to air.

20 Banks of Tubes

Banks of tubes are important in heating and cooling equipment (heat exchangers). Such banks are typically in one of two configurations: aligned or staggered; see Fig. 20.1. In either configuration, all tubes have the same external diameter D, and one fluid flows over the tubes, while another fluid flows inside the tubes. By such flows, heat is exchanged between the external and internal fluids which have different temperatures. We identify the temperature of the external fluid entering the bank as $T_i = T_\infty$ and that leaving the bank as T_o. Of primary interest is the average convection heat transfer coefficient for the entire bank. Since the speed of the internal and external flows are relatively low, the flows are assumed to be incompressible.

Figure 20.1: Banks of tubes.

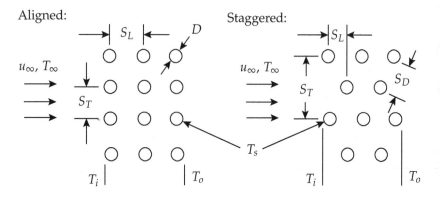

Associated with a bank of tubes, there are two geometrical parameters that are connected with the dimensions indicated in the figure:

$$P_L = \frac{S_L}{D} = \text{longitudinal pitch} \quad \text{and} \quad P_T = \frac{S_T}{D} = \text{transverse pitch.} \tag{20.1}$$

Note that in the staggered tube configuration we have that

$$S_D = \left[S_L^2 + \left(\frac{S_T}{2} \right)^2 \right]^{1/2}. \tag{20.2}$$

In addition, in either configuration, N_L represents the number of tubes in the longitudinal direction, N_T the number of tubes in the transverse direction, and N the total number of tubes in the bundle.

To characterize the flow over the tube bundle, we define the Reynolds number

$$Re_{D,max} = \frac{u_{max} D}{\nu},$$

(20.3)

where u_{max} is the maximum fluid velocity outside the tubes. For incompressible flow, using the mass balance equation we can estimate the maximum velocity:

aligned

$$u_{max} = \frac{S_T}{S_T - D} u_\infty;$$

(20.4)

staggered

$$u_{max} = \begin{cases} \dfrac{S_T}{S_T - D} u_\infty, & \text{for} \quad S_D \geq \dfrac{S_T + D}{2}, \\[2ex] \dfrac{S_T}{2(S_T - D)} u_\infty, & \text{for} \quad S_D < \dfrac{S_T + D}{2}. \end{cases}$$

(20.5)

20.1 Correlations for Banks of Tubes

For airflow through a bundle, Grimison provides the following correlation:

$$\overline{Nu}_D = 1.13 \, C_1 \, Re_{D,max}^m \, Pr^{1/3}, \quad N_L \geq 10, \; Pr \geq 0.7,$$
$$2 \times 10^3 < Re_{D,max} < 4 \times 10^4,$$

(20.6)

where C_1 and m are given in Table 20.1 as functions of P_L and P_T for aligned and staggered bundles. All properties required by the correlation are evaluated at the film temperature T_f. If $N_L < 10$, then the following modified correlation is used:

$$\overline{Nu'}_D = C_2 \, \overline{Nu}_D,$$

(20.7)

where $\overline{Nu}_D$ is given by (20.6) and C_2 is given in Table 20.2 as a function of N_L for aligned and staggered bundles.

A different correlation is provided by Zukauskas:

$$\overline{Nu}_D = C \, Re_{D,max}^m \, Pr^{0.36} \left(\frac{Pr_\infty}{Pr_s} \right)^{1/4}, \quad N_L \geq 20, \, 0.7 < Pr < 500,$$
$$10^3 < Re_{D,max} < 2 \times 10^6,$$

(20.8)

where the constants C and m are given in Table 20.3. For $N_L < 20$, equation (20.7) is used, where in this case C_2 is given in Table 20.4. In this correlation, all properties, except Pr_s (which is evaluated at T_s), are evaluated at T_∞.

Table 20.1: Constants for correlation (20.6).

P_L	P_T							
	1.25		1.5		2.0		3.0	
	C_1	m	C_1	m	C_1	m	C_1	m
Aligned								
1.25	0.348	0.592	0.275	0.608	0.100	0.704	0.0633	0.752
1.50	0.367	0.586	0.250	0.620	0.101	0.702	0.0678	0.744
2.00	0.418	0.570	0.299	0.602	0.229	0.632	0.198	0.648
3.00	0.290	0.601	0.357	0.584	0.374	0.581	0.286	0.608
Staggered								
0.600	—	—	—	—	—	—	0.213	0.636
0.900	—	—	—	—	0.446	0.571	0.401	0.581
1.000	—	—	0.497	0.558	—	—	—	—
1.125	—	—	—	—	0.478	0.565	0.518	0.560
1.250	0.518	0.556	0.505	0.554	0.519	0.556	0.522	0.562
1.500	0.451	0.568	0.460	0.562	0.452	0.568	0.488	0.568
2.000	0.404	0.572	0.416	0.568	0.482	0.556	0.449	0.570
3.000	0.310	0.592	0.356	0.580	0.440	0.562	0.428	0.574

Table 20.2: Correlation factor C_2 for equation (20.7).

N_L	Aligned	Staggered
1	0.64	0.68
2	0.80	0.75
3	0.87	0.83
4	0.90	0.89
5	0.92	0.92
6	0.94	0.95
7	0.96	0.97
8	0.98	0.98
9	0.99	0.99

Table 20.3: Constants for correlation (20.8).

Table 20.4: Correlation factor C_2 for equation (20.7).

Configuration	$Re_{D,max}$	C	m
Aligned	$10\text{-}10^2$	0.80	0.40
Staggered	$10\text{-}10^2$	0.90	0.40
Aligned	$10^2\text{-}10^3$	approx. as single cylinder	
Staggered	$10^2\text{-}10^3$	approx. as single cylinder	
Aligned ($S_T/S_L > 0.7$)	$10^3\text{-}2 \times 10^5$	0.27	0.63
Staggered ($S_T/S_L < 2$)	$10^3\text{-}2 \times 10^5$	$0.35(S_T/S_L)^{1/5}$	0.60
Staggered ($S_T/S_L > 2$)	$10^3\text{-}2 \times 10^5$	0.40	0.60
Aligned	$2 \times 10^5\text{-}2 \times 10^6$	0.021	0.84
Staggered	$2 \times 10^5\text{-}2 \times 10^6$	0.022	0.84

N_L	Aligned	Staggered
1	0.70	0.64
2	0.80	0.76
3	0.86	0.84
4	0.90	0.89
5	0.92	0.92
7	0.95	0.95
10	0.97	0.97
13	0.98	0.98
16	0.99	0.99

20.2   Log-mean Temperature Difference

As the fluid moves through the bundle of tubes, fairly quickly the temperature difference between the air and the tubes becomes much smaller than $\Delta T = T_s - T_\infty$ and so $q \neq \bar{h} A_s \Delta T$. In this case, as will be justified later, use of the following *log-mean temperature difference* is more appropriate:

$$\Delta T_{lm} = \frac{(T_s - T_i) - (T_s - T_o)}{\ln\left(\dfrac{T_s - T_i}{T_s - T_o}\right)}, \qquad (20.9)$$

where $T_i = T_\infty$ is the initial, or inlet, temperature, and T_o is the final, or outlet, temperature. Subsequently, we write

$$q' = \bar{h}\,(N\,\pi\,D)\,\Delta T_{lm}. \qquad (20.10)$$

Now, since q' is also given by

$$q' = \dot{m}' c_p (T_o - T_i) = (\rho \, u_\infty \, N_T \, S_T) \, c_p \, (T_o - T_i) , \qquad (20.11)$$

we see that, equating (20.10) and (20.11), the outlet temperature is subsequently given by

$$\frac{T_s - T_o}{T_s - T_i} = \exp\left(-\frac{N_L \, \pi \, D \, \overline{h}}{\rho \, u_\infty \, S_T \, c_p} \right). \qquad (20.12)$$

The pressure drop through a tube bundle has been experimentally determined and is given by

$$\Delta P = N_L \, \chi \left(\frac{\rho \, u_{max}^2}{2} \right) f, \qquad (20.13)$$

where f is the friction factor and $\chi = \chi \, (P_T, P_L)$ is a correlation factor. The friction and correlation factors are given as functions of $Re_{D,max}$ for aligned and staggered tube bundles in Figs. 20.2 and 20.3, respectively. Note that the empirical correlations given in the figures are limited to $P_L = P_T$ in the aligned case and $S_D = S_T$ in the staggered case.

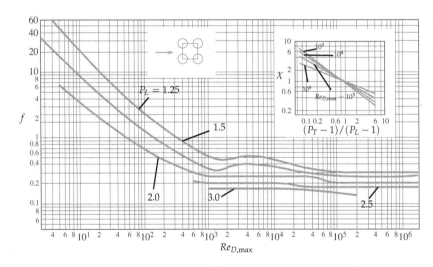

Figure 20.2: Friction factor f vs. $Re_{D,max}$ and correction factor χ for aligned tube bundle with $P_L = P_T$.

Example 20.1:
An aligned tube bundle consists of 19 rows of 2.5 cm outside diameter tubes with 12 tubes in each row (in the direction of flow). The tube spacing is 3.75 cm in the direction normal to the flow and 5.0 cm parallel to it. The tube surfaces are maintained at 127°C. Air at 27°C and 1 atm pressure flows through the bundle with a maximum velocity of 9 m/s.

Figure 20.3: Friction factor f vs. $Re_{D,\text{max}}$ and correction factor χ for for staggered tube bundle with $S_D = S_T$.

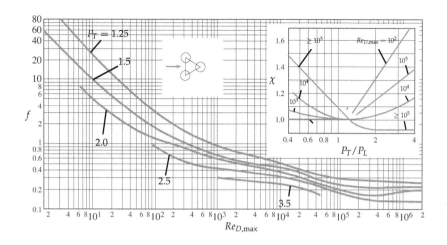

Known: The size and number of tubes in an aligned configuration; the temperature of the tubes; free stream temperature and maximum velocity within bundle.

Find: The total heat transfer from the bundle per unit length.

Assumptions: Steady state conditions, uniform temperatures, and constant properties.

Properties: For air at $P_\infty = 1$ atm and $T_f = (T_\infty + T_s)/2 = 77°C$: $\rho = 0.998$ kg/m^3, $c_p = 1.0090 \times 10^3$ J/kg·°C, $\nu = 20.76 \times 10^{-6}$ m^2/s, $k = 0.030$ W/m·°C, and $Pr = 0.697$.

Analysis: The maximum Reynolds number is

$$Re_{D,\text{max}} = \frac{u_{\text{max}} D}{\nu} = \frac{(9\,\text{m/s})\,(0.025\,\text{m})}{20.76 \times 10^{-6}\,\text{m}^2/\text{s}} = 1.0838 \times 10^4,$$

so that Eq. (20.6) applies. Note that the free stream velocity, from Eq. (20.4), is

$$u_\infty = \frac{S_T - D}{S_T} u_{\text{max}} = \frac{(3.75 - 2.5)\,\text{cm}}{(3.75\,\text{cm})} (9\,\text{m/s}) = 3\,\text{m/s}.$$

From Fig. 20.1 and Eqs. 20.1 we see that

$$P_L = \frac{S_L}{D} = \frac{5.0\,\text{cm}}{2.5\,\text{cm}} = 2 \quad \text{and} \quad P_T = \frac{S_T}{D} = \frac{3.75\,\text{cm}}{2.5\,\text{cm}} = 1.5.$$

Table 20.1 gives $C_1 = 0.299$ and $m = 0.602$. Thus, from Eq. (20.6) we have

$$\bar{h} = \frac{k}{D}\, 1.13\, C_1\, Re_{D,\text{max}}^{m}\, Pr^{1/3}$$

$$= \frac{0.030\,\text{W/m}\cdot^\circ\text{C}}{0.025\,\text{m}}\,(1.13)(0.299)(1.0838\times10^4)^{0.602}(0.697)^{1/3}$$

$$= 96.64\,\text{W/m}^2\cdot^\circ\text{C}.$$

Next, the final, or outlet, temperature is given by Eq. (20.12):

$$T_o = T_s + (T_i - T_s)\,\exp\left(-\frac{N_L\,\pi\,D\,\bar{h}}{\rho\,u_\infty\,S_T\,c_p}\right)$$

$$= 127^\circ\text{C} + (27 - 127)^\circ\text{C}\times$$

$$\exp\left(-\frac{(12)\,\pi\,(0.025\,\text{m})(96.64\,\text{W/m}^2\cdot^\circ\text{C})}{(0.998\,\text{kg/m}^3)(3\,\text{m/s})(0.0375\,\text{m})(1009\,\text{J/kg}\cdot^\circ\text{C})}\right)$$

$$= 82.25^\circ\text{C}.$$

Finally, the total heat transfer per unit length is then given by Eq. (20.11):

$$q' = (\rho\,u_\infty\,N_T\,S_T)\,c_p\,(T_o - T_i),$$

$$= (0.998\,\text{kg/m}^3)(3\,\text{m/s})(19)(0.0375\,\text{m})(1009\,\text{J/kg}\cdot^\circ\text{C})(55.25^\circ\text{C})$$

$$= 1.189\times10^5\,\text{W/m}.$$

Comments: Note that the log-mean temperature difference, as given by Eq. (20.9), is

$$\Delta T_{lm} = \frac{(T_s - T_i) - (T_s - T_o)}{\ln\left(\dfrac{T_s - T_i}{T_s - T_o}\right)}$$

$$= \frac{(127 - 27)^\circ\text{C} - (127 - 82.25)^\circ\text{C}}{\ln\left(\dfrac{(127 - 27)^\circ\text{C}}{(127 - 82.25)^\circ\text{C}}\right)}$$

$$= 68.71\,^\circ\text{C}$$

and subsequently, from Eq. (20.10), we obtain the identical result:

$$q' = \bar{h}\,(N\,\pi\,D)\,\Delta T_{lm}$$

$$= (96.64\,\text{W/m}^2\cdot^\circ\text{C})(19)(12)\,\pi\,(0.025\,\text{m})(68.71\,^\circ\text{C})$$

$$= 1.189\times10^5\,\text{W/m}.$$

Exercises 20:

1. Water at 37°C flows at 3 m/s across at 6 cm outside diameter tube that is held at 97°C. In a second configuration, 37°C water flows

at an average velocity of 3 m/s through a bundle of 6 cm outside diameter tubes that are held at 97°C. The bundle is staggered, with $S_T/S_L = 2$. Compare the heat transfer coefficients for the two situations.

2. Determine the average heat transfer coefficient in a staggered tube bundle having twelve 20 mm outside diameter tubes per row spaced 40 mm apart in both directions. Water at 20°C flows over the 100°C tubes at a free stream velocity of 0.20 m/s.

3. Air is to be cooled in the evaporator section of a refrigerator by passing it over a bank of 0.8 cm outer diameter and 0.4 m long tubes inside which the refrigerant is evaporating at 20°C. The tubes are in an aligned configuration with longitudinal and transverse pitches of $S_L = S_T = 1.5$ cm. There are 30 rows in the flow direction with 15 tubes in each row. Air approaches the tube bank in the normal direction at 0°C and 1 atm with a mean velocity of 4 m/s. Determine (a) the refrigeration capacity of this system, and (b) the pressure drop across the tube bank.

21 *Internal Flow – Circular Tube*

21.1 *Circular Tube*

We consider the flow inside a circular tube of diameter D. As indicated in Fig. 21.1, assuming that the flow enters with the uniform velocity u_∞ and with a temperature lower than the tube's surface temperature, $T_\infty < T_s$, we would like to study the flow characteristics within the tube and the heat transferred to the fluid. Assuming the flow is axisymmetric, we have that $u = u(r, x)$ and $T = T(r, x)$. The flow is characterized by the Reynolds number

$$Re_D = \frac{u_m\, D}{\nu},\tag{21.1}$$

where u_m is the (generally unknown) mean velocity, and ν is the fluid's kinematic viscosity. An important characteristic is that the flow is laminar for $Re_D \lesssim 2300$ and turbulent for $Re_D \gtrsim 4000$; for $2300 \lesssim Re_D \lesssim 4000$ the flow transitions from laminar to turbulent.

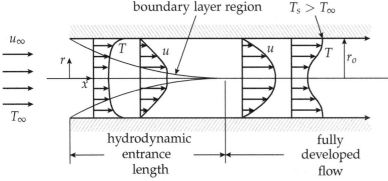

Figure 21.1: Flow in circular tube.

As indicated in the figure, at the tube's entrance, a boundary layer develops along the wall until a certain distance. We call this flow developing distance the hydrodynamic entrance length, $x_{e,u}$. After this entrance length, the flow becomes fully developed. It should be noted that the distance which the thermal field develops, $x_{e,T}$, and subsequently becomes fully developed, is in general different than that of the velocity field. The entry lengths in the laminar regime are approximately given by

$$\left(\frac{x_{e,u}}{D}\right)_{lam} \approx 0.05\, Re_D, \quad \text{and} \quad \left(\frac{x_{e,T}}{D}\right)_{lam} \approx 0.05\, Re_D\, Pr, \quad (21.2)$$

while in the turbulent regime both entrance lengths are basically the same and approximately given by

$$\left(\frac{x_e}{D}\right)_{turb} \gtrsim 10. \qquad (21.3)$$

A quantity of primary interest to us is the tube surface's heat flux:

$$q_s'' = h\left(T_s - T_m\right), \qquad (21.4)$$

where T_m is the mean (generally unknown) temperature.

The flow rate through the tube is given by

$$\dot{m} = \int_{A_c} \rho\, u\, dA, \qquad (21.5)$$

where the cross-sectional area is $A_c = \pi r_o^2$, where $r_o = D/2$ is the tube's radius. Assuming the flow to be incompressible, the flow rate is related to the mean flow as follows:

$$\dot{m} = \rho\, u_m\, A_c, \qquad (21.6)$$

Lastly, for fully developed flow, the mean velocity is given by

$$u_m = \frac{1}{\rho\, A_c} \int_{A_c} \rho\, u\, dA = \frac{2}{r_o^2} \int_0^{r_o} u\, r\, dr, \qquad (21.7)$$

the friction factor by

$$f = \frac{-\left(dP/dx\right) D}{\rho\, u_m^2/2}, \qquad (21.8)$$

where dP/dx is the pressure gradient along the pipe, the friction coefficient by

$$c_f = \frac{\tau_s}{\rho\, u_m^2/2} = \frac{-\mu\,\left(du/dr\right)|_{r_o}}{\rho\, u_m^2/2}, \qquad (21.9)$$

where τ_s is the shear stress on the pipe's surface, and the pressure drop between two points along the pipe, using Eq. (21.8), by

$$\Delta P = P_1 - P_2 = -\int_{P_1}^{P_2} dP = \frac{\rho\, u_m}{2\, D} \int_{x_1}^{x_2} f\, dx. \qquad (21.10)$$

Note:

- In fully developed flow, $u = u\,(r)$ and $T = T\,(r, x)$; subsequently, $u_m = \text{const.}$ and $T_m = T_m\,(x)$.

- We can also write the Reynolds number as

$$Re_D = \frac{4\,\dot{m}}{\pi\, D\, \mu},$$

where μ is the fluid's kinematic viscosity.

It is important to clarify the meaning of fully developed flow. It is clear that in such case the flow should only be in the longitudinal direction and it should not vary in this direction (we will say more about this in the next Lecture). On the other hand, since the fully developed temperature field varies along the tube as heat continues to warm the flowing fluid, a reasonable condition for the energy field is

$$\frac{\partial}{\partial x}\left[\frac{T_s\left(x\right)-T\left(r,x\right)}{T_s\left(x\right)-T_m\left(x\right)}\right]=0, \tag{21.11}$$

where $T_m(x)$ is the *bulk temperature* defined as

$$\dot{m}\,c_v\,T_m(x)=\int_{A_c}\rho\,c_v\,u\,T\,dA. \tag{21.12}$$

To appreciate the physical meaning of (21.11), we see that

$$\frac{\partial}{\partial r}\left[\frac{T_s(x)-T(r,x)}{T_s(x)-T_m(x)}\right]\Bigg|_{r=r_o}=\frac{-\left(\partial T/\partial r\right)|_{r=r_o}}{T_s(x)-T_m(x)}=\frac{q_s''/k}{q_s''/h}=\frac{h}{k}. \tag{21.13}$$

Subsequently, the fully developed condition (21.11) amounts to nothing more than requiring that the convection heat transfer coefficient h be constant along the tube!

From the energy balance moving with the mean velocity, as illustrated in Fig. 21.2, we have

$$dq_{st}=dq_{conv}, \tag{21.14}$$

where

$$dq_{st}=\dot{m}\,c_p\,dT_m \quad\text{and}\quad dq_{conv}=q_s''\,\mathcal{P}\,dx, \tag{21.15}$$

and $\mathcal{P}=\pi D$ is the tube's perimeter. Thus,

$$\frac{dT_m}{dx}=\frac{q_s''\,\mathcal{P}}{\dot{m}\,c_p}=\frac{\mathcal{P}}{\dot{m}\,c_p}\,h\left[T_s(x)-T_m(x)\right]. \tag{21.16}$$

There are two types of boundary conditions that are typically applied: i) $q_s''=$ const. or ii) $T_s=$ const.; the solution obviously depends on the boundary condition selected. We next consider the two distinct cases.

i) If $q_s''=$ const., then from Eq. (21.16) it follows that $dT_m/dx=$ const. and therefore

$$T_m\left(x\right)=T_{m,i}+\frac{q_s''\,\mathcal{P}}{\dot{m}\,c_p}\,x, \tag{21.17}$$

where $T_{m,i}=T_m(0)$ is the initial bulk temperature. Note that from Eq. (21.16) it also follows that T_s and T_m must have the same linear variation with x in the fully developed region.

ii) If $T_s=$ const., we take $\Delta T=T_s-T_m$ so that Eq. (21.16) is rewritten as

$$-\frac{d\left(\Delta T\right)}{dx}=\frac{\mathcal{P}}{\dot{m}\,c_p}\,h\,\Delta T. \tag{21.18}$$

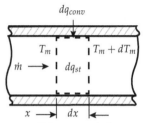

Figure 21.2: Tube energy balance.

Note:

- For a tube of length L with $q_s''=$ const.,

$$T_{m,o}-T_{m,i}=\Delta T_o=\frac{\mathcal{P}\,L}{\dot{m}\,c_p}\,q_s'',$$

where $T_{m,o}=T_m(L)$.

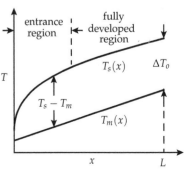

Figure 21.3: Temperature distributions for $q_s''=$ const.

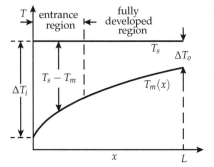

Figure 21.4: Temperature distributions for $T_s = $ const.

Note:

- For a tube of length L with $T_s = $ const.,

$$\ln\left(\frac{\Delta T_o}{\Delta T_i}\right) = -\frac{\mathcal{P} L}{\dot{m} c_p} \bar{h}_L,$$

where $\Delta T_o = T_s - T_{m,o}$.

Subsequently, we obtain

$$\ln\left(\frac{\Delta T}{\Delta T_i}\right) = -\frac{\mathcal{P} x}{\dot{m} c_p} \bar{h}_x, \qquad (21.19)$$

where $\Delta T_i = T_s - T_{m,i}$ and

$$\bar{h}_x = \frac{1}{x}\int_0^x h(x')\, dx'. \qquad (21.20)$$

We conclude by observing that for a tube of length L, upon integrating Eq. (21.14), we have that

$$q_{conv} = q_{st} = \dot{m}\, c_p\left(T_{m,o} - T_{m,i}\right)$$

or

$$q_{conv} = \dot{m}\, c_p\left[(T_s - T_{m,i}) - (T_s - T_{m,o})\right] = \dot{m}\, c_p\left(\Delta T_i - \Delta T_o\right). \quad (21.21)$$

Eliminating $\dot{m}\, c_p$ between Eq. (21.19) for $x = L$ and Eq. (21.20), we have that

$$q_{conv} = \bar{h}_L\, A_s\, \Delta T_{lm} \qquad (21.22)$$

where $A_s = \mathcal{P}\, L$ is the tube's surface area, and

$$\Delta T_{lm} = \frac{\Delta T_o - \Delta T_i}{\ln\left(\dfrac{\Delta T_o}{\Delta T_i}\right)} \qquad (21.23)$$

is the log-mean temperature difference introduced in Eq. (20.9).

Example 21.1:

Water enters a 2.5 cm internal diameter thin copper tube of a heat exchanger at 15°C at a rate of 0.3 kg/s, and is heated by steam condensing outside at 120°C. If the average heat transfer coefficient is 800 W/m²·°C, what is the length of the tube required in order to heat the water to 115°C.

Known: Water is heated by steam in a circular copper tube of given size and temperature; inlet and outlet temperatures; mass flow rate; average heat transfer coefficient.

Find: The tube length required to heat the water to 115°C.

Assumptions: Steady state conditions, constant properties, constant convection heat transfer coefficient, conduction resistance of copper tube is negligible.

Properties: For water at the bulk temperature of $T_m = (15 + 115)°C/2 = 65°C$: $c_p = 4.187$ kJ/kg·°C.

Analysis: Knowing the inlet and exit temperatures of water, the rate of heat transfer is given by Eq. (21.21):

$$q_{conv} = \dot{m} \, c_p \, (T_{m,o} - T_{m,i})$$
$$= (0.3 \, \text{kg/s})(4.187 \, \text{kJ/kg} \cdot^\circ \text{C})(115 - 15)^\circ \text{C} = 125.6 \, \text{kW}.$$

From Eq. (21.23) the logarithmic mean temperature difference is

$$\Delta T_{lm} = \frac{(T_s - T_{m,o}) - (T_s - T_{m,i})}{\ln \left(\dfrac{T_s - T_{m,o}}{T_s - T_{m,i}} \right)}$$
$$= \frac{(120 - 115)^\circ \text{C} - (120 - 15)^\circ \text{C}}{\ln \left(\dfrac{(120 - 115)^\circ \text{C}}{(127 - 15)^\circ \text{C}} \right)} = 32.85 \,^\circ \text{C}.$$

Subsequently, from Eq. (21.22), we obtain the surface area:

$$A_s = \frac{q_{conv}}{h_L \, \Delta T_{lm}} = \frac{125.6 \, \text{kW}}{(0.8 \, \text{kW/m}^2 \cdot^\circ \text{C})(32.85^\circ \text{C})} = 4.78 \, \text{m}^2,$$

and thus the length of the tube

$$L = \frac{A_s}{\pi D} = \frac{4.78 \, \text{m}^2}{\pi \, (0.025 \, \text{m})} = 61 \, \text{m}.$$

Comments: The bulk mean temperature of water is 65°C, and thus the arithmetic mean temperature difference is $\Delta T = (120 - 65)^\circ \text{C} = 55^\circ \text{C}$. Using ΔT instead of ΔT_{lm} would give $L = 36$ m, which is grossly in error.

Exercises 21:

1. Consider the flow of oil in a tube. How will the hydrodynamic and thermal entry lengths compare if the flow is laminar? How would they compare if the flow is turbulent?

2. Air enters a 20 cm diameter 12 m long underwater duct at 50°C and 1 atm at a mean velocity of 7 m/s, and is cooled by the water outside. If the average heat transfer coefficient is 85 W/m²·°C and the tube temperature is nearly equal to the water temperature of 5°C, determine the exit temperature of air and the rate of heat transfer.

3. Combustion gases passing through a 3 cm internal diameter circular tube are used to vaporize waste water at atmospheric pressure. Hot gases enter the tube at 115 kPa and 250°C at a mean velocity of 5 m/s, and leave at 150°C. If the average heat transfer coefficient is 120 W/m²·°C and the inner surface temperature of the tube is 110°C, determine the tube length and the rate of evaporation of water.

22 Internal Flow – More on Circular Tube

22.1 Velocity and Temperature Distributions

From Sec. 13.2 we recall the equations for incompressible flow with negligible buoyancy and viscous dissipation effects:

$$\nabla \cdot v = 0, \tag{22.1}$$

$$\dot{v} = -\frac{1}{\rho} \nabla P + \nu \nabla^2 v, \tag{22.2}$$

$$\dot{T} = \alpha \nabla^2 T. \tag{22.3}$$

We consider the flow in a tube where we use cylindrical polar coordinates $x = (r, \theta, x)$ with velocity components $v = (u_r, u_\theta, u_x)$, where the r-direction measures the distance from the tube's central axis which points in the x-direction. Assuming the flow is steady and axisymmetric with $u_\theta = \partial g / \partial \theta = 0$ (g represents any of the dependent variables), the above equations become

$$\frac{1}{r} \frac{\partial r u_r}{\partial r} + \frac{\partial u_x}{\partial x} = 0, \tag{22.4}$$

$$u_r \frac{\partial u_r}{\partial r} + u_x \frac{\partial u_r}{\partial x} = -\frac{1}{\rho} \frac{\partial P}{\partial r} + \nu \left[\frac{\partial}{\partial r} \left(\frac{1}{r} \frac{\partial r u_r}{\partial r} \right) + \frac{\partial^2 u_r}{\partial x^2} \right], \tag{22.5}$$

$$u_r \frac{\partial u_x}{\partial r} + u_x \frac{\partial u_x}{\partial x} = -\frac{1}{\rho} \frac{\partial P}{\partial x} + \nu \left[\frac{1}{r} \frac{\partial}{\partial r} \left(r \frac{\partial u_x}{\partial r} \right) + \frac{\partial^2 u_x}{\partial x^2} \right], \tag{22.6}$$

$$u_r \frac{\partial T}{\partial r} + u_x \frac{\partial T}{\partial x} = \alpha \left[\frac{1}{r} \frac{\partial}{\partial r} \left(r \frac{\partial T}{\partial r} \right) + \frac{\partial^2 T}{\partial x^2} \right]. \tag{22.7}$$

Note:

- The linear momentum equation in the θ-direction becomes trivial.

- In fully developed flow we have that $dP/dx = $ const., $v = (0, 0, u_x(r))$, and $T = T(r, x)$.

Furthermore, assuming that the flow is fully developed, *i.e.*, $u_r = \partial s / \partial x = 0$, where s represents either u_x or T, the above equations reduce to

$$0 = \frac{\partial P}{\partial r}, \quad 0 = -\frac{\partial P}{\partial x} + \frac{\mu}{r} \frac{\partial}{\partial r} \left(r \frac{\partial u}{\partial r} \right) \quad \text{and} \quad u \frac{\partial T}{\partial x} = \frac{\alpha}{r} \frac{\partial}{\partial r} \left(r \frac{\partial T}{\partial r} \right), \tag{22.8}$$

where, to simplify the notation, we have written $u_x \to u$. From the first two equations above, we conclude that $P = P(x)$ and $dP/dx = $ const., which we assume is given. In addition, the corresponding boundary conditions for the last two equations are

$$u(0) < \infty, \quad u(r_o) = 0, \quad \text{and} \quad T(0) < \infty, \quad T(r_o) = T_s \quad \text{or} \quad q''(r_o) = q''_s.$$
(22.9)

Since the first equation is decoupled from the second equation, we solve it first. The solution for u is easily obtained by integrating twice:

$$u(r) = \frac{1}{\mu}\left(\frac{dP}{dx}\right)\frac{r^2}{4} + C_1 \ln r + C_2.$$
(22.10)

Applying the corresponding boundary conditions in Eq. (22.9), we see that u has the following parabolic distribution (called Poiseuille flow):

$$u(r) = -\frac{1}{4\mu}\left(\frac{dP}{dx}\right) r_o^2 \left[1 - \left(\frac{r}{r_o}\right)^2\right].$$
(22.11)

Subsequently, using Eq. (21.7), we find that

$$u_m = -\frac{2}{4\mu}\frac{dP}{dx}\int_0^{r_o}\left[1 - \left(\frac{r}{r_o}\right)^2\right] r\,dr = -\frac{r_o^2}{8\mu}\frac{dP}{dx}$$
(22.12)

and Eq. (22.11) can be rewritten as

$$\frac{u(r)}{u_m} = 2\left[1 - \left(\frac{r}{r_o}\right)^2\right].$$
(22.13)

Subsequently, using the definition Eq. (21.1), from Eqs. (21.8)-(21.10), we have that the friction factor is given by

$$f = \frac{64}{Re_D},$$
(22.14)

the friction coefficient by

$$c_f = \frac{16}{Re_D} = \frac{f}{4},$$
(22.15)

and the pressure drop by

$$\Delta P = \frac{\rho\,u_m^2}{2\,D} f\,(x_2 - x_1).$$
(22.16)

Now we recall that the condition Eq. (21.11) for a fully developed thermal field,

$$\frac{\partial}{\partial x}\left[\frac{T_s(x) - T(r,x)}{T_s(x) - T_m(x)}\right] = 0,$$
(22.17)

or, more explicitly,

$$\frac{\partial T}{\partial x} = \left(1 - \frac{T_s - T}{T_s - T_m}\right)\frac{dT_s}{dx} + \left(\frac{T_s - T}{T_s - T_m}\right)\frac{dT_m}{dx},$$
(22.18)

is equivalent to $h = \text{const}$. Now, since $q''_s = h(T_s - T_m)$, we pursue the two different cases corresponding to

Note:

- For flow in the positive x-direction, $dP/dx < 0$.

- The maximum velocity is $u_{max} = u(0) = 2\,u_m$.

i) $q''(r_o) = q_s'' = $ const., in which case, from Eq. (22.18), we see that

$$\frac{dT_s}{dx} = \frac{dT_m}{dx} \quad \rightarrow \quad \frac{\partial T}{\partial x} = \frac{dT_m}{dx}, \tag{22.19}$$

and

ii) $T(r_o) = T_s = $ const., in which case, from Eq. (22.18), we see that

$$\frac{dT_s}{dx} = 0 \quad \rightarrow \quad \frac{\partial T}{\partial x} = \left(\frac{T_s - T}{T_s - T_m} \right) \frac{dT_m}{dx}. \tag{22.20}$$

22.2   *Constant Heat Flux*

When $q''(r_o) = q_s'' = $ const., Eq. (22.8), upon using Eqs. (22.13) and (22.19), becomes

$$\frac{2\,u_m}{\alpha} \left[1 - \left(\frac{r}{r_o} \right)^2 \right] \frac{dT_m}{dx} = \frac{1}{r} \frac{\partial}{\partial r} \left(r \frac{\partial T}{\partial r} \right). \tag{22.21}$$

Now, integrating twice in r, we obtain

$$T(r, x) = \frac{2\,u_m}{\alpha} \left(\frac{dT_m}{dx} \right) \left[\frac{r^2}{4} - \frac{r^4}{16\,r_o^2} \right] + C_1 \ln r + C_2. \tag{22.22}$$

Subsequently, using the boundary conditions Eq. (22.9), we have

$$T(r, x) = T_s(x) - \frac{u_m\,r_o^2}{2\,\alpha} \frac{dT_m}{dx} \left[\frac{3}{4} - \left(\frac{r}{r_o} \right)^2 + \frac{1}{4} \left(\frac{r}{r_o} \right)^4 \right]. \tag{22.23}$$

From the definition of the bulk temperature Eq. (21.12), we have that

$$T_m(x) = \frac{2}{u_m\,r_o^2} \int_0^{r_o} u\,T\,r\,dr = T_s(x) - \frac{11}{48} \left(\frac{u_m\,r_o^2}{\alpha} \right) \frac{dT_m}{dx}. \tag{22.24}$$

But, using Eq. (21.6), from Eq. (21.16) we also have that

$$\frac{dT_m}{dx} = \frac{q_s''\,P}{\dot{m}\,c_p} = \frac{q_s''\,(\pi D)}{(\rho\,u_m\,\pi\,D^2/4)\,c_p}, \tag{22.25}$$

thus Eq. (22.24) becomes

$$T_m(x) - T_s(x) = -\frac{11}{48} \frac{q_s''\,D}{k} = \text{const.}, \tag{22.26}$$

and since $q_s'' = h\,(T_s - T_m)$, we have

$$h = \frac{48}{11} \left(\frac{k}{D} \right) \tag{22.27}$$

and

$$Nu_D = \frac{h\,D}{k} = \frac{48}{11} \approx 4.36. \tag{22.28}$$

Note:

- In this case, as well as the next, k is evaluated at T_m.

22.3   Constant Temperature

When $T(r_0) = T_s = $ const., Eq. (22.8), upon using Eqs. (22.13) and (22.20), becomes

$$\frac{2\,u_m}{\alpha}\left[1-\left(\frac{r}{r_o}\right)^2\right]\left(\frac{T_s-T}{T_s-T_m}\right)\frac{dT_m}{dx}=\frac{1}{r}\frac{\partial}{\partial r}\left(r\frac{\partial T}{\partial r}\right). \qquad (22.29)$$

This is a linear equation for $T(r,x)$ as a function of r, but the solution requires knowledge of $T_m(x)$ which is given by

$$T_m(x)=\frac{2}{u_m\,r_o^2}\int_0^{r_o} u\,T\,r\,dr, \qquad (22.30)$$

where the solution Eq. (22.13) is used, but Eq. (22.30) also depends on $T(r,x)$! Subsequently, Eqs. (22.29) and (22.30) are solved iteratively, numerically. Upon obtaining converged solutions of $T(r,x)$ and $T_m(x)$ and noting that $q_s'' = -k\,\partial T/\partial r|_{r=r_o} = h(T_s-T_m)$, we obtain h and subsequently it is found that

$$Nu_D \approx 3.66. \qquad (22.31)$$

> Example 22.1:
> For flow of a liquid metal through a circular tube of diameter D, the velocity and temperature profiles at a particular axial location may be approximated as being uniform and parabolic, respectively ($u(r) = c_1$ and $T(r) = T_s - c_2\left[1-(r/r_o)^2\right]$, where c_1 and c_2 are positive constants).
>
> Known: Diameter of tube, and velocity and temperature distributions at a particular axial location.
>
> Find: What is the value of the Nusselt number, Nu_D, at the location?
>
> Assumptions: Steady state conditions, constant properties, constant tube wall temperature, incompressible flow.
>
> Analysis: Since $Nu_D = hD/k$, we need to obtain the convection coefficient $h = q_s''/(T_s-T_m)$. First, the heat flux may be obtained from Fourier's law:
>
> $$q_s'' = -k\left.\frac{dT}{dr}\right|_{r=r_o} = -2\,c_2\,\frac{k}{r_o}.$$
>
> Second, we note that since the velocity is constant, the mean velocity is simply $u_m = c_1$. Knowing the mean velocity and temper-

ature distribution, the mean temperature can be obtained from Eq. (22.30):

$$
\begin{aligned}
T_m &= \frac{2}{u_m\, r_0^2} \int_0^{r_0} u\, T\, r\, dr \\
&= \frac{2}{r_0^2} \int_0^{r_0} \left\{ T_s + c_2 \left[1 - \left(\frac{r}{r_0} \right)^2 \right] \right\} r\, dr \\
&= \frac{2}{r_0^2} \left[T_s\, \frac{r^2}{2} + c_2\, \frac{r^2}{2} - \frac{c_2}{4}\, \frac{r^4}{r_0^2} \right]_0^{r_0} \\
&= T_s + \frac{c_2}{2}.
\end{aligned}
$$

Subsequently,

$$
h = \frac{-2\, c_2\, (k/r_0)}{-c_2/2} = -\frac{4\, k}{r_0} \qquad \text{and} \qquad Nu_D = 8.
$$

Exercises 22:

1. Consider fully developed laminar flow in a circular pipe. If the viscosity of the fluid is reduced by half by heating while the flow rate is held constant, how will the pressure drop change?

2. In fully developed laminar flow in a circular pipe, the velocity at $r_0/2$ (midway between the wall surface and the centerline) is measured to be 6 m/s. Determine the velocity at the center of the pipe.

3. Water at 10°C ($\rho = 999.7$ kg/m^3 and $\mu = 1.307 \times 10^{-3}$ kg/m·s) is flowing in a 0.20 cm diameter 15 m long pipe steadily at an average velocity of 1.2 m/s. Determine (a) the pressure drop and (b) the pumping power requirement to overcome this pressure drop.

23 Internal Flow – Miscellaneous Topics

23.1 Entry Region

For constant temperature and constant heat flux conditions, the local as well as the average Nusselt numbers, Nu and $\overline{Nu}$, respectively, as functions of the scaled distance from the entrance of a pipe of diameter D, given by the inverse of the local Graetz number defined as

$$Gz_x \equiv \frac{Re_D\,Pr}{x/D}, \qquad (23.1)$$

are provided in Fig. 23.1. The thermal entrance length corresponds to that given in Eq. (21.2). For the constant temperature case (T_s = const.) we can use the following correlation, provided by Sieder and Tate, in the region where momentum and energy are simultaneously developing:

$$\overline{Nu}_D = 1.86\,Gz_L^{1/3} \left(\frac{\mu}{\mu_s}\right)^{0.14}, \qquad \begin{array}{c} 0.48 < Pr < 16{,}700 \\[4pt] 0.0044 < \dfrac{\mu}{\mu_s} < 9.75 \end{array} \qquad (23.2)$$

with all properties except μ_s evaluated at $\overline{T}_m \equiv \frac{1}{2}\left(T_{m,i} + T_{m,o}\right)$.

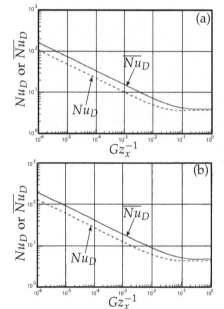

Figure 23.1: Local and average Nusselt numbers for tube at uniform surface (a) temperature, and (b) heat flux.

23.2 Turbulent Correlations

The laminar flow becomes unstable when $Re_D \gtrsim 2100$ and starts becoming turbulent when $Re_D \gtrsim 4000$. In the range of $4000 \lesssim Re_D \lesssim 9000$ we have a transition region where the flow is intermittently turbulent. A quantity of interest is the pressure drop across a length of pipe. Recall from Eq. (22.16) that if the friction coefficient is constant, then for a pipe of length L we have

$$\Delta P = \frac{1}{2}\,f\,\rho\,u_m^2\left(\frac{L}{D}\right), \qquad (23.3)$$

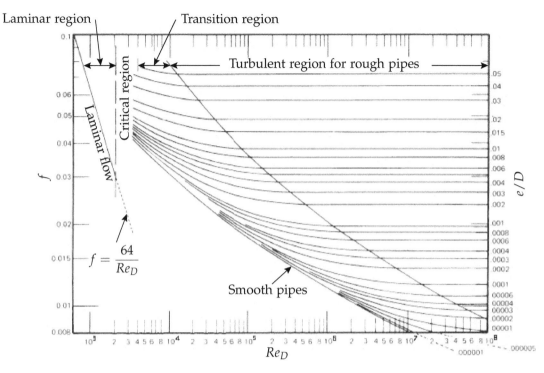

Figure 23.2: Friction factors for pipe of diameter D.

where in the laminar case $f = 64/Re_D$ (see Eq. (22.14)). In the turbulent case f depends on the roughness e. The friction factor, f, as a function of the Reynolds number, Re_D, for different values of relative roughness, e/D, is illustrated in Fig. 23.2, referred to as the Moody chart.

In addition, from the modified Reynolds, or Chilton-Colburn, analogy Eqs. (15.8) and (15.9), and assuming that the relation Eq. (22.15) (*i.e.*, $c_f = f/4$) remains valid in the turbulent regime, we have that

$$Nu_D = \frac{f}{8} Re_D Pr^{1/3}. \tag{23.4}$$

23.2.1   *Smooth Pipes*

For smooth pipes we have that

$$f = \begin{cases} 0.316\, Re_D^{-1/4}, & Re_D < 2 \times 10^4, \\ 0.184\, Re_D^{-1/5}, & Re_D \gtrsim 2 \times 10^4. \end{cases} \tag{23.5}$$

Now, using Eq. (23.5) in Eq. (23.4) we obtain the Colburn equation

$$Nu_D = 0.023\, Re_D^{4/5} Pr^{1/3}, \quad Re_D \gtrsim 2 \times 10^4. \tag{23.6}$$

The equation is extended by the Dittus-Boelter equation for $|T_s - T_m| \lesssim 0.2$:

$$Nu_D = 0.023\, Re_D^{4/5}\, Pr^n, \quad n = \begin{cases} 0.4, & T_s > T_m, \\ 0.3, & T_s < T_m, \end{cases} \quad \begin{array}{l} 0.7 \leq Pr \leq 160, \\ Re_D \gtrsim 10^4, \\ L/D \gtrsim 10, \end{array} \quad (23.7)$$

with all properties evaluated at T_m. For $|T_s - T_m| \gtrsim 0.2$ the following Sieder and Tate equation is appropriate:

$$Nu_D = 0.027\, Re_D^{4/5}\, Pr^{1/3} \left(\frac{\mu}{\mu_s}\right)^{0.14}, \quad \begin{array}{l} 0.7 \leq Pr \leq 16{,}700, \\ Re_D \gtrsim 10^4, \\ L/D \gtrsim 10. \end{array} \quad (23.8)$$

If we require $\overline{Nu_D}$, then all properties, except μ_s, are evaluated at $\overline{T}_m$.

23.2.2   Rough Pipes

For rough pipes, it is necessary to use the appropriate friction factor f from the Moody chart Fig. 23.2 in conjunction with Eq. (23.4).

23.2.3   Liquid Metals

For liquid metals with $3 \times 10^{-3} \lesssim Pr \lesssim 5 \times 10^{-2}$ and for pipes sufficiently long so that $L/D \gtrsim 10$, when $q_s'' = $ const., we have

$$Nu_D = 4.82 + 0.0185\, Pe_D^{0.827}, \quad \begin{array}{l} 10^2 < Pe_D < 10^4, \\ 3.6 \times 10^3 < Re_D < 9.05 \times 10^5, \end{array} \quad (23.9)$$

while for $T_s = $ const., we have

$$Nu_D = 5.0 + 0.025\, Pe_D^{0.8}, \quad Pe_D > 100. \quad (23.10)$$

23.2.4   Non-Circular Tubes

For non-circular tubes, we define the hydraulic diameter as

$$D_h \equiv \frac{4 A_c}{\mathcal{P}}, \quad (23.11)$$

Note:

- The hydraulic diameter is defined in such a way as to reduce to the diameter in circular tubes.

where A_c is the flow cross-sectional area, and $\mathcal{P}$ is the tube's wetted perimeter. Subsequently, we use D_h in place of D in Re_D and Nu_D and use the friction factor and Nusselt number correlations given above for turbulent flow in circular tubes. For fully developed laminar flow we correspondingly use Table 23.1.

Table 23.1: Nusselt numbers and friction factors for fully developed laminar flow in tubes of varying cross sections.

Cross Section	$\dfrac{b}{a}$	$q_s'' = $ const.	$T_s = $ const.	$f\,Re_{D_h}$
◯	—	4.36	3.66	64
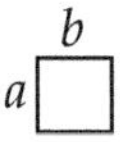 $a\,\square\ ^b$	1.0	3.61	2.98	57
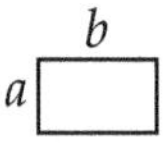 $a\,\square\ ^b$	1.43	3.73	3.08	59
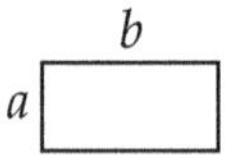 $a\,\square\ ^b$	2.0	4.12	3.39	62
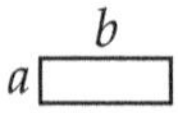 $a\,\square\ ^b$	3.0	4.79	3.96	69
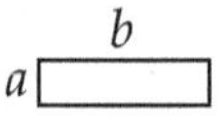 $a\,\square\ ^b$	4.0	5.33	4.44	73
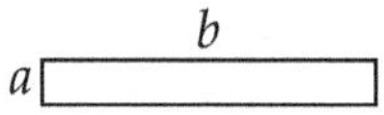 $a\,\square\ ^b$	8.0	6.49	5.60	82
 ▭	∞	8.23	7.54	96
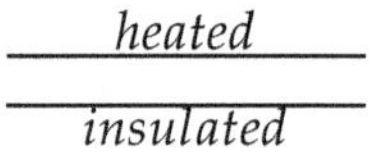 heated / insulated	∞	5.39	4.86	96
 △	—	3.11	2.47	53

The header NuD_h spans the columns for $q_s'' = $ const. and $T_s = $ const.

23.3 Fully Developed Annular Flow

The flow within annular circular pipes is illustrated in Fig. 23.3, where the subscripts "o" and "i" label corresponding quantities associated with the outer and inner surfaces of the annular region, respectively. We correspondingly write the hydraulic diameter as

$$D_h = \frac{4\,A_c}{\mathcal{P}} = D_o - D_i, \qquad (23.12)$$

and the heat fluxes and Nusselt numbers associated with the outer and inner surfaces of the annular region by

$$q_o'' = h_o\,(T_{s,o} - T_m) \qquad \text{and} \qquad q_i'' = h_i\,(T_{s,i} - T_m) \qquad (23.13)$$

and

$$Nu_o = \frac{h_o\,D_h}{k} \qquad \text{and} \qquad Nu_i = \frac{h_i\,D_h}{k}. \qquad (23.14)$$

For laminar flow, if one surface is insulated, $q_s'' = 0$, and the other surface is at constant temperature, $T_s = $ const., we use Table 23.2 to obtain the Nusselt numbers corresponding to the outer and inner surfaces. If the heat flux is specified on both tube surfaces, $q_s'' = $ const.,

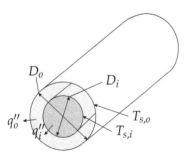

Figure 23.3: Annular flow.

then we have

$$Nu_o = \frac{Nu_{oo}}{1 - \left(q_i''/q_o''\right)\theta_o^*} \quad \text{and} \quad Nu_i = \frac{Nu_{ii}}{1 - \left(q_o''/q_i''\right)\theta_i^*}, \quad (23.15)$$

where the influence coefficients Nu_{oo}, Nu_{ii}, θ_o^*, θ_i^*, are obtained from Table 23.3.

For turbulent flow in the annular region, we assume that $h_i \approx h_o$ and use the Dittus-Boelter equation (23.7) with D_h substituted for D in the Reynolds and Nusselt numbers.

Table 23.2: Nusselt number for fully developed laminar flow in circular annulus with one surface insulated and the other at constant temperature.

D_i/D_o	Nu_o	Nu_i
0.00	3.66	—
0.05	4.06	17.46
0.10	4.11	11.56
0.25	4.23	7.37
0.50	4.43	5.74
1.00	4.86	4.86

Example 23.1:

Hot air at atmospheric pressure and 80°C enters an 8 m long uninsulated square duct of cross section 0.2 m × 0.2 m that passes through at a rate of 0.15 m³/s. The duct is observed to be nearly isothermal at 60°C.

Known: The shape, size, and length of duct, inlet air temperature, pressure, and flow rate, and duct temperature.

Find: Determine the exit temperature of the air and the rate of heat loss from the duct to the surroundings.

Assumptions: Steady state conditions, constant properties, the inner surfaces of the duct are smooth, air is an ideal gas.

Properties: We do not know the exit temperature of the air in the duct, and thus we cannot determine the bulk mean temperature of air. We evaluate the properties at the inlet temperature of 80°C even though we expect the temperature to be a little lower due to heat loss. At 80°C and 1 atm we have: $\rho = 0.9994$ kg/m³, $c_p = 1.008$ kJ/kg·°C, $\nu = 2.097 \times 10^{-5}$ m²/s, $k = 0.02953$ W/m·°C, $Pr = 0.7154$.

Analysis: The hydraulic diameter, mean velocity, and Reynolds number are

$$D_h = \frac{4\,A_c}{\mathcal{P}} = \frac{4\,a^2}{4\,a} = a = 0.2\,\text{m},$$

$$u_m = \frac{\dot{V}}{A_c} = \frac{0.15\,\text{m}^3/\text{s}}{(0.2\,\text{m})^2} = 3.75\,\text{m/s},$$

$$Re_{D_h} = \frac{u_m\,D_h}{\nu} = \frac{(3.75\,\text{m/s})(0.2\,\text{m})}{2.097 \times 10^{-5}\,\text{m}^2/\text{s}} = 3.5765 \times 10^4,$$

which is greater than 10^4. Therefore, the flow is turbulent and the

Table 23.3: Influence coefficients for fully developed laminar flow in circular annulus with uniform heat flux on both surfaces.

D_i/D_o	Nu_{oo}	Nu_{ii}	θ_o^*	θ_i^*
0.00	4.364	—	0.0000	∞
0.05	4.792	17.81	0.0294	2.180
0.10	4.834	11.91	0.0562	1.383
0.20	4.833	8.499	0.1041	0.905
0.40	4.979	6.583	0.1823	0.603
0.60	5.099	5.912	0.2455	0.473
0.80	5.240	5.580	0.2990	0.401
1.00	5.385	5.385	0.3460	0.346

entry length in this case is roughly

$$x_e \approx 10\,D_h = 10 \times 0.2\,\mathrm{m} = 2\,\mathrm{m},$$

which is much shorter than the total length of the duct. Therefore, we will assume fully developed turbulent flow in the entire duct and determine the Nusselt number from

$$Nu_{D_h} = 0.023\,Re_{D_h}^{4/5}Pr^{1/3} = 0.023(35,765)^{4/5}(0.7154)^{1/3} = 90.4.$$

Then

$$\bar{h} = \frac{k}{D_h}\,Nu_{D_h} = \frac{0.02953\,\mathrm{W/m\cdot^\circ C}}{0.2\,\mathrm{m}}\,(90.4) = 13.3\,\mathrm{W/m^2\cdot^\circ C},$$
$$A_s = \mathcal{P}\,L = 4\,a\,L = 4\,(0.2\,\mathrm{m})(8\,\mathrm{m}) = 6.4\,\mathrm{m^2},$$
$$\dot{m} = \rho\,\dot{V} = (1.009\,\mathrm{kg/m^3})(0.15\,\mathrm{m^3/s}) = 0.151\,\mathrm{kg/s}.$$

Next, we determine the exit temperature of air from

$$T_{m,o} = T_s - (T_s - T_{m,i})\exp\left(-\frac{A_s\,\bar{h}}{\dot{m}\,c_p}\right)$$

$$= 60^\circ C - \left[(60-80)^\circ C\right]\exp\left[-\frac{(6.4\,\mathrm{m^2})\left(13.3\,\mathrm{W/m^2\cdot^\circ C}\right)}{(0.151\,\mathrm{kg/s})(1008\,\mathrm{J/kg\cdot^\circ C})}\right]$$

$$= 71.4^\circ C.$$

Then the logarithmic mean temperature difference and the rate of heat loss from the air become

$$\Delta T_{lm} = \frac{(T_s - T_{m,o}) - (T_s - T_{m,i})}{\ln\left(\dfrac{T_s - T_{m,o}}{T_s - T_{m,i}}\right)}$$

$$= \frac{(60-71.4)^\circ C - (60-80)^\circ C}{\ln\left(\dfrac{(60-71.4)^\circ C}{(60-80)^\circ C}\right)} = -15.3^\circ C,$$

$$q = \bar{h}\,A_s\,\Delta T_{lm}$$

$$= \left(13.3\,\mathrm{W/m^2\cdot^\circ C}\right)\left(6.4\,\mathrm{m^2}\right)(-15.3^\circ C) = -1302\,\mathrm{W}.$$

Air will lose heat at a rate of 1302 W as it flows through the duct.

Comments: The average fluid temperature $(80+71.4)/2 = 75.7^\circ C$ is sufficiently close to $80^\circ C$ so that it is not necessary to re-evaluate the properties and repeat the calculations.

Exercises 23:

1. What is the pressure drop in a 600 m length of 0.15 m inside di-

ameter galvanized iron pipe with relative roughness of 1.01×10^{-3} when 40°C water ($v = 0.658 \times 10^{-6}$ m^2/s) flows through it at a velocity of 0.173 m/s?

2. A 21.5 kg/s flow of water is dynamically and thermally developed in a 12 cm inside diameter smooth pipe. The pipe is held at 90°C. Find h and f where the bulk temperature of the fluid has reached 50°C. ($\rho = 977$ kg/m^3, $v = 4.07 \times 10^{-7}$ m^2/s, $Pr = 2.47$.)

3. Air at 1 atm and 12°C enters a 2 m long rectangular duct with cross section 75 mm × 150 mm. The duct is maintained at a constant surface temperature of 127°C, and the air mass flow rate is 0.10 kg/s. Determine the heat transfer rate from the duct to the air and the air outlet temperature.

24 Free Convection – Similarity Solution

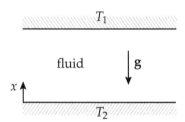

Figure 24.1: Thermal layer.

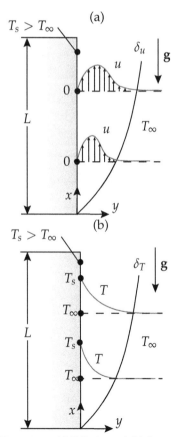

Figure 24.2: (a) Velocity and (b) thermal boundary layers.

In free, or natural, convection the flow is due entirely by the body force, *.i.e., gravity*, acting on the presence of density gradients with no external forcing present. If we have a fluid layer, such as indicated in Fig. 24.1 and $T_2 > T_1$, then the situation is such that $\rho_2 < \rho_1$ and if the difference in density is sufficiently large to overcome diffusion effects, then the lighter fluid will tend to rise, while the heavier fluid will tend to fall. In this case, we have a thermal instability that will give rise to a flow and thus convective heat transfer. If, on the other hand, $T_2 < T_1$, then $\rho_2 > \rho_1$ and in this case the lighter fluid is on top of the heavier fluid. This situation is stable and thus not lead to an instability and subsequent flow. Heat transfer in this case will occur purely by conduction.

24.1 Boundary Layer on Vertical Flat Plate

We now consider boundary layer flow developing along the vertical flat surface indicated in Fig. 24.2. We note that when $T_s > T_\infty$, the fluid next to the surface is lighter than that away from it and thus would tend to rise and lead to free convection. If instead $T_s < T_\infty$, then the fluid next to the surface would be colder than that away from it and thus would tend to fall. So, we see that as long as T_s is different than T_∞ we have an unstable situation that would lead to convective flow.

The velocity resulting from such flow is typically small and thus viscous dissipation is negligible ($Ec \approx 0$). Such flow presents a peculiar situation. First we note that in this case $P_\infty = $ const. and thus $dP_\infty^*/dx^* = 0$ in Eq. (14.3). In addition, in free convection we have that $u_\infty = 0$; we recall that in Eq. (14.1) u_∞ was used as a velocity scale and it subsequently appears in the dimensionless parameters in Eq. (14.6). In the present problem, we need to use a different reference velocity scale, say u_r, which can be constructed from our available physical parameters. The three possible choices, representing different physical aspects, are:

$$u_r = \begin{cases} [\beta g (T_s - T_\infty) L]^{1/2}, & \text{free buoyancy speed,} \\ \nu/L, & \text{viscous diffusion speed,} \\ \alpha/L, & \text{thermal diffusion speed.} \end{cases} \quad (24.1)$$

For the problem under consideration, the most appropriate reference speed would be $u_r = [\beta g (T_s - T_\infty) L]^{1/2}$. Nevertheless, from convention, most authors use $u_r = \nu/L$ for the reference velocity; we will follow convention. In addition, in this case it is more convenient to take

$$T^* = \frac{T - T_\infty}{T_s - T_\infty} \quad (24.2)$$

to normalize the temperature. Thus, taking $u_\infty \to \nu/L$ in Eq. (14.1), noting from Eq. (14.6) that in such case $Re_L \to 1$ and $Pe_L \to Pr$, and considering the above modifications and simplifications, Eqs. (14.2)-(14.5) become

$$\frac{\partial u^*}{\partial x^*} + \frac{\partial v^*}{\partial y^*} = 0, \quad (24.3)$$

$$u^* \frac{\partial u^*}{\partial x^*} + v^* \frac{\partial u^*}{\partial y^*} = \frac{\partial^2 u^*}{\partial y^{*2}} + Gr_L T^*, \quad (24.4)$$

$$u^* \frac{\partial T^*}{\partial x^*} + v^* \frac{\partial T^*}{\partial y^*} = \frac{1}{Pr} \frac{\partial^2 T^*}{\partial y^{*2}}, \quad (24.5)$$

Note:

- In contrast to forced convection, when buoyancy is important we have full coupling between the momentum and energy equations!

with boundary conditions

$$v^* (x^*, 0) = \mathbf{0}, \; T^* (x^*, 0) = 1, \; u^* (x^*, \infty) = 0, \; T^* (x^*, \infty) = 0, \; (24.6)$$

and dimensionless parameters

$$Gr_L = \frac{\beta g (T_s - T_\infty) L^3}{\nu^2} \quad \text{and} \quad Pr = \frac{\nu}{\alpha}. \quad (24.7)$$

Subsequently, we see that in free convection

$$Nu_L = f (Gr_L, Pr). \quad (24.8)$$

In summary, from the above discussion, we see that when

$$\begin{aligned} \frac{Gr_L}{Re_L^2} &\ll 1, & \text{forced convection,} & \quad Nu_L = f (Re_L, Pr), \\ \frac{Gr_L}{Re_L^2} &\gg 1, & \text{free convection,} & \quad Nu_L = f (Gr_L, Pr), \quad (24.9) \\ \frac{Gr_L}{Re_L^2} &= O(1), & \text{mixed convection,} & \quad Nu_L = f (Re_L, Gr_L, Pr). \end{aligned}$$

It is understood that in forced and mixed convection u_∞ is used as the velocity scale and Eqs. (14.2)-(14.6) provide the relevant equations.

24.2 Similarity Solution

For 2-D incompressible flow we can always introduce a stream function, ψ^*, such that the continuity equation (24.3) is automatically satisfied:

$$u^* = \frac{\partial \psi^*}{\partial y^*} \quad \text{and} \quad v^* = -\frac{\partial \psi^*}{\partial x^*}, \qquad (24.10)$$

where the normalization $\psi = \nu \, \psi^*$ is used. Now, the basic assumption is that the laminar boundary layer is similar:

$$u^* = \phi \left(\frac{y}{\delta_u(x)} \right) \quad \text{and} \quad T^* = \theta \left(\frac{y}{\delta_u(x)} \right),$$

where we note that ϕ and θ are dimensionless functions of the dimensionless quantity $y/\delta_u(x)$, where $\delta_u(x)$ is given from the scaling arguments in Sec. 13.3:

$$\delta_u(x) \sim \sqrt{\frac{\nu x}{u_r}}.$$

In this particular case, the appropriate reference velocity, as indicated earlier, would be the local driving buoyancy speed, $u_r = [\beta g (T_s - T_\infty) x]^{1/2}$, so that

$$\delta_u \sim x \, Gr_x^{-1/4}, \qquad (24.11)$$

where

$$Gr_x = \frac{\beta g (T_s - T_\infty) x^3}{\nu^2}, \qquad (24.12)$$

is the local Grashof number. Subsequently, accounting for the normalizations and introducing factors of 4 for convenience, we define the new independent (similarity) variable and dependent variables as

$$\eta = \frac{y^*}{x^*} \left(\frac{Gr_x}{4} \right)^{1/4}, \qquad (24.13)$$

$$\psi^* (x^*, y^*) = 4 \left(\frac{Gr_x}{4} \right)^{1/4} f(\eta), \qquad (24.14)$$

$$T^* = T^* (\eta), \qquad (24.15)$$

where we use the similarity variable η in lieu of the independent variable y^*. It then follows that

$$u^* = \frac{\partial \psi^*}{\partial y^*} = \frac{\partial \psi^*}{\partial \eta} \frac{\partial \eta}{\partial y^*} = \frac{2}{x^*} Gr_x^{1/2} f'(\eta), \qquad (24.16)$$

$$v^* = -\frac{\partial \psi^*}{\partial x^*} = \frac{3}{x^*} \left(\frac{Gr_x}{4} \right)^{1/4} \left[f(\eta) - \frac{1}{3} \eta f'(\eta) \right], \qquad (24.17)$$

and evaluating all other derivatives in Eqs. (24.4) and (24.5), as done in Sec. 17.2, we arrive at the following system of fully coupled ordinary differential equations:

$$f''' + 3 f f'' - 2 (f')^2 + T^* = 0, \qquad (24.18)$$

$$T^{*\prime\prime} + 3 \, Pr \, f \, T^{*\prime} = 0, \qquad (24.19)$$

where prime superscripts denote derivatives with respect to η. In addition, as done in Sec. 17.2, the boundary conditions Eq. (24.6) lead to the following conditions for f and T^* at $\eta = 0$ and $\eta \to \infty$:

$$f(0) = f'(0) = 0, \; T^*(0) = 1 \quad \text{and} \quad f'(\infty) = 0, \; T^*(\infty) = 0. \quad (24.20)$$

The numerical solution showing f' and T^* as functions of η for $Pr = 0.7$ is provided in Fig. 24.3. Now, since

$$q_s'' = -k \left. \frac{\partial T}{\partial y} \right|_{y=0} = -\frac{k}{x} (T_s - T_\infty) \left(\frac{Gr_x}{4} \right)^{1/4} \left. \frac{dT^*}{d\eta} \right|_{\eta=0}, \qquad (24.21)$$

it follows that

$$Nu_x = \frac{h \, x}{k} = \frac{[q_s'' / (T_s - T_\infty)] \, x}{k} = \left(\frac{Gr_x}{4} \right)^{1/4} g \, (Pr), \qquad (24.22)$$

where

$$g \, (Pr) \equiv -T^{*\prime}(0) \qquad (24.23)$$

is shown in Fig. 24.4. To an error of less than 0.5% we can write

$$g \, (Pr) = \frac{0.75 \, Pr^{1/2}}{\left(0.609 + 1.221 \, Pr^{1/2} + 1.238 \, Pr \right)^{1/4}}, \quad 0 \le Pr < \infty. \quad (24.24)$$

Lastly, it follows that

$$\overline{Nu}_L = \frac{\overline{h} \, L}{k} = \frac{4}{3} \left(\frac{Gr_L}{4} \right)^{1/4} g \, (Pr) = \frac{4}{3} Nu_L, \qquad (24.25)$$

where

$$\overline{h} = \frac{1}{L} \int_0^L h \, dx. \qquad (24.26)$$

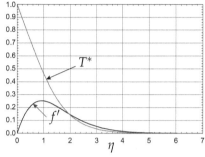

Figure 24.3: f' and T^* as functions of η for $Pr = 0.7$.

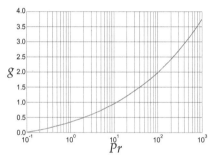

Figure 24.4: Values of g as a function of Pr.

Example 24.1:

Water at 20°C is heated by a 15 cm by 15 cm vertical flat plate which is maintained at 52°C.

Known: The size and temperature of the plate, and the temperature of the water.

Find: Use the similarity solution to find the heat transfer rate.

Assumptions: Steady state conditions, constant properties, incompressible flow.

Properties: At 40°C we have: $\rho = 995$ kg/m^3, $\beta = 1.8 \times 10^{-4}$ 1/°C, $\nu = 0.658 \times 10^{-6}$ m^2/s, $k = 0.628$ W/m·°C, $Pr = 4.34$.

Analysis: From Fig. 24.4 or Eq. (24.24) we see that for $Pr = 4.34$ we have $g(Pr) = -T^{*\prime}(0) \approx 0.9$. In addition, we have

$$Gr_L = \frac{\beta g \, (T_s - T_\infty)L^3}{\nu^2}$$

$$= \frac{(1.8 \times 10^{-4} \, 1/°C)(9.8 \, \text{m/s}^2)[(52-20)°C](0.15 \, \text{m})^3}{(0.658 \times 10^{-6} \, \text{m}^2/\text{s})^2}$$

$$= 4.40 \times 10^8$$

so that from Eq. (24.25) we have

$$\bar{h} = \frac{4}{3} \frac{k}{L} \left(\frac{Gr_L}{4}\right)^{1/4} g\,(Pr)$$

$$= \frac{4}{3} \left(\frac{0.628 \, \text{W/m} \cdot°\text{C}}{0.15 \, \text{m}}\right) \left(\frac{4.40 \times 10^8}{4}\right)^{1/4} (0.9)$$

$$= 515 \, \text{W/m}^2 \cdot°\text{C}.$$

The heat transfer is then

$$q = \bar{h} \, A_s \, (T_s - T_\infty)$$

$$= (515 \, \text{W/m}^2 \cdot°\text{C})(0.15 \, \text{m})^2 [(52-20)°\text{C}]$$

$$= 371 \, \text{W}.$$

Exercises 24:

1. Derive Eqs. (24.18)-(24.20) from Eqs. (24.3)-(24.6).

2. Estimate the heat loss from a vertical wall exposed to nitrogen at 1 atm and 4°C. The wall is 1.8 m high and 2.45 m wide. It is maintained at 50°C.

3. What is the maximum vertical velocity in the boundary layer of Exercise 2 at $x = 0.9$ m (from the bottom of the wall)?

25 Free Convection – Miscellaneous Topics

25.1 Transition and Turbulence on Vertical Flat Plate

A dimensionless parameter that is useful in free or natural convection flows is the Rayleigh number. It is related to the Grashof number as follows:

$$Ra_L = Gr_L \, Pr = \frac{\beta \, g \, (T_s - T_\infty) \, L^3}{\alpha \, \nu}. \tag{25.1}$$

For a heated vertical flat plate, the free convecting flow transitions at the local Rayleigh number of

$$Ra_{x,c} \approx 10^9. \tag{25.2}$$

For larger values, the flow becomes turbulent. A useful empirical correlation for the average Nusselt number is given by

$$\overline{Nu_L} = \begin{cases} 0.59 \, Ra_L^{1/4}, & \text{for} \quad 10^4 \lesssim Ra_L \lesssim 10^9 \\ 0.10 \, Ra_L^{1/3}, & \text{for} \quad 10^9 \lesssim Ra_L \lesssim 10^{13}. \end{cases} \tag{25.3}$$

A correlation provided by Churchill and Chu that is valid over the entire range of Rayleigh number is given by

$$\overline{Nu_L} = \left\{ 0.825 + \frac{0.387 \, Ra_L^{1/6}}{\left[1 + (0.492/Pr)^{9/16} \right]^{8/27}} \right\}^2, \quad \text{for } Ra_L \lesssim 10^{13}. \tag{25.4}$$

All properties in the above correlations are evaluated at the film temperature $T_f = \frac{1}{2} (T_s + T_\infty)$.

25.2 Horizontal Plate

For a horizontal heated or cooled plate, the free or natural convection correlations for the top and bottom surfaces are different. The correlation for the upper surface of a heated plate or lower surface of a cooled plate is given by

$$\overline{Nu_L} = \begin{cases} 0.54\, Ra_L^{1/4}, & \text{for} \quad 10^4 \lesssim Ra_L \lesssim 10^7 \\ 0.15\, Ra_L^{1/3}, & \text{for} \quad 10^7 \lesssim Ra_L \lesssim 10^{11}, \end{cases} \tag{25.5}$$

while for the lower surface of a heated plate or upper surface of a cooled plate by

$$\overline{Nu_L} = 0.27\, Ra_L^{1/4}, \qquad \text{for} \quad 10^5 \lesssim Ra_L \lesssim 10^{10}, \tag{25.6}$$

where in the above correlations the length scale is given by

$$L \equiv \frac{A_s}{\mathcal{P}}. \tag{25.7}$$

and A_s and $\mathcal{P}$ are the surface area and perimeter of the plate, respectively. The above correlations are valid for $Pr \gtrsim 0.7$.

25.3   Long Horizontal Cylinder

For a heated long horizontal cylinder of diameter D, the empirical heat transfer correlation is given by

$$\overline{Nu_D} = \frac{\overline{h}\, D}{k} = C\, Ra_D^n \tag{25.8}$$

where C and n are given in Table 25.1. A more complicated correlation that remains continuous over a large range of Ra_D is given by

$$\overline{Nu_D} = \left\{ 0.60 + \frac{0.387\, Ra_D^{1/6}}{\left[1 + (0.559/Pr)^{9/16}\right]^{8/27}} \right\}^2, \quad \text{for } Ra_D \lesssim 10^{12}. \tag{25.9}$$

Table 25.1: Constants for Eq. (25.8) for free convection from a horizontal circular cylinder.

Ra_D	C	n
10^{-10}–10^{-2}	0.675	0.058
10^{-2}–10^2	1.020	0.148
10^2–10^4	0.850	0.188
10^4–10^7	0.480	0.250
10^7–10^{12}	0.125	0.333

25.4   Spheres

The following empirical correlation, due to Churchill, applies to the natural convection flow of fluids with $Pr \gtrsim 0.7$ due to heated or cooled spheres:

$$Nu_D = 2 + \frac{0.589\, Ra_D^{1/4}}{\left[1 + (0.469/Pr)^{9/14}\right]^{4/9}}, \quad \text{for } Ra_D \lesssim 10^{11}. \tag{25.10}$$

25.5   Channels and Enclosures

Many other empirical correlations exist for channels and enclosures. Here we provide a sampling of the most useful ones.

a) Vertical channels — For channels of length L composed of two vertical parallel plates separated by a horizontal distance H, with the top and bottom of the channel exposed to a quiescent fluid, Bar-Cohen and Rohsenow provide the correlation

$$\overline{Nu}_H = \left[\frac{c_1}{(A\,Ra_H)^2} + \frac{c_2}{(A\,Ra_H)^{1/2}} \right]^{-1/2}, \qquad (25.11)$$

where

$$A = \frac{H}{L} \quad \text{and} \quad Ra_H = \frac{\beta g\,(T_s - T_\infty)\,H^3}{\alpha\,\nu}, \qquad (25.12)$$

while for constant flux surfaces they provide the correlation

$$Nu_H = \left[\frac{c_1}{(A\,Ra_H^*)} + \frac{c_2}{(A\,Ra_H^*)^{2/5}} \right]^{-1/2}, \qquad (25.13)$$

where the modified Rayleigh number is given by

$$Ra_H^* = \frac{\beta g\,q_s''\,H^4}{k\,\alpha\,\nu}. \qquad (25.14)$$

The constants in the above correlations are

$$c_1,\, c_2 = \begin{cases} 576,\ 2.87 & \text{if} \quad T_{s,1} = T_{s,2} = \text{const.,} \\ 144,\ 2.87 & \text{if} \quad T_{s,1} = \text{const}, \ q_{s,2}'' = 0, \\ 48,\ 2.51 & \text{if} \quad q_{s,1}'' = q_{s,2}'' = \text{const.,} \\ 24,\ 2.51 & \text{if} \quad q_{s,1}'' = q_{s,2}'' = 0. \end{cases} \qquad (25.15)$$

The limits of fully developed flow and flow isolated to each plate are given by $A\,Ra_H$ (or Ra_H^*) $\lesssim 10$ and $A\,Ra_H$ (or Ra_H^*) $\gtrsim 100$, respectively.

b) Rectangular cavities — Most of the cavities considered have two opposing walls separated by a distance H at different temperatures T_1 and T_2, with $T_1 > T_2$, and all other walls insulated. The aspect ratios of $A_1 = L/H$ and $A_2 = W/H$, where the length, L, and width, W, dimensions of the cavity also play important roles in the natural convection flow, along with the dimensionless parameters of relevance which are the Rayleigh and Prandtl numbers defined as

$$Ra_H = \frac{\beta g\,(T_1 - T_2)\,H^3}{\alpha\,\nu} \quad \text{and} \quad Pr = \frac{\nu}{\alpha}. \qquad (25.16)$$

The cavity is said to be horizontal, vertical or at an angle depending if the isothermal walls are horizontal, vertical or the isothermal wall with temperature T_1 is tilted at an angle θ from the horizontal. Thus, all empirical correlations for cavities have the following average Nusselt number dependence:

$$\overline{Nu}_H = \overline{Nu}_H\,(Ra_H, Pr, A_1, A_2, \theta). \qquad (25.17)$$

Horizontal cavity: If the wall with the higher temperature is on top ($\theta = 180°$), then heat transfer is purely by conduction. On the other hand, if the wall with the higher temperature is at the bottom ($\theta = 0°$), convection proceeds if the Rayleigh number is sufficiently large. Globe and Dropkin provide the following empirical correlation valid when A_1 is sufficiently large and $A_2 \gg 1$:

$$\overline{Nu}_H = 0.069\, Ra_H^{1/3} Pr^{0.074}, \quad \text{for } 3 \times 10^5 \lesssim Ra_H \lesssim 7 \times 10^9, \quad (25.18)$$

where all properties are evaluated at the average temperature of $(T_1 + T_2)/2$.

Vertical cavity: For a vertical cavity ($\theta = 90°$) with $A_2 \gg 1$, the following correlation is suggested:

$$\overline{Nu}_H = 0.046\, Ra_H^{1/3}, \quad \text{for } 1 \le Pr \le 20,\ 1 \le A_1 \le 40,$$
$$10^6 \le Ra_H \le 10^9, \quad (25.19)$$

where all properties are evaluated at the average temperature of $(T_1 + T_2)/2$.

Table 25.2: Critical angle for inclined rectangular cavity.

A_1	θ^*
1	25°
3	53°
6	60°
12	67°
> 12	70°

Inclined cavity: For an inclined cavity, there is a critical angle beyond which natural convection flow proceeds. For $A_2 \gg 1$, the critical angle is given in Table 25.2 as a function of A_1. The suggested correlations is subsequently given by

$$\overline{Nu}_H = \begin{cases} \overline{Nu}_H\,(\theta = 90°)\,(\sin\theta)^{1/4}, & \theta^* \le \theta \le 90°, \\ 1 + \left[\overline{Nu}_H\,(\theta = 90°) - 1\right]\sin\theta, & 90° \le \theta \le 180°, \end{cases}$$
$$(25.20)$$

c) Concentric cylinders — For natural convection flow between two long horizontal concentric circular cylinders of radii r_i and r_o, and constant surface temperatures of T_i and T_o, where the subscripts "i" and "o" refer to the inner and outer cylinders, respectively, the heat transfer rate per unit length is given by

$$q' = \frac{2\pi k_e |T_i - T_o|}{\ln(r_o/r_i)}, \quad (25.21)$$

where the effective thermal conductivity is

$$\frac{k_e}{k} = 0.386 \left(\frac{Pr}{0.861 + Pr}\right)^{1/4} Ra_{L_c}^{1/4} \ge 1, \quad (25.22)$$

and the length scale on the Rayleigh number Ra_{L_c} is given by

$$L_c = \frac{2\left[\ln(r_o/r_i)\right]^{4/3}}{\left(r_i^{-3/5} + r_o^{-3/5}\right)^{5/3}}. \quad (25.23)$$

All properties are evaluated at the mean temperature of $(T_i + T_o)/2$, $Ra_{L_c} \lesssim 10^7$, and $0.7 \lesssim Pr \lesssim 6000$.

d) Concentric spheres — For natural convection flow between two concentric spheres of radii r_i and r_o, and constant surface temperatures of T_i and T_o, where the subscripts "i" and "o" refer to the inner and outer spheres, respectively, the heat transfer rate is given by

$$q = \frac{4 \pi k_e |T_i - T_o|}{r_i^{-1} - r_o^{-1}}, \tag{25.24}$$

where the effective thermal conductivity is

$$\frac{k_e}{k} = 0.74 \left(\frac{Pr}{0.861 + Pr} \right)^{1/4} Ra_{L_s}^{1/4} \geq 1, \tag{25.25}$$

and the length scale on the Rayleigh number Ra_{L_s} is given by

$$L_s = \frac{\left(r_i^{-1} - r_o^{-1} \right)^{4/3}}{2^{1/3} \left(r_i^{-7/5} + r_o^{-7/5} \right)^{5/3}}. \tag{25.26}$$

All properties are evaluated at the mean temperature of $(T_i + T_o)/2$, $Ra_{L_s} \lesssim 10^4$, and $0.7 \lesssim Pr \lesssim 4000$.

25.6   Combined Natural and Forced Convection

There are many situations in which we have forced convection while at the same time free or natural convection might also be important. This would be the case when the buoyancy force and the inertial force become of the same order. We recall from our non-dimensionalization in Lecture 14.1 and the discussion in reference to Eq. (24.9) that this situation occurs when the dimensionless ratio of Gr_L / Re_L^2 is of $O(1)$.

In such case, the following correlation is recommended:

$$Nu^n = Nu_F^n \pm Nu_N^n \quad \text{with} \quad n = 3, \tag{25.27}$$

where Nu_F corresponds to the Nusselt number due to the forced convection component, Nu_N the Nusselt number due to the natural convection components, the plus sign when the two components are in the same directions (assisting flows), and minus sign when the two components are in the opposite directions (opposing flows). Lastly, it is noted that the power of $n = 3$ is only approximate.

Example 25.1:

The two concentric spheres of radii $r_i = 10$ cm and $r_o = 15$ cm are separated by air at 1 atm pressure. The surface temperatures of the two spheres enclosing the air are $T_i = 320$ K and $T_o = 280$ K, respectively.

Known: Concentric spheres of given radii and temperatures separated by air at a given pressure.

Find: Determine the rate of heat transfer from the inner sphere to the outer sphere by natural convection.

Assumptions: Steady state conditions, constant properties, air is an ideal gas.

Properties: Properties of air at $(T_i + T_o)/2 = (320 + 280)\,\text{K}/2 = 300$ K and 1 atm are: $\nu = 1.580 \times 10^{-5}$ m^2/s, $k = 0.02566$ W/m·K, $Pr = 0.7290$, $\beta = 1/300$ K^{-1}.

Analysis: From Eq. (25.26) the characteristic length in this case is

$$L_s = \frac{\left(r_i^{-1} - r_o^{-1}\right)^{4/3}}{2^{1/3}\left(r_i^{-7/5} + r_o^{-7/5}\right)^{5/3}}$$

$$= \frac{\left((0.1\,\text{m})^{-1} - (0.15\,\text{m})^{-1}\right)^{4/3}}{2^{1/3}\left((0.1\,\text{m})^{-7/5} + (0.15\,\text{m})^{-7/5}\right)^{5/3}} = 0.047\,\text{m}.$$

The Rayleigh number is then

$$Ra_{L_s} = \frac{\beta g (T_i - T_o) L_s^3}{\nu^2} Pr$$

$$= \frac{(1/300\,\text{K}^{-1})(9.81\,\text{m/s}^2)[(320 - 280)\,\text{K}](0.047\,\text{m})^3}{(1.580 \times 10^{-5}\,\text{m}^2/\text{s})^2}(0.7290)$$

$$= 3.966 \times 10^5.$$

The effective thermal conductivity, from Eq. (25.25), is

$$k_e = 0.74\,k \left(\frac{Pr}{0.861 + Pr}\right)^{1/4} Ra_{L_s}^{1/4}$$

$$= 0.74\,(0.02566\,\text{W/m}\cdot\text{K})\left(\frac{0.7290}{0.861 + 0.7290}\right)^{1/4}(3.966 \times 10^5)^{1/4}$$

$$= 0.3921\,\text{W/m}\cdot\text{K}.$$

Lastly, the rate of heat transfer between the spheres is given by

Eq. (25.24):

$$q = \frac{4\,\pi\,k_e\,|T_i - T_o|}{r_i^{-1} - r_o^{-1}}$$

$$= \frac{4\,\pi\,(0.3921\,\text{W/m}\cdot\text{K})\,|320 - 280|\,\text{K}}{(0.1\,\text{m})^{-1} - (0.15\,\text{m})^{-1}} = 59.1\,\text{W}.$$

Comments: Note that the air in the spherical enclosure will act like a stationary fluid whose thermal conductivity is $k_e/k = 15.3$ times that of air as a result of natural convection currents.

Exercises 25:

1. You have been asked to design a vertical wall panel heater, 1.5 m high, for a dwelling. What should the heat flux be if no part of the wall should exceed 33°C? How much heat will be added to the room if the panel is 7 m in width?

2. The vertical 0.8 m high, 2 m wide double-pane window consists of two sheets of glass separated by a 2 cm air gap at atmospheric pressure. If the glass surface temperatures across the air gap are measured to be 12°C and 2°C, determine the rate of heat transfer through the window.

3. A solar collector consists of a horizontal copper tube of outer diameter 5 cm enclosed in a concentric thin glass tube of 9 cm diameter. Water is heated as it flows through the tube, and the annular space between the copper and glass tube is filled with air at 1 atm pressure. During a clear day, the temperatures of the tube surface and the glass cover are measured to be 60°C and 32°C, respectively. Determine the rate of heat loss from the collector by natural convection per meter length of the tube.

Part IV

Thermal Radiation

26 Basic Concepts

26.1 Definitions and Geometry

Radiation is the propagation of electromagnetic waves. As opposed to conduction and convection, no medium is required for transfer of energy via radiation. Energy related to thermal radiation (or radiation for short) is mostly a surface phenomenon, except in high temperature transparent or semi-transparent mediums, where it is a volumetric phenomenon.

Radiation is transmitted through waves of different wavelengths within the electromagnetic spectrum illustrated in Fig. 26.1. The wavelength λ is given by

$$\lambda = \frac{c}{f} \tag{26.1}$$

and is given in units of $1\mu m = 10^{-6}$ m, where c is the speed of light $(3 \times 10^8$ m/s in vacuum) and f is the frequency of the wave with units of 1/s or Hertz. Our focus is on thermal radiation which is comprised of waves in the range of approximately 0.1–100 μm of the spectrum. The visible spectrum extends from $\lambda_1 = 0.40\,\mu m$ to $\lambda_2 = 0.76\,\mu m$.

The study of thermal radiation is complicated due to the following:

a) *directional distribution* – radiation intensity is a function of the angle it makes with a surface upon which it strikes,

b) *spectral distribution* – radiation depends on wavelength.

We examine these aspects next.

We first illustrate in Fig. 26.2 the thermal radiation from a point on area A_1 striking area A_2. We note that the areas are not normal to each other. In such case, area A_1 sees area A_2 as

$$A_{2,n} = A_2 \cos\theta_2. \tag{26.2}$$

When $A/r \ll 1$ in two dimensions, or $A/r^2 \ll 1$ in three dimensions, we approximate the areas as differential surfaces. Thus, in two dimensions, we quantify the circular section illustrated in Fig. 26.3(a) by the

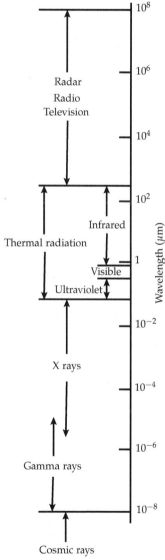

Figure 26.1: Electromagnetic spectrum.

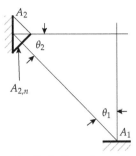

Figure 26.2: Projection of area A_2 normal to the direction of radiation from point on area A_1.

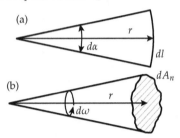

Figure 26.3: (a) Plane angle and (b) solid angle.

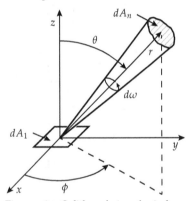

Figure 26.4: Solid angle in spherical coordinates.

Note:

• The limits on the integrals in Eqs. (26.12) and (26.13) depend on the extents of the area and spectral range selected.

differential angle

$$da = \frac{dl}{r}, \tag{26.3}$$

where dl is the differential arc length of the circular segment of radius r. The angle da is measured in radians (rad). Equivalently, in three dimensions, we quantify the spherical portion illustrated in Fig. 26.3(b) by the differential angle

$$d\omega = \frac{dA_n}{r^2}, \tag{26.4}$$

where dA_n is the differential area of the spherical sector of radius r. The angle $d\omega$ is a solid angle measure in steradians (sr).

In general, in three dimensions, we have the situation as pictured in Fig. 26.4 where radiation from the differential area segment dA_1 centered at the origin strikes the differential area segments dA_n located at a distance r and at angle ϕ from the x-axis and angle θ from the z-axis, where $0 \leq \varphi \leq 2\pi$ and $0 \leq \theta \leq \pi/2$. It should be noted that since

$$dA_n = r^2 \sin\theta \, d\theta \, d\varphi, \tag{26.5}$$

it follows that

$$d\omega = \sin\theta \, d\theta \, d\varphi. \tag{26.6}$$

We define the *spectral intensity* of radiation as

$$I_\lambda\left(\lambda, \theta, \varphi\right) \equiv \frac{dq_\lambda}{dA_1 \cos\theta \, d\omega}, \tag{26.7}$$

where

$$q_\lambda \equiv \frac{dq}{d\lambda} \tag{26.8}$$

is the rate at which thermal radiation of wavelength λ, with units of W/μm, propagates from dA_1 to dA_n. A diffusive surface is a surface that radiates equally in all hemispherical directions. For a *diffusive surface*

$$I_\lambda\left(\lambda, \theta, \varphi\right) = I_\lambda\left(\lambda\right), \tag{26.9}$$

and in such case

$$I = \int_0^\infty I_\lambda\left(\lambda\right) d\lambda \tag{26.10}$$

is the *total intensity*.

Now, the differential spectral heat flux from radiation is given by

$$dq_\lambda'' = I_\lambda\left(\lambda, \theta, \varphi\right) \cos\theta \, \sin\theta \, d\theta \, d\varphi, \tag{26.11}$$

the spectral heat flux by

$$q_\lambda'' = \iint I_\lambda\left(\lambda, \theta, \varphi\right) \cos\theta \, \sin\theta \, d\theta \, d\varphi \quad \left(\text{W/m}^2 \cdot \mu\text{m}\right), \tag{26.12}$$

and the heat flux by

$$q'' = \int q''_\lambda (\lambda)\, d\lambda \quad \left(\text{W/m}^2\right). \qquad (26.13)$$

In what follows, since we have to keep track of several thermal radiation sources, we will be using different symbols for these sources. In each case, it should be kept in mind that they represent spectral or total heat fluxes which we have represented as q''_λ or q'' up to now. These different sources are noted in Fig. 26.5.

26.2   Emission

Emission is the rate at which radiation that a surface at a finite temperature issues. The *hemispherical spectral emissive power* of a surface is given by

$$E_\lambda (\lambda) = \int_0^{2\pi} \int_0^{\pi/2} I_{\lambda,e}(\lambda,\theta,\varphi) \cos\theta\, \sin\theta\, d\theta\, d\varphi, \qquad (26.14)$$

where $I_{\lambda,e}$ is the *spectral intensity of emitted radiation*. The *total emissive power* is given by

$$E = \int_0^{\infty} E_\lambda (\lambda)\, d\lambda. \qquad (26.15)$$

For diffusive surfaces we have

$$E_\lambda (\lambda) = \pi\, I_{\lambda,e}(\lambda) \qquad \text{and} \qquad E = \pi\, I_e, \qquad (26.16)$$

where I_e is the *total emitted intensity*.

26.3   Irradiation

Irradiation is the rate at which radiation is incident on a surface. Analogously, we define the *hemispherical spectral irradiation* as

$$G_\lambda (\lambda) = \int_0^{2\pi} \int_0^{\pi/2} I_{\lambda,i}(\lambda,\theta,\varphi) \cos\theta\, \sin\theta\, d\theta\, d\varphi, \qquad (26.17)$$

where $I_{\lambda,i}$ is the *spectral intensity of irradiation*. The *total irradiation* is subsequently given by

$$G = \int_0^{\infty} G_\lambda (\lambda)\, d\lambda. \qquad (26.18)$$

For diffusive surfaces we have

$$G_\lambda = \pi\, I_{\lambda,i}(\lambda) \qquad \text{and} \qquad G = \pi\, I_i, \qquad (26.19)$$

where I_i is the *total irradiated intensity*.

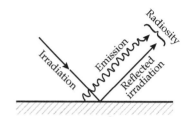

Figure 26.5: Radiations associated with a surface.

Note:

- *Hemispherical spectral* quantities include radiation from all hemispherical directions.

- Spectral quantities depend on the wavelength of the radiation.

- The corresponding *total* quantities include radiation from all wavelengths.

26.4 Radiosity

Radiosity is the rate at which radiation leaves a surface. As illustrated in Fig. 26.5, it's composed of emitted radiation plus the reflected portion of irradiation. We define the *hemispherical spectral radiosity* as

$$J_\lambda (\lambda) = \int_0^{2\pi} \int_0^{\pi/2} I_{\lambda,e+r} (\lambda, \theta, \varphi) \cos \theta \, \sin \theta \, d\theta \, d\varphi, \qquad (26.20)$$

where $I_{\lambda,e+r}$ is the *spectral intensity of radiosity*. Subsequently, the *total radiosity* is given by

$$J = \int_0^\infty J_\lambda (\lambda) \, d\lambda. \qquad (26.21)$$

For diffusive surfaces (reflectors and emitters), we have

$$J_\lambda (\lambda) = \pi \, I_{\lambda,e+r} \qquad \text{and} \qquad J = \pi \, I_{e+r}, \qquad (26.22)$$

where I_{e+r} is the *total radiosity intensity*.

Example 26.1:

What is the total irradiation for the spectral distribution of surface irradiation given by

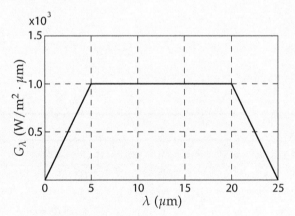

Known: Spectral distribution of surface irradiation.

Find: Total irradiation.

Analysis: The total irradiation is given by Eq. (26.18), thus

$$G = \int_{0\,\mu m}^{5\,\mu m} G_\lambda \, d\lambda + \int_{5\,\mu m}^{20\,\mu m} G_\lambda \, d\lambda + \int_{20\,\mu m}^{25\,\mu m} G_\lambda \, d\lambda.$$

Subsequently,

$$G = \frac{1}{2}\left(1000\,\text{W/m}^2 \cdot \mu m\right)(5-0)\,\mu m+$$
$$\left(1000\,\text{W/m}^2 \cdot \mu m\right)(20-5)\,\mu m+$$
$$\frac{1}{2}\left(1000\,\text{W/m}^2 \cdot \mu m\right)(25-20)\,\mu m$$
$$= (2500 + 15000 + 2500)\,\text{W/m}^2 = 2 \times 10^4\,\text{W/m}^2.$$

Comments: In general, the spectral distribution is not so regular. Nevertheless, the procedure of computing the total irradiation remains the same.

Exercises 26:

1. A microwave oven is designed to operate at a frequency of 2.8×10^9 Hz. Determine the wavelength of these microwaves and the energy of each microwave.

2. A small surface of area $A = 1\,\text{cm}^2$ is subjected to incident radiation of constant intensity $I_i = 2.2 \times 10^4\,\text{W/m}^2\cdot\text{sr}$ over the entire hemisphere. Determine the rate at which radiation energy is incident on the surface through (a) $0° \leq \theta \leq 45°$ and (b) $45° \leq \theta \leq 90°$, where θ is the angle a radiation beam makes with the normal of the surface.

3. Determine the fraction of the total, hemispherical emissive power that leaves a diffuse surface in the directions $\pi/4 \leq \theta \leq \pi/2$ and $0 \leq \phi \leq \pi$.

27 Radiation Physics

27.1 Blackbody Radiation

A *blackbody radiator* is considered an ideal surface since

a) it absorbs all incident radiation,

b) its emissivity is unity (see below), *i.e.* $\epsilon = 1$, and

c) it is a diffusive emitter, *i.e.* emitted radiation is independent of directionality.

Blackbody radiators are perfect absorbers and emitters. While no real surface is truly a blackbody radiator, such a surface serves as a reference for comparison purposes. A cavity with a very small opening has properties that are closest to a blackbody radiator. Any radiation entering the opening is reflected indefinitely or absorbed inside and is unlikely to re-emerge, making the hole a nearly perfect absorber.

The spectral intensity of a blackbody radiator is given by Plank's distribution

$$I_{\lambda,b}\left(\lambda, T\right) = \frac{2\,\hbar\,c_0^2}{\lambda^5\left[\exp\left(\hbar\,c_0/\lambda\,\kappa\,T\right) - 1\right]}, \tag{27.1}$$

where $\hbar = 6.6256 \times 10^{-34}$ J·s is Plank's constant, $\kappa = 1.3805 \times 10^{-23}$ J/K is Boltzmann's constant, $c_0 = 2.998 \times 10^8$ m/s is the speed of light in vacuum, and T K is the absolute temperature. Since a blackbody is a diffusive emitter, then from (26.16) we see that the spectral emissive power is given by

$$E_{\lambda,b}\left(\lambda, T\right) = \pi\,I_{\lambda,b}\left(\lambda, T\right) = \frac{C_1}{\lambda^5\left[\exp\left(C_2/\lambda\,T\right) - 1\right]}, \tag{27.2}$$

where $C_1 = 2\,\pi\,\hbar\,c_0^2 = 3.742 \times 10^8$ W·μm^4/m^2, and $C_2 = \hbar\,c_0/\kappa = 1.439 \times 10^4$ μm·K. This blackbody spectral emissive power is illustrated in Fig. 27.1 for different values of temperature.

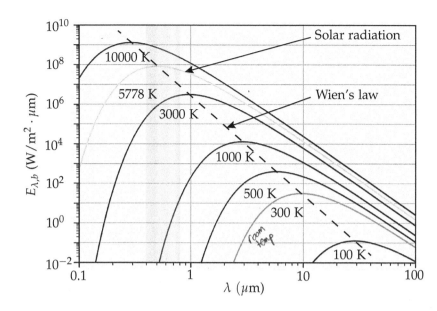

27.1.1 Wien's Displacement Law

Wien's displacement law states that the black body radiation curve for different temperatures peaks at a wavelength inversely proportional to the temperature. This result is obtained by finding the frequency at which the maximum of (27.2) occurs, resulting in

$$\lambda_{\max} T = C_3 = 2897.8 \ \mu\text{m} \cdot \text{K}. \tag{27.3}$$

The shift of the peak, noted on Fig. 27.1, is a direct consequence of the Planck radiation law.

27.1.2 Stefan-Boltzmann Law

The total emissive power of a blackbody is obtained by using (26.15):

$$E_b(T) = \int_0^\infty E_{\lambda,b}(\lambda, T) \, d\lambda = \sigma T^4, \tag{27.4}$$

where σ is the Stefan–Boltzmann constant which is equal to 5.670×10^{-8} W/m²·K⁴. This is called the Stefan-Boltzmann law and corresponds to the power radiated by a blackbody over all wavelengths and in all directions as a function of temperature.

Note:

- The total intensity of a blackbody is given by (26.16), *i.e.* $I_b = E_b/\pi$.

27.1.3 Band Emission of Blackbody

Band emission is the fraction of the total emission from a blackbody that is in a certain wavelength interval or band. For a prescribed temperature T and the spectral interval from 0 to λ, it is the ratio of the total emissive power of a black body from 0 to λ to the total emissive power over the entire spectrum:

$$F_{(0\to\lambda)} = \frac{\int_0^\lambda E_{\lambda,b}\,d\lambda}{\int_0^\infty E_{\lambda,b}\,d\lambda} = \frac{\int_0^\lambda E_{\lambda,b}\,d\lambda}{E_b(T)}. \qquad (27.5)$$

Values of this fractional function of blackbody radiation are usually given in figure or table form as a function of λT. Nevertheless, it has been shown that its value is exactly given by

$$F_{(0\to\lambda)} = \frac{15}{\pi^4}\sum_{n=1}^\infty\left[\frac{e^{-nx}}{n}\left(x^3 + \frac{3x^2}{n} + \frac{6x}{n^2} + \frac{6}{n^3}\right)\right], \qquad (27.6)$$

where $x = \hbar c_0/\lambda\kappa T$. A truncation of the sum to $n = 3$ provides an excellent approximation. Subsequently, the total emission from the spectral band from λ_1 to λ_2 is given by

$$F_{(\lambda_1\to\lambda_2)} = F_{(0\to\lambda_2)} - F_{(0\to\lambda_1)}. \qquad (27.7)$$

27.1.4 Real Surface Emission

The emissivity of a material surface is its effectiveness in emitting energy as thermal radiation. Real surfaces do not behave as blackbody surfaces. Quantitatively, the spectral emissivity $\epsilon_{\lambda,\theta}$ is the ratio of the spectral intensity of the emitted radiation from such a surface to the spectral intensity of blackbody radiation from a blackbody surface at the same temperature:

$$\epsilon_{\lambda,\theta}(\lambda,\theta,\varphi,T) = \frac{I_{\lambda,e}(\lambda,\theta,\varphi,T)}{I_{\lambda,b}(\lambda,T)}. \qquad (27.8)$$

Subsequently, for a diffuse surface, we can rewrite the spectral it as

$$\epsilon_\lambda(\lambda,T) = \frac{E_\lambda(\lambda,T)}{E_{\lambda,b}(\lambda,T)} \qquad (27.9)$$

and the total hemispherical emissivity as

$$\epsilon(T) = \frac{E(T)}{E_b(T)}. \qquad (27.10)$$

While the spectral emissivity of a real surface surely depends on the angles at which emissions occur, it is usually a good approximation to take the spectral emissivity corresponding to the normal direction of the surface and write $\epsilon_{\lambda,\theta} \approx \epsilon_{\lambda,n}$. Subsequently, we also see that the total emissivity is given by $\epsilon \approx \epsilon_n$. For values of ϵ_n for common materials, see Table 27.1.

Table 27.1: Emissivity of common materials.

Surface Material	ϵ_n
Aluminum, foil	0.04
Aluminum, oxidized	0.2 - 0.31
Aluminum, polished	0.039–0.057
Asbestos, paper	0.93–0.945
Asphalt	0.93
Brass, polished	0.03
Brick, fireclay	0.75
Cement	0.54
Clay	0.91
Coal	0.80
Concrete	0.85
Copper, polished	0.023–0.052
Glass, smooth	0.92–0.94
Gold, not polished	0.47
Gold, polished	0.025
Granite	0.45
Gravel	0.28
Gypsum	0.85
Iron, polished	0.14–0.38
Iron, rough ingot	0.87–0.95
Limestone	0.90–0.93
Marble, white	0.95
Masonry, plastered	0.93
Mild steel	0.20–0.32
Mortar	0.87
Oak, planed	0.89
Paint	0.96
Paper	0.93
Pine	0.84
Plaster	0.98
Plaster board	0.91
Plastics	0.90–0.97
PVC	0.91–0.93
Roofing paper	0.91
Salt	0.34
Sand	0.76
Sandstone	0.59
Sawdust	0.75
Silica	0.79
Soil	0.90–0.95
Steel, oxidized	0.79
Steel, polished	0.07
Tile	0.97
Tin, unoxidized	0.04
Water	0.95–0.963
Wood, beech planed	0.935
Wood, oak planed	0.885
Wood, pine	0.95

27.1.5 Irradiation

Irradiation is the process by which an object is struck or impacted by radiation. As illustrated in Fig. 27.2, when incident radiation strikes a *semi-transparent medium* with a certain intensity, a fraction is absorbed, a fraction is reflected and a fraction is transmitted, thus we write

$$G_\lambda = G_{\lambda,a} + G_{\lambda,r} + G_{\lambda,t}, \tag{27.11}$$

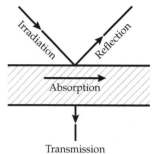

Figure 27.2: Irradiation on semi-transparent medium.

where G_λ is the spectral irradiation. Obviously, these fractions depend on the type of surface, as well as the angle and wavelength of radiation. The spectral absorptivity, reflectivity and transmissivity properties are respectively defined as follows:

$$\alpha_{\lambda,\theta}(\lambda,\theta,\varphi) = \frac{I_{\lambda,i,a}(\lambda,\theta,\varphi)}{I_{\lambda,i}(\lambda,\theta,\varphi)}, \tag{27.12}$$

$$\rho_{\lambda,\theta}(\lambda,\theta,\varphi) = \frac{I_{\lambda,i,r}(\lambda,\theta,\varphi)}{I_{\lambda,i}(\lambda,\theta,\varphi)}, \tag{27.13}$$

$$\tau_{\lambda,\theta}(\lambda,\theta,\varphi) = \frac{I_{\lambda,i,t}(\lambda,\theta,\varphi)}{I_{\lambda,i}(\lambda,\theta,\varphi)}, \tag{27.14}$$

where $I_{\lambda,i}(\lambda,\theta,\varphi)$ is the spectral intensity of irradiation. The corresponding spectral hemispherical properties are subsequently given by

$$
\begin{aligned}
\alpha_\lambda(\lambda) &= \frac{G_{\lambda,a}(\lambda)}{G_\lambda(\lambda)} \\
&= \frac{\int_0^{2\pi}\int_0^{\pi/2} \alpha_{\lambda,\theta}(\lambda,\theta,\varphi)\, I_{\lambda,i}(\lambda,\theta,\varphi) \cos\theta \sin\varphi\, d\theta\, d\varphi}{\int_0^{2\pi}\int_0^{\pi/2} I_{\lambda,i}(\lambda,\theta,\varphi) \cos\theta \sin\varphi\, d\theta\, d\varphi},
\end{aligned} \tag{27.15}
$$

$$
\begin{aligned}
\rho_\lambda(\lambda) &= \frac{G_{\lambda,r}(\lambda)}{G_\lambda(\lambda)} \\
&= \frac{\int_0^{2\pi}\int_0^{\pi/2} \rho_{\lambda,\theta}(\lambda,\theta,\varphi)\, I_{\lambda,i}(\lambda,\theta,\varphi) \cos\theta \sin\varphi\, d\theta\, d\varphi}{\int_0^{2\pi}\int_0^{\pi/2} I_{\lambda,i}(\lambda,\theta,\varphi) \cos\theta \sin\varphi\, d\theta\, d\varphi},
\end{aligned} \tag{27.16}
$$

$$
\begin{aligned}
\tau_\lambda(\lambda) &= \frac{G_{\lambda,t}(\lambda)}{G_\lambda(\lambda)} \\
&= \frac{\int_0^{2\pi}\int_0^{\pi/2} \tau_{\lambda,\theta}(\lambda,\theta,\varphi)\, I_{\lambda,i}(\lambda,\theta,\varphi) \cos\theta \sin\varphi\, d\theta\, d\varphi}{\int_0^{2\pi}\int_0^{\pi/2} I_{\lambda,i}(\lambda,\theta,\varphi) \cos\theta \sin\varphi\, d\theta\, d\varphi}.
\end{aligned} \tag{27.17}
$$

Furthermore, the corresponding total absorptivity, reflectivity and transmissivity properties are respectively given by

$$\alpha = \frac{G_a}{G} = \frac{\int_0^\infty \alpha_\lambda(\lambda) G_\lambda(\lambda) d\lambda}{\int_0^\infty G_\lambda(\lambda) d\lambda}, \tag{27.18}$$

$$\rho = \frac{G_r}{G} = \frac{\int_0^\infty \rho_\lambda(\lambda) G_\lambda(\lambda) d\lambda}{\int_0^\infty G_\lambda(\lambda) d\lambda}, \tag{27.19}$$

$$\tau = \frac{G_t}{G} = \frac{\int_0^\infty \tau_\lambda(\lambda) G_\lambda(\lambda) d\lambda}{\int_0^\infty G_\lambda(\lambda) d\lambda}. \tag{27.20}$$

Note that $\alpha_\lambda + \rho_\lambda + \tau_\lambda = 1$ and $\alpha + \rho + \tau = 1$. In addition, if the medium is opaque then $\tau_\lambda = \tau = 0$.

Example 27.1:

The temperature of the filament of an incandescent lightbulb is 2500 K. Assuming the filament to be a blackbody, determine the fraction of the radiant energy emitted by the filament that falls in the visible range. Also, determine the wavelength at which the emission of radiation from the filament peaks.

Known: Temperature of lightbulb filament.

Find: Determine the fraction of the radiant energy emitted by the filament that falls in the visible range and the wavelength at which the emission of radiation from the filament peaks.

Assumptions: The filament behaves as a blackbody.

Analysis: As can be observed from Fig. 26.1, the visible range of the electromagnetic spectrum extends from $\lambda_1 = 0.40\,\mu$m to $\lambda_2 = 0.76\,\mu$m. Noting that $T = 2500$ K, the blackbody radiation functions corresponding to $\lambda_1 T$ and $\lambda_2 T$ are determined from Eq. (27.6) to be

$$\lambda_1 T = (0.40\,\mu\text{m})(2500\,\text{K}) = 1000\,\mu\text{m} \cdot \text{K} \rightarrow F_{(0\to\lambda_1)} = 0.000321,$$

$$\lambda_2 T = (0.76\,\mu\text{m})(2500\,\text{K}) = 1900\,\mu\text{m} \cdot \text{K} \rightarrow F_{(0\to\lambda_2)} = 0.053035.$$

Then the fraction of radiation emitted between these two wavelengths is

$$F_{(\lambda_1\to\lambda_2)} = F_{(0\to\lambda_2)} - F_{(0\to\lambda_1)} = 0.053035 - 0.000321 = 0.0527135.$$

Therefore, only about 5% of the radiation emitted by the filament of the lightbulb falls in the visible range. The remaining 95% appears in the infrared region in the form of radiant heat.

The wavelength at which the emission of radiation from the filament peaks is easily determined from Wien's displacement law, Eq. (27.3), to be

$$\lambda_{max} T = 2897.8 \, \mu m \cdot K \quad \rightarrow \quad \lambda_{max} = \frac{2897.8 \, \mu m \cdot K}{2500 \, K} = 1.16 \, \mu m.$$

Comments: This is not a very efficient way of converting electric energy to light. From Fig. 26.1, we see that the radiation emitted from the filament peaks in the infrared region.

Exercises 27:

1. Derive Wien's law, Eq. (27.3), from Planck's formula, Eq. (27.1).

2. Using the definitions of total emissive power and total absorptivity, show that ϵ and α are not necessarily equal for irradiation of a surface at temperature T from a source at a different temperature, T^*.

3. For a blackbody maintained at 115°C, determine (a) the total emissive power, (b) the wavelength at which the maximum monochromatic emissive power occurs, and (c) the maximum monochromatic emissive power.

28 Kirchhoff's Law and Solar Radiation

28.1 Kirchhoff's Law

Kirchhoff's law of thermal radiation refers to wavelength-specific radiative emission and absorption by a material body in thermodynamic equilibrium, including radiative exchange equilibrium. A body at temperature T radiates electromagnetic energy. A black body in thermodynamic equilibrium absorbs all radiation that strikes it, and radiates energy according to a unique law of radiative emissive power for temperature T, universal for all perfect black bodies. Kirchhoff's law states that for an arbitrary body emitting and absorbing thermal radiation in thermodynamic equilibrium, the emissivity is equal to the absorptivity.

To see how this result is arrived at, consider a number of small bodies inside a large isothermal enclosure, as illustrated in Fig. 28.1. Under steady-state conditions, we must have that $T_1 = T_2 = \cdots = T_s$. Now consider the body labeled "1". An energy balance for this body says that the energy from irradiation absorbed by the body must be equal to the energy emitted:

$$\alpha_1 \, G \, A_1 = E_1 \, A_1. \tag{28.1}$$

In the situation considered, the cavity's radiation is effectively that of a blackbody, and thus

$$G = E_b \left(T_s \right). \tag{28.2}$$

Subsequently, the energy balance becomes

$$\alpha_1 \, E_b = E_1 \tag{28.3}$$

or

$$\alpha_1 = \frac{E_1}{E_b} = \epsilon_1, \tag{28.4}$$

and similarly $\alpha_2 = \epsilon_2 = \ldots$ or more generally $\alpha = \epsilon$. A similar argument applied for each wavelength results in $\alpha_\lambda = \epsilon_\lambda$.

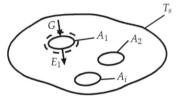

Figure 28.1: Small bodies inside a large enclosure.

We recall that a diffuse surface has properties that are independent of direction. We call a surface a *gray surface* if the properties are independent of wavelength over the spectral region of interest. The combined gray and diffuse approximations are commonly used to perform radiation calculations on real surfaces.

28.2   *Radiation Between the Sun and the Earth*

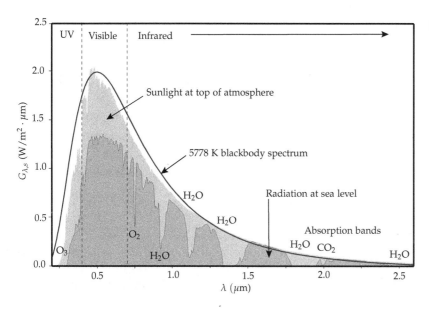

Figure 28.2: Solar irradiation spectrum.

As indicated in Fig. 28.2, the sun emits approximately as a blackbody at 5778 K. Irradiance is a function of distance from the sun, the solar cycle, and cross-cycle changes. Solar irradiance is the power per unit area received by the earth from the sun. The irradiance may be measured at the top of the atmosphere or at the earth's surface after atmospheric absorption and scattering. It is measured perpendicular to the incoming sunlight. Interaction of solar radiation with different molecules present in the atmosphere is also noted in Fig. 28.2.

The total solar irradiance is a measure of the solar power over all wavelengths per unit area incident on the earth's upper atmosphere. As indicated on Fig. 28.3, the *solar constant* is a conventional measure of total solar irradiance at the edge of the atmosphere when the earth is at a mean distance from the sun:

$$G_s = S_c f \cos\theta, \qquad (28.5)$$

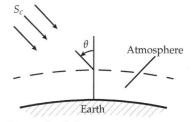

Figure 28.3: Solar constant.

where $S_c = 1368 \text{ W/m}^2$ is the solar constant, f is a correction factor that accounts for the eccentricity of the earth's orbit with a value of

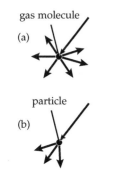

Figure 28.4: (a) Rayleigh scattering and (b) Mie scattering.

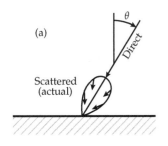

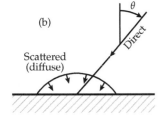

Figure 28.5: Direct radiation (a) actual and (b) diffuse.

Table 28.1: Solar absorptance and emissivity of common materials.

Substance	α	ϵ
Aluminum	0.1 - 0.15	0.05
Copper	0.2 - 0.5	0.05
Glass	0.1	0.9
Ice	0.3 - 0.5	0.92
Iron	0.3	0.2 - 0.7
Nickel	0.2	0.05
Paper	0.3	0.95
Sand & soil	0.4 - 0.7	0.5 - 0.8
Steel (carbon)	0.2	0.2 - 0.6

$0.97 \lesssim f \lesssim 1.03$, and θ is the zenith angle which is relative to the surface normal.

Absorption and *scattering* of the sun's irradiation occurs in the atmosphere. The scattering is of the two types illustrated in Fig. 28.4. Molecular (or Rayleigh) scattering in which the sun's rays interact with small molecules and result in fairly uniform scattering in all directions. Subsequently, some of this radiation is re-directed back outside the atmosphere. Particle (or Mie) scattering occurs when a sun's ray interacts with a dust or soot particle. Subsequently, the radiation, while more diffused, is concentrated in the same direction of the incident ray.

The portion of irradiation that penetrates the atmosphere without being absorbed or scattered and is in the direction of the zenith angle is called direct radiation and is illustrated in Fig. 28.5(a). On the other hand, we often assume such radiation to be diffuse, as illustrated in Fig. 28.5(b) when it strikes the earth's surface. Scattered radiation is usually assumed to be diffuse and varies from 10% to 90% between a clear day and a cloudy day.

On the other hand, the earth's radiation emission at temperature T is given by

$$E = \epsilon \sigma T^4, \qquad (28.6)$$

where, being that 2/3 of the earth's surface is composed of water, we have that the surface emissivity is $\epsilon \approx 0.97$. The average temperature of the earth is approximately 290 K. Similar to solar irradiation, radiation emission from the earth is also modified by absorption and scattering as it propagates through the atmosphere.

Due to absorption and scattering of solar irradiation and terrestrial emission as they propagate through the atmosphere, the atmosphere itself becomes warm. Thus, the earth is also a recipient of irradiation from atmospheric emission. This atmospheric irradiation is approximated by

$$G_{atm} = \sigma T_{sky}^4, \qquad (28.7)$$

where the effective sky temperature is in the range $230\,\text{K} < T_{sky} < 285\,\text{K}$ depending on wether we have a cold and clear sky or a warm cloudy sky.

We note regarding the energy balance between solar irradiation, sky irradiation and earth emission, that we cannot use the gray approximation since the irradiations mostly occur at short wavelengths while the emission occurs at long wavelengths. This is verified in Table 28.1 where solar absorptivity and emissivity of some common surfaces are listed.

Example 28.1:

The sun has a diameter of 1.391×10^9 m. The earth has a diameter of 1.274×10^7 m and its center lies at a mean distance of 1.496×10^{11} m from the center of the sun. Use the measured solar irradiation of 1368 W/m^2 to show that the effective black body temperature of the sun is approximately 5778 K.

Known: Diameter of the sun, diameter of the earth, the distance between the sun and the earth, and the solar irradiation.

Find: The effective black body temperature of the sun.

Assumptions: The sun is spherical and emits radiation as a blackbody; the solar energy experiences no variation on its way through the vacuum between the sun and the earth; the earth is spherical and the sun's irradiation is normal to the earth (from Eq. (28.5) we subsequently have that $G_s = S_c$).

Analysis: The conservation of energy principle requires that the total solar energy passing through a spherical surface whose radius is the mean earth-sun distance must be equal to the total energy that leaves the sun's outer surface. Thus

$$\left[4\pi (L-r)^2 \right] G_s = \left(4\pi R^2 \right) \sigma T_s^4,$$

where L is the mean distance between the sun's center and the earth center, R is the radius of the sun, and r is the radius of the earth. Note that the radius of the earth is negligible compared to the distance between the sun and the earth. Subsequently, we have that

$$T_s = \left[\left(\frac{L}{R} \right)^2 \frac{G_s}{\sigma} \right]^{1/4}$$

$$= \left[\left(\frac{1.496 \times 10^{11}\,\text{m}}{0.6955 \times 10^9\,\text{m}} \right)^2 \frac{1368\,\text{W/m}^2}{5.670 \times 10^{-8}\,\text{W/m}^2 \cdot \text{K}^4} \right]^{1/4}$$

$$= 5780\,\text{K}.$$

Comments: This result is also confirmed by measurements of the spectral distribution of the solar radiation just outside the atmosphere plotted in Fig. 28.2, which shows only small deviations from the idealized blackbody behavior.

Exercises 28:

1. Explain why surfaces usually have quite different absorptivities for

solar radiation and for radiation originating from the surrounding bodies.

2. The air temperature on a clear night is observed to remain at about 4°C. Yet water is reported to have frozen that night due to radiation effect. Taking the convection heat transfer coefficient to be 18 W/m^2·°C, determine the value of the maximum effective sky temperature that night.

3. A radiometer is calibrated to indicate the temperature of a blackbody. A steel billet having a diffuse, gray surface of emissivity 0.8 is heated in a furnace whose walls are at 1500 K. Estimate the temperature of the billet when the radiometer viewing the billet through a small hole in the furnace indicates 1160 K.

29 Radiation Exchange and View Factor

29.1   Radiation Exchange Between Two Surfaces

Consider the radiation exchange between the two arbitrarily oriented differential surfaces dA_i and dA_j corresponding to surfaces A_i, at temperature T_i, and A_j, at temperature T_j, as illustrated in Fig. 29.1. We assume that the media between the two surfaces are non-participating (*i.e.* it is transparent to radiation). We recall from Eq. (26.7) that

$$dq_\lambda = I_\lambda\, dA_1 \cos\theta\, d\omega, \tag{29.1}$$

where from Eq. (26.4) the solid angle is given by

$$d\omega = \frac{dA_n}{r^2}. \tag{29.2}$$

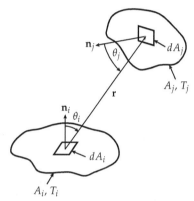

Figure 29.1: Radiation exchange between two differential surfaces.

In our specific case, assuming that the surfaces are gray, the differential rate at which radiation leaving dA_i strikes dA_j is denoted as

$$dq_{i\to j} = I_i \cos\theta_i\, dA_i\, d\omega_{j-i}, \tag{29.3}$$

where I_i is the radiation intensity (from emission and reflection) of dA_i and $d\omega_{j-i}$, given by

$$d\omega_{j-i} = \frac{\cos\theta_j\, dA_j}{r^2}, \tag{29.4}$$

corresponds to the solid angle subtended by dA_j when viewed from dA_i. Now assuming that A_i emits and reflects diffusely, then $J_i = \pi I_i$, where J_i is the radiosity of dA_i. Subsequently we can write

$$dq_{i\to j} = J_i \frac{\cos\theta_i \cos\theta_j}{\pi r^2}\, dA_i\, dA_j. \tag{29.5}$$

Assuming that the radiosity J_i is constant over the surface A_i (*i.e.* the surface is isothermal at temperature T_i), the total rate of radiation leaving A_i that is intercepted by A_j is given by

$$q_{i\to j} = J_i \int_{A_i} \int_{A_j} \frac{\cos\theta_i \cos\theta_j}{\pi r^2}\, dA_i\, dA_j. \tag{29.6}$$

29.2   *View Factor*

Now, we define the view factor (also called the shape factor) F_{ij} as the proportion of the rate of thermal radiation which leaves surface A_i that strikes surface A_j:

$$F_{ij} = \frac{q_{i \to j}}{A_i J_i} = \frac{1}{A_i} \int_{A_i} \int_{A_j} \frac{\cos \theta_i \cos \theta_j}{\pi r^2} \, dA_i \, dA_j. \qquad (29.7)$$

Analogously, the view factor F_{ji} is the proportion of the rate of thermal radiation which leaves surface A_j that strikes surface A_i:

$$F_{ji} = \frac{q_{j \to i}}{A_j J_j} = \frac{1}{A_j} \int_{A_i} \int_{A_j} \frac{\cos \theta_i \cos \theta_j}{\pi r^2} \, dA_i \, dA_j. \qquad (29.8)$$

From Eqs. (29.7) and (29.8) we see that view factors obey the *reciprocity relation*

$$A_i F_{ij} = A_j F_{ji}. \qquad (29.9)$$

Such relation allows us to calculate F_{ji} with knowledge of F_{ij} using the two surface areas A_i and A_j.

For the enclosure composed of n surfaces illustrated in Fig. 29.2, it follows that the radiation leaving a surface must be deposited on the other surfaces. Thus, the sum of all view factors from a given surface, say A_i, is unity. This provides the following *summation rule*:

$$\sum_{j=1}^{n} F_{ij} = 1. \qquad (29.10)$$

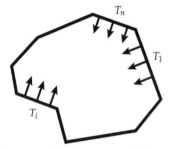

Figure 29.2: Cavity composed of n surfaces.

Furthermore, since this must be true for each of the individual surfaces that form the cavity, we have that

$$\sum_{j=1}^{n} F_{ij} = 1 \qquad \text{for} \quad i = 1, \dots, n. \qquad (29.11)$$

Note that the number of unknown view factors for the enclosure are $n(n-1)/2$. For simple geometries, the above rules may be utilized to compute the view factors. For more complicated geometries, (29.7) is used directly.

For a flat or convex surface, no radiation can leave the surface and strike itself. For a concave surface, radiation leaving the surface can indeed strike itself. Thus, we have the following rule for the view factors:

$$F_{ii} = 0 \qquad \text{for plane or convex surfaces, and} \qquad (29.12)$$

$$F_{ii} > 0 \qquad \text{for concave surfaces.} \qquad (29.13)$$

View factors can also be summed. Consider thermal radiation from surface A_i to surface A_j which is composed of m subsurfaces. Then it is obvious that

$$F_{i(j)} = \sum_{k=1}^{m} F_{ik},\qquad(29.14)$$

where the parentheses around j indicates that A_j is composed of m subsurfaces. Now multiplying the above equation by A_i and using the reciprocal relation Eq. (29.9) we have that

$$F_{(j)i} = \frac{\displaystyle\sum_{k=1}^{m} A_k F_{ki}}{A_j} = \frac{\displaystyle\sum_{k=1}^{m} A_k F_{ki}}{\displaystyle\sum_{k=1}^{m} A_k}.\qquad(29.15)$$

29.3   *Blackbody Radiation Exchange*

Consider radiation exchange between two arbitrary blackbodies with corresponding surfaces A_i at temperature T_i and A_j at temperature T_j. Since radiosity from a blackbody equals its emissive power, *i.e.* $J_i = E_{b,i} = \sigma T_i^4$, it follows from Eqs. (29.7) and (29.8) that the rates of radiation transfer from A_i to A_j and vice versa are given by $q_{i\to j} = A_i F_{ij} E_{b,i}$ and $q_{j\to i} = A_j F_{ji} E_{b,j}$. This makes the net rate of radiation exchange equal to

$$
\begin{aligned}
q_{ij} &= q_{i\to j} - q_{j\to i} \\
&= A_i F_{ij} E_{b,i} - A_j F_{ji} E_{b,j} \\
&= A_i F_{ij} E_{b,i} - A_i F_{ij} E_{b,j} \\
&= A_i F_{ij} \left(E_{b,i} - E_{b,j} \right) \\
&= A_i F_{ij} \, \sigma \left(T_i^4 - T_j^4 \right),
\end{aligned}
\qquad(29.16)
$$

where we have utilized the reciprocal relation Eq. (29.9).

In a blackbody enclosure composed of n surfaces at different temperatures the *net* transfer of radiation from surface A_i is equal to

$$q_i = \sum_{j=1}^{n} A_i F_{ij} \, \sigma \left(T_i^4 - T_j^4 \right).\qquad(29.17)$$

View factors for hundreds of common geometries have been evaluated and the results are given in analytical, graphical, and tabular forms. They are easily available through various sources.

Example 29.1:

We illustrate different techniques to calculate view factors for (a) two concentric cylinders, (b) two coaxial parallel circular surfaces with $A_i/A_j \ll 1$, and (c) the closed cavity within a truncated cone:

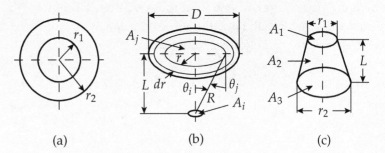

(a)   (b)   (c)

Known: Dimensions of surfaces.

Find: View factors.

Analysis: (a) We first illustrate the use of simple view factor algebra applied to two concentric cylinders. Since the surface of the interior cylinder A_1 is convex, we have from Eq. (29.12) that $F_{11} = 0$, so from the summation rule Eq. (29.11) for this surface we have that $F_{12} = 1$. Now using the reciprocal relation Eq. (29.9) we obtain

$$F_{21} = F_{12} \frac{A_1}{A_2} = \frac{A_1}{A_2} = \frac{r_1}{r_2} ,$$

and using the summation rule Eq. (29.11) for surface A_2 we finally have

$$F_{22} = 1 - \frac{r_1}{r_2}.$$

(b) In this case we use the integral definition Eq. (29.7):

$$F_{ij} = \frac{1}{A_i} \int_{A_i} \int_{A_j} \frac{\cos\theta_i \cos\theta_j}{\pi R^2} dA_i \, dA_j.$$

Since $A_i/A_j \ll 1$, the integral associated with dA_i is approximately equal to A_i. As a consequence, θ_i, θ_j and R are effectively independent of positions within area A_i. Subsequently, $\theta_i = \theta_j = \theta$ and the remaining integral is rewritten as

$$F_{ij} = \frac{1}{\pi} \int_{A_j} \frac{\cos^2\theta}{R^2} dA_j.$$

Using the fact that $R^2 = L^2 + r^2$, $\cos\theta = L/R$, and $dA_j = 2\pi r\, dr$, we obtain

$$F_{ij} = 2L^2 \int_0^{D/2} \frac{r\, dr}{(L^2 + r^2)^2} = \frac{D^2}{D^2 + 4L^2}.$$

(c) This last illustration demonstrates the use of closed form parametric relationships to obtain a single view factor and the other values using view factor algebra. We begin by noting that the surface area, A, of a cone of base radius r, and perpendicular height, h is given by the expression $A = \pi r (r^2 + h^2)^{1/2}$. The surface area of a truncated cone is the difference between the surface area of the larger cone to that of the smaller one.

Using the integral procedure described above, but for the case where A_i is not much smaller than A_j, it can be shown that the view factor for two coaxial parallel circular surfaces of radii r_1 and r_2 separated by a distance L is given by

$$F_{12} = \frac{1}{2}\left\{ S - \left[S^2 - 4\left(\frac{r_2}{r_1}\right)^2 \right]^{1/2} \right\},$$

where

$$R_1 = \frac{r_1}{L}, \quad R_2 = \frac{r_2}{L}, \quad \text{and} \quad S = 1 + \frac{1 + R_2^2}{R_1^2}.$$

In addition, we have from Eq. (29.12) that $F_{11} = 0$, so from Eq. (29.11) for $i = 1$ we have that $F_{13} = 1 - F_{12}$. Also, from the reciprocal relation Eq. (29.9) we can write that

$$F_{21} = F_{12}\,\frac{A_1}{A_2}.$$

Now, again, from Eq. (29.12) that $F_{22} = 0$ and from Eq. (29.11) for $i = 2$ we have that $F_{23} = 1 - F_{21}$. Lastly, from the reciprocal relation Eq. (29.9) we can write that

$$F_{31} = F_{13}\,\frac{A_1}{A_3}, \qquad F_{32} \qquad = F_{23}\,\frac{A_2}{A_3},$$

and from Eq. (29.11) for $i = 3$ we have that $F_{33} = 1 - F_{31} - F_{32}$.

Exercises 29:

1. For the configuration of two coaxial circular cylinders of finite length, where A_1 is the inner surface area of the outer cylinder, A_2 is the outer surface of the inner cylinder, and A_3 is the flat annular surface area between the two cylinders at one end, obtain expressions for

F_{13}, F_{31}, F_{32}, and F_{33} in terms of F_{11}, F_{12}, and the three areas A_1, A_2, and A_3. F_{33} is the view factor between the two annular areas at opposite ends.

2. Two parallel infinite black planes are maintained at 200°C and 300°C. (a) Determine the net rate of heat transfer per unit area. (b) Repeat for the case where both temperatures are lowered by 100°C and determine the ratio of the reduced heat transfer to the original value.

3. Suppose that two concentric parallel disks are 3 m apart, with disk 1 (1 m radius) being at 200°C and disk 2 (1.5 m radius) being at 400°C. Calculate q_i and q_{ij} for the two disks being blackbodies.

30 Surfaces and Enclosures

30.1 Radiation Exchange in an Enclosure

We consider an enclosure composed of n surfaces containing a fluid. We make the following assumptions regarding each surface of the enclosure and the contained fluid: i) surfaces are isothermal, opaque, diffuse and gray; ii) the irradiation received by and radiosity emanating from each surface is uniform; and iii) the fluid is non-participating.

30.1.1 Energy Analysis of Single Surface

From the energy balance at the single surface having area A_i, illustrated in Fig. 30.1(a), we have that the net heat rate is due to the difference between radiation leaving the surface (radiosity) and that received by the surface (irradiation):

$$q_i = A_i \left(J_i - G_i \right). \tag{30.1}$$

From the definition, the radiosity of a surface consists of emitted radiation from the surface and the reflected portion of the irradiation reaching the surface (see Fig. 30.1(b)):

$$J_i = E_i + \rho_i \, G_i. \tag{30.2}$$

Since the surface is assumed to be opaque ($\tau_i = 0$), we have that $\alpha_i + \rho_i = 1$ (see Fig. 30.1(b)), and thus

$$q_i = A_i \left(E_i - \alpha_i \, G_i \right). \tag{30.3}$$

In addition, for a diffuse gray surface we have that $\epsilon_i = E_i / E_{b,i}$ and $\alpha_i = \epsilon_i$. Substituting these relations into (30.2) and solving the resulting equation for the irradiation, we have

$$G_i = \frac{J_i - \epsilon_i \, E_{b,i}}{1 - \epsilon_i}. \tag{30.4}$$

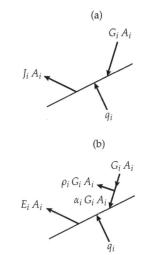

(a)

$G_i \, A_i$

$J_i \, A_i$

q_i

(b)

$G_i \, A_i$

$\rho_i \, G_i \, A_i$

$E_i \, A_i$

$\alpha_i \, G_i \, A_i$

q_i

Figure 30.1: Energy balance at surface.

Subsequently, substituting (30.4) into (30.3), we obtain the rate of net radiation transfer for the surface:

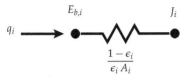

$$q_i = \frac{E_{b,i} - J_i}{(1 - \epsilon_i) / \epsilon_i A_i}. \tag{30.5}$$

Figure 30.2: Surface resistance.

Equation (30.5) is very convenient since it can be represented by the resistance shown in Fig. 30.2. As indicated in the figure, $E_{b,i} - J_i$ is the driving potential and $(1 - \epsilon_i)/\epsilon_i A_i$ is the *surface radiative resistance*.

30.1.2   Radiation Exchange Between Surfaces

Given the surface temperature T_i, the surface area A_i, and the surface emissivity ϵ_i, to evaluate Eq. (30.5) one must know the radiosity J_i. It can be obtained by solving the system of equations arising from the energy balances of all surfaces of the cavity illustrated in Fig. 30.3.

We start by noting that the irradiation of surface A_i is due to the radiosity of all surfaces comprising the cavity composed of n surfaces:

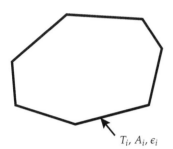

$$A_i G_i = \sum_{j=1}^{n} F_{ji} A_j J_j = \sum_{j=1}^{n} A_i F_{ij} J_j, \tag{30.6}$$

Figure 30.3: Cavity composed of isothermal surfaces.

where the reciprocity relation Eq. (29.9) was used to arrive at the last expression. Subsequently, we can write the irradiation as

$$G_i = \sum_{j=1}^{n} F_{ij} J_j. \tag{30.7}$$

Substituting this result in Eq. (30.1) and making use of the summation rule Eq. (29.11), we have that

$$q_i = A_i \left(\sum_{j=1}^{n} F_{ij} J_i - \sum_{j=1}^{n} F_{ij} J_j \right) = \sum_{j=1}^{n} A_i F_{ij} \left(J_i - J_j \right) = \sum_{j=1}^{n} q_{ij}, \tag{30.8}$$

which is the sum of the net radiative exchanges.

We finally write

$$q_i = \sum_{j=1}^{n} \frac{J_i - J_j}{\left(A_i F_{ij} \right)^{-1}} \tag{30.9}$$

$$= \frac{E_{b,i} - J_i}{(1 - \epsilon_i) / \epsilon_i A_i}, \tag{30.10}$$

where $\left(A_i F_{ij} \right)^{-1}$ is known as the *geometrical radiative resistance*. We make the following important observations. If the surface heat rate q_i of area A_i is given, then Eq. (30.9) represents an equation for the unknown J_i. If the surface temperature T_i of area A_i is given, then Eq. (30.10) represents an equation for the unknown J_i. Subsequently,

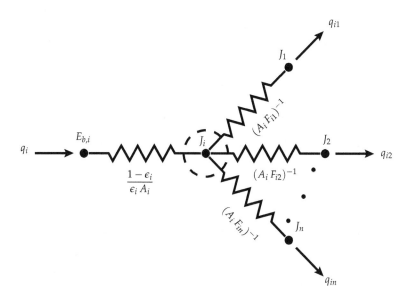

the interaction between surface A_i and all other surfaces can be represented by the resistance network illustrated in Fig. 30.4.

We note that for each surface of area A_i we have one equation. For the n surfaces we n equations which can be written as

$$\mathbf{A} \cdot \mathbf{J} = \mathbf{C}, \tag{30.11}$$

where $\mathbf{A}$ is an $n \times n$ matrix whose elements consist of reciprocal surface or geometrical resistances, $\mathbf{J}$ is an n dimensional vector of the unknown radiosities, and $\mathbf{C}$ is an n dimensional vector whose elements consist of known information arising from prescribed heat fluxes or temperatures. These quantities take the form

$$\mathbf{A} = \begin{bmatrix} a_{11} & a_{12} & \cdots & a_{1n} \\ a_{21} & a_{22} & \cdots & \vdots \\ \vdots & \vdots & \ddots & \vdots \\ a_{n1} & \cdots\cdots\cdots & a_{nn} \end{bmatrix}, \quad \mathbf{J} = \begin{bmatrix} J_1 \\ J_2 \\ \vdots \\ J_n \end{bmatrix}, \quad \mathbf{C} = \begin{bmatrix} C_1 \\ C_2 \\ \vdots \\ C_n \end{bmatrix}. \tag{30.12}$$

Solving for $\mathbf{J}$ directly or by iteration, we obtain the radiosities:

$$\mathbf{J} = \mathbf{A}^{-1} \cdot \mathbf{C}. \tag{30.13}$$

30.2   Two Surface Cavities

The simplest cavity is one consisting of two surfaces. Consider the two-surfaces enclosure illustrated in Fig. 30.5. At steady state we must have that $q_1 = -q_2 = q_{12}$, so that it is easiest to construct the resistance network illustrated in Fig. 30.6:

Figure 30.5: Cavity composed of two surfaces.

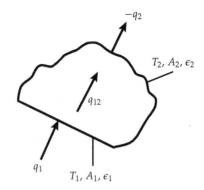

Figure 30.6: Resistance network for two-surfaces cavity.

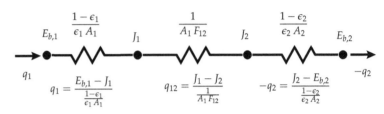

Subsequently, we have that

$$q_1 = -q_2 = q_{12} = \frac{E_{b,1} - E_{b,2}}{\dfrac{1-\epsilon_1}{\epsilon_1 A_1} + \dfrac{1}{A_1 F_{12}} + \dfrac{1-\epsilon_2}{\epsilon_2 A_2}}$$

$$q_{12} = \frac{\sigma \left(T_1^4 - T_2^4\right)}{\dfrac{1-\epsilon_1}{\epsilon_1 A_1} + \dfrac{1}{A_1 F_{12}} + \dfrac{1-\epsilon_2}{\epsilon_2 A_2}}. \tag{30.14}$$

This result applies to any cavity consisting of two surfaces using the appropriate values of the two surface areas, their emissivities, and the view factor F_{12}. For example, if we consider the cavity between two concentric spheres or radii r_1 and $r_2 > r_1$, then $A_1/A_2 = r_1^2/r_2^2$, and $F_{12} = 1$. Subsequently,

$$q_{12} = \frac{\sigma A_1 \left(T_1^4 - T_2^4\right)}{\dfrac{1}{\epsilon_1} + \dfrac{1-\epsilon_2}{\epsilon_2}\left(\dfrac{r_1}{r_2}\right)^2}. \tag{30.15}$$

Example 30.1:

Two very large parallel plates are maintained at uniform temperatures $T_1 = 800$ K and $T_2 = 500$ K and have emissivities $\epsilon_1 = 0.2$ and $\epsilon_2 = 0.7$, respectively. Determine the net rate of radiation heat transfer between the two surfaces per unit surface area.

Known: The plates are maintained at uniform temperatures.

Find: The net rate of radiation heat transfer per unit area.

Assumptions: The surfaces have the same area; both surfaces are opaque, diffuse, and gray.

Properties: Emissivities of the surfaces are $\epsilon_1 = 0.2$ and $\epsilon_2 = 0.7$.

Analysis: Since $A_1 = A_2 = A$, and $F_{11} = F_{22} = 0$ and $F_{12} = F_{21} = 1$, from Eq. (30.14 we have that net rate of radiation heat transfer between the two plates per unit area is given by

$$q''_{12} = \frac{\sigma \left(T_1^4 - T_2^4 \right)}{\dfrac{1}{\epsilon_1} + \dfrac{1}{\epsilon_2} - 1}$$

$$= \frac{5.67 \times 10^{-8}\,\text{W/m}^2 \cdot \text{K}^4 \left[(800\,\text{K})^4 - (500\,\text{K})^4 \right]}{\dfrac{1}{0.2} + \dfrac{1}{0.7} - 1} = 3625\,\text{W/m}^2$$

Comments: Heat at a net rate of 3625 W is transferred from plate 1 to plate 2 by radiation per unit surface area of either plate.

Exercises 30:

1. Consider a cylindrical furnace with radius r_0 and height H of 1 m. The top (surface 1) and the base (surface 2) of the furnace have emissivities $\epsilon_1 = 0.8$ and $\epsilon_2 = 0.4$, respectively, and are maintained at uniform temperatures $T_1 = 700$ K and $T_2 = 500$ K. The side surface closely approximates a blackbody and is maintained at a temperature of $T_3 = 400$ K. Determine the net rate of radiation heat transfer at each surface during steady operation and explain how these surfaces can be maintained at specified temperatures.

2. A furnace is shaped like a long equilateral triangular duct. The width of each side is 1 m. The base surface has an emissivity of 0.7 and is maintained at a uniform temperature of 600 K. The heated left-side surface closely approximates a blackbody at 1000 K. The right-side surface is well insulated. Determine the rate at which heat must be supplied to the heated side externally per unit length of the duct in order to maintain these operating conditions.

3. Consider a hemispherical furnace of diameter $D = 5$ m with a flat base. The dome of the furnace is black, and the base has an emissivity of 0.7. The base and the dome of the furnace are maintained at uniform temperatures of 400 K and 1000 K, respectively. Determine the net rate of radiation heat transfer from the dome to the base surface during steady operation.

31 Miscellaneous Topics

31.1   Radiation Shields

Radiation shields are a type of thermal (heat) insulations that inhibits heat transfer by thermal radiation. A radiation shield reflects radiation heat, preventing transfer from one side to another due to a highly reflective ($\rho \gg 1$) (or low emittance ($\epsilon \ll 1$)) opaque ($\tau = 0$) surface.

To illustrate how this is accomplished, consider the thermal radiation transfer between two large parallel plates with temperatures $T_1 > T_2$, areas $A_1 = A_2 = A$ and $F_{12} = 1$. In this case, from Eq. (30.14), we have that

$$q_{12} = \frac{\sigma A \left(T_1^4 - T_2^4\right)}{\dfrac{1}{\epsilon_1} + \dfrac{1}{\epsilon_2} - 1}. \tag{31.1}$$

If we now insert a third thin highly reflective (low emissivity) surface between the two plates, as illustrated in Fig. 31.1,

Figure 31.1: Radiation shield between parallel planes.

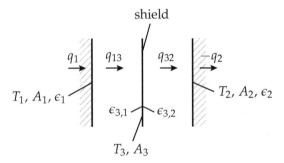

where now $A_1 = A_2 = A_3 = A$ and $F_{13} = F_{32} = 1$, we now have that

$$q_{12} = \frac{\sigma A \left(T_1^4 - T_2^4\right)}{\left(\dfrac{1}{\epsilon_1} + \dfrac{1}{\epsilon_2} - 1\right) + \left(\dfrac{1}{\epsilon_{3,1}} + \dfrac{1}{\epsilon_{3,2}} - 1\right)}. \tag{31.2}$$

The corresponding resistance network is illustrated in Fig. 31.2. When $\epsilon_{3,1} \ll 1$ and $\epsilon_{3,2} \ll 1$ the thermal resistances are large. Indeed, the reduction ratio, R, is obtained by dividing Eq. (31.2) by Eq. (31.1), which in this limit becomes

$$R \approx \frac{\frac{1}{\epsilon_1} + \frac{1}{\epsilon_2} - 1}{\frac{1}{\epsilon_{3,1}} + \frac{1}{\epsilon_{3,2}}}. \tag{31.3}$$

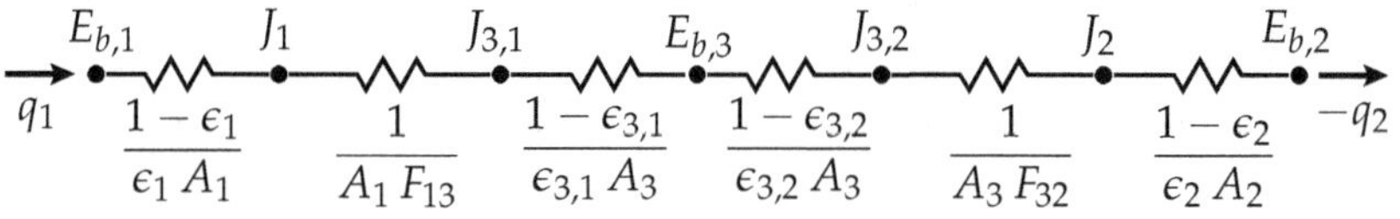

Figure 31.2: Resistance network for radiation shield illustrated in Fig. 31.1.

The appearance of Eq. (31.2) suggests that parallel plates involving multiple radiation shields can be handled by adding a group of terms like those in the second set of parentheses to the denominator for each radiation shield. Then the radiation heat transfer through large parallel plates separated by N radiation shields becomes

$$q_{12,N} = \frac{\sigma A \left(T_1^4 - T_2^4\right)}{\left(\frac{1}{\epsilon_1} + \frac{1}{\epsilon_2} - 1\right) + \left(\frac{1}{\epsilon_{3,1}} + \frac{1}{\epsilon_{3,2}} - 1\right) + \cdots + \left(\frac{1}{\epsilon_{N,1}} + \frac{1}{\epsilon_{N,2}} - 1\right)}. \tag{31.4}$$

If the emissivities of all surfaces are equal, Eq. (31.4) reduces to

$$q_{12,N} = \frac{\sigma A \left(T_1^4 - T_2^4\right)}{(N+1)\left(\frac{1}{\epsilon} + \frac{1}{\epsilon} - 1\right)} = \frac{1}{N+1} q_{12,0}, \tag{31.5}$$

where $q_{12,0}$ is the heat transfer rate without a shield.

31.2 Reradiating Surfaces

A reradiating surface is an idealized surface that has zero net radiation transfer, *i.e.* $q_i = 0$, and thus no surface resistance. The equilibrium temperature is independent of the surface emissivity. It is approximated by a surface that is insulated on one side and negligible or no thermal convection occurs on the other side. At steady-state, for such surface we have from Eqs. (30.1) and (30.5) that

$$G_i = J_i = E_{b,i}. \tag{31.6}$$

In this case, if G_i or J_i is known, we can readily determine T_i. In a cavity, the radiosity of the reradiating surface is determined by its interaction with the other surfaces comprising the cavity using the first equation in Eq. (30.10).

31.3 *Participating Media*

Up to this point, we have neglected the presence of gases on radiation transfer between surfaces. For nonpolar gases (such as O_2 and N_2) this is an excellent approximation since these gases are essentially transparent to radiation transfer. On the other hand, polar gases (such as CO_2, H_2O, NH_3, and hydrocarbons) emit and absorb radiation over a wide temperature range. In such case, radiation is effectively volumetric in character and not a surface phenomena, and occurs in specific wavelength intervals or bands (see Fig. 28.2).

Spectral radiation in a gas (or semi-transparent liquid or solid) layer of thickness L (m), illustrated in Fig. 31.3, follows *Beer's law*:

$$\tau_\lambda = \frac{I_{\lambda,L}}{I_{\lambda,0}} = e^{-\kappa_\lambda L}, \tag{31.7}$$

where τ_λ is the spectral transmissivity, $I_{\lambda,x}$ is the spectral intensity of wavelength λ at location x within the layer, and κ_λ (1/m) is the absorption coefficient. Note that the spectral intensity at $x = 0$ corresponds to the value incident on the layer and that at $x = L$ to the value exiting the layer.

With no radiation reflection, we have that the absorptivity is given by $\alpha_\lambda = 1 - \tau_\lambda$. Furthermore, assuming Kirchhoff's law, we have that $\alpha_\lambda = \epsilon_\lambda$ so that we can use Eq. (31.7) to also obtain the spectral emissivity of the layer.

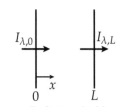

Figure 31.3: Radiation shield.

Example 31.1:
A thin aluminum sheet with an emissivity of 0.1 on both sides is placed between two very large parallel plates that are maintained at uniform temperatures $T_1 = 800$ Kand $T_2 = 500$ K and have emissivities $\epsilon_1 = 0.2$ and $\epsilon_2 = 0.7$, respectively. Determine the net rate of radiation heat transfer between the two plates per unit surface area of the plates and compare the result to that without the shield.

Known: Large parallel plates with given temperatures and emissivities; thin shield with given and equal emissivity on both sides.

Find: The net rate of radiation heat transfer between the two plates per unit surface area of the plates and compare the result to that without the shield.

Assumptions: The surfaces are opaque, diffuse, and gray.

Properties: The plate emissivities are $\epsilon_1 = 0.2$ and $\epsilon_2 = 0.7$, and the shield's emissivity is $\epsilon_3 = 0.1$ on both sides.

Analysis: The net rate of radiation heat transfer between these two plates without the shield was determined in Example 30.2 to be 3625 W/m^2. The heat transfer in the presence of one shield is determined from Eq. (31.2) to be

$$
\begin{aligned}
q_{12}'' &= \frac{\sigma \left(T_1^4 - T_2^4 \right)}{\dfrac{1}{\epsilon_1} + \dfrac{1}{\epsilon_2} + \dfrac{1 - \epsilon_{3,1}}{\epsilon_{3,1}} + \dfrac{1 - \epsilon_{3,2}}{\epsilon_{3,2}}} \\[2mm]
&= \frac{\left(5.67 \times 10^{-8} \, \text{W/m}^2 \cdot \text{K}^4 \right) \left[(800 \, \text{K})^4 - (500 \, \text{K})^4 \right]}{\left(\dfrac{1}{0.2} \right) + \left(\dfrac{1}{0.7} \right) + \left(\dfrac{1 - 0.1}{0.1} \right) + \left(\dfrac{1 - 0.1}{0.1} \right)} \\[2mm]
&= 806 \, \text{W/m}^2 .
\end{aligned}
$$

Comments: Note that the rate of radiation heat transfer reduces to about one-fourth of what it was as a result of placing a radiation shield between the two parallel plates.

Exercises 31:

1. A thin aluminum sheet with an emissivity of 0.15 on both sides is placed between two very large parallel plates, which are maintained at uniform temperatures $T_1 = 900$ K and $T_2 = 650$ K and have emissivities $\epsilon_1 = 0.5$ and $\epsilon_2 = 0.8$, respectively. Determine the net rate of radiation heat transfer between the two plates per unit surface area of the plates and compare the result with that without the shield.

2. A radiation shield that has the same emissivity ϵ_3 on both sides is placed between two large parallel plates, which are maintained at uniform temperatures of $T_1 = 650$ K and $T_2 = 400$ K and have emissivities of $\epsilon_1 = 0.6$ and $\epsilon_2 = 0.9$, respectively. Determine the emissivity of the radiation shield if the radiation heat transfer between the plates is to be reduced to 15 percent of that without the radiation shield.

3. Two very large parallel plates are maintained at uniform temperatures of $T_1 = 1000$ K and $T_2 = 800$ K and have emissivities of $\epsilon_1 = \epsilon_2 = 0.2$, respectively. It is desired to reduce the net rate of radiation heat transfer between the two plates to one-fifth by placing thin aluminum sheets with an emissivity of 0.15 on both sides between the plates. Determine the number of sheets that need to be inserted.

Index

CPSIA information can be obtained
at www.ICGtesting.com
Printed in the USA
LVHW101037200120
644156LV00009B/360

9 781098 530969